MORE PRAISE FOR
MORE THAN THE TROUBLES

"This book is a guide through the deadly landscape of Northern Ireland, but only for those whose minds are brave enough to seek beyond the bloodshed and tragedy for the silver dove of peace that is hidden among the thorns of conflict."

—*Dr. Dennis Clark*

"They [the authors] have produced an excellent reference work providing concise factual information on every aspect of the problem: the power structure (all organizations, legal, illegal, official, unofficial); the issues, Irish history to 1967; year-by-year chronology, 1967-1983; alternative solutions; U.S. and Irish-American involvement; appendices on the various peace groups, 'facts and figures', organizational addresses; plus an extensive annotated bibliography. Recommended for most libraries."

—*Library Journal*

"A well-documented, balanced, and very readable analysis of the conflict, it should provide a proper perspective for interested Americans who have tended to view the Northern Ireland tragedy as nothing more than a religious war between Protestants and Catholics.... There are many lessons to be learned from reading this excellent book, not least that understanding, forgiveness, respect, trust and co-operation are necessary elements for peace and reconciliation in Northern Ireland between the Unionist and Nationalist traditions and that the road to peace is a long one."

—*DAWN*

"Not every attempt at reconciliation has been successful, but it is the people of Northern Ireland who share their humanity and work for peaceful change that offer hope for the difficult days ahead."

—*Currents in Books,*
The San Diego Union

"No school or college that studies Ireland should be without this book."

—*Irish Edition*

ABOUT THE AUTHORS

Lynne Shivers has visited Northern Ireland numerous times since 1970. She has written articles for the Northern Irish magazines *Fortnight* and *Dawn*. Her writings have also appeared in *Christianity and Crisis*, *WIN Magazine*, *Friends Journal*, and *Fellowship*, as well as in two anthologies, *Tell the American People: Perspectives on the Iranian Revolution* (1980) and *Reweaving the Web of Life: Feminism and Nonviolence* (New Society Publishers, 1982). A member of the Religious Society of Friends (Quakers), Ms. Shivers teaches at the Community College of Philadelphia.

In 1972, David Bowman, S.J. became liason-staff with the Irish Council of Churches, and in July of 1975 became Director of the Ireland Program of the Division of Overseas Ministries, National Council of Churches. In 1979, he returned to the U.S. as Secretary for Ministries of the Jesuit Conference. Fr. Bowman is a member of the Catholic Theological Society of America, the National Association of Ecumenical Staff, and the Commission on Regional and Local Ecumenicism of the National Council of Churches, for which he is also Consultant on Ireland and Northern Ireland. He also serves as Director of the Jesuit International Ecumenist Committee.

Denis P. Barritt (foreword writer) is a former secretary of the Belfast Council of Social Welfare and chairman of the Fellowship of Reconciliation of Northern Ireland. He is co-chair of the Protestant and Catholic Encounter Movement (PACE), and author of *Northern Ireland: A Problem to Every Solution*, and co-author of *Orange and Green* and *The Northern Ireland Problem*.

more than the troubles

a common sense view of the northern ireland conflict

By Lynne shivers
and David Bowman, sj

foreword By
Denis p. Barritt

new society publishers

Cover design by Dion Lerman
Book design by Nina Huizinga

ISBN: 0-86571-025-2 Hardbound
      0-86571-061-9 Paperback
Printed in the United States

New Society Publishers is a project of New Society Educational Foundation and a collective of Movement for a New Society. New Society Educational Foundation is a non-profit, tax-exempt public foundation. Movement for a New Society is a network of small groups and individuals working for fundamental social change through nonviolent action. To learn more about MNS write: Movement for a New Society, 4722 Baltimore Avenue, Philadelphia, PA 19143. Opinions expressed in this book do not necessarily represent positions of either New Society Educational Foundation or Movement for a New Society.

DEDICATION

This book is dedicated
to the memory of Will Warren of the Society of Friends
and all others who have lived
for justice-peace-reconciliation
in Northern Ireland.

Lynne Shivers

Will Warren

Because this book is dedicated to the memory of Will Warren (1906-80), we would like to share more of the kind of person he was. People admired Will for his straightforwardness and commitment. He showed us what peacemaking can really be like without the romance or fantasy. Real peacemaking can be hard and exacting work that demands real sacrifice. But its successful accomplishment can mean the prevention of conflicts and misery, and the saving of lives.

Will thought that since he believed in nonviolence, he should locate himself in a violent place. Will lived in Derry from 1971 to 1977 on his own, though his wife visited from time to time. Will had been active in the British Campaign for Nuclear Disarmament in the fifties and sixties. His goals in Derry were clear: to do what he could to try to reconcile groups by helping them talk to each other and to try to reduce the killing in Northern Ireland.

Rumors about Will often preceded meeting him. The rumor that Will stopped riots was legend. For a time, daily riots occurred between schoolchildren and soldiers; people said you could set your clock by them. Stones, plastic bullets, and gas were often used. For all the six years Will lived in Derry, he walked down the middle of the street between the sides, effectively though only temporarily ending the fighting.

His affection for the children was also legend. He loved to fill his station wagon with the "wains" and drive them out into the country. Little boys would come up to Will to have their noses tweaked. Children seem to be the first to suffer from fear in a society. To have a playful grandfather meant a great deal to many children and to their parents.

The biggest rumor of all was that Will helped to prevent the development of sectarian assassinations in Derry, something that has devastated Belfast for some years. An example: a member of one community had been killed. Some men from the other community published a list, saying that if the murderer did not confess in twenty-four hours, they would proceed to kill people whose names were on the list. Will offered to find out if any of the men on the list were responsible. He asked, "If I discover that none are responsible, then can the murders be called off?" The men agreed. Will asked for forty-eight hours and brought back the word that none of the other community were responsible. Sectarian assassinations did not develop in Derry.

The incredible thing about Will Warren is that all the rumors were true. He did save lives; he did prevent sectarian murders from developing in Derry; children adored him. He remained steadfastly committed to his work, supported by individuals and peace groups. He taught many people important lessons. He said, "You can't expect to reconcile people unless you talk to the people you are trying to reconcile," and he meant it. He refused to judge a person even though he disagreed with that person. Derry people learned that Will had "no axes to grind," as Will himself put it.

Independently of Will's work, in the mid-1970s, the Northwest Centre for Learning and Development formed cooperative programs to develop training and jobs for unemployed youth. Part of this program is the Inner City Trust, a program to rebuild the bombed part of the city inside the walls. It also provides workshops for craft work to give maximum employment and develop attraction for future tourists.

In April 1982, the Derry Inner City Project opened the first renovated house and called it the "Will Warren House." It was "a tribute to Will's work that his name be remembered in this way where young people and unemployed adults are creating a new future in the town, where he worked and gave so generously of his time."

In a society where trust diminishes with each killing, Will was trusted by all sides—Republican, Loyalist, police, army, women, non-combatants, and children. May we be inspired by his example.

FOREWORD

People who have lived all their lives in Northern Ireland find that they have been born into one or other of the two main cultures and will have, almost inevitably, absorbed much of the outlook of their group. Even those who consider themselves unbiased and who make positive efforts to act as reconcilers or bridge-builders still are at times surprised how easily they can feel that a book or statement is unfair and prejudiced against their group.

Born in Belfast, I know from experience just how difficult it is to arrive at a balanced judgment when writing about—"that place apart"—Northern Ireland. There are such complex and at times seemingly contradictory allegiances and susceptibilities that it is necessary to have a firsthand knowledge of life in this province to catch all the necessary nuances. The two authors themselves come from two very different backgrounds and have spent much time on numerous extended visits, so that they write from no ivory tower. The chapter on first impressions gives a hint of how their knowledge was built up.

I commend this book to its American readers feeling that the authors have made a very worthy job of striking a balanced judgment. This judgment is not just a balancing act that says little; when the authors find things which they feel are wrong or unjust they do not hesitate to say so. Sharing a deep commitment to a nonviolent way of life, they are also united in their concern for and love of the people of Northern Ireland.

It soon becomes obvious that we are a people trapped by our history, and so the view of past developments should not just be skimmed over. The next section is a careful review of the unfolding of recent events which in itself forms a useful resource reference. Above all, however, the book will perform a valuable service in making it crystal clear that the Northern Irish people are made up of two differing traditions, cultures and allegiances which are a stronger divisive element than the differing denominational tenets. Failure to realize this leads to the acceptance of simplistic solutions, such as the belief that if only the British were to sever the link with Northern Ireland, all would be well. Such thinking, even if it does not lead to direct or indirect support of organizations linked with violence, in the words of President Carter, "delays the day when the people of Northern Ireland can live and work together in harmony free from fear."

What then can be done to ameliorate the situation? In spite of the terrible events which take place, those coming to live in Northern Ireland from overseas find, paradoxically, that people on all sides are remarkably friendly. On this one can build, and the authors show in chapter 6 what voluntary organizations in Northern Ireland are doing in an attempt to heal the wounds and to replace conflict with cooperation. If tribal fear is removed, both sides find that so many of the problems of modern life are shared in common and many things can be done together. Little of this work is known even in Great Britain, and still less in the United States. The writers then make suggestions as to how citizens of the United States and Canada can help.

I commend also the balanced answers to the "Final Questions" based on actual queries addressed to the writers.

Finally may I say how pleased I am that the book is dedicated to the memory of Will Warren, and that it includes a short note about him. After a lifetime of working for disarmament and peace in England, on retirement he gave six years of dedicated service to try to bring peace in Ulster. He did not achieve the "ceasefire" in Derry for which he hoped in the early years, but with great tact and at considerable personal risk he achieved trust not only from the army and the police, but also from the extreme groups on both sides which were engaged in violent confrontation. No one will ever know how many actual lives he saved, but we do know that he brought comfort and support to those who were harassed and whose lives were at times in danger—and happiness and hope to countless numbers of children. He lives on the hearts of so many in the city of Londonderry, to give it its official title, and today a community center for voluntary reconciling agencies in that city bears his name.

—Denis P. Barritt

ACKNOWLEDGMENTS

We wish to acknowledge with gratitude the support and assistance of people associated with the following organizations in Northern Ireland and the Republic of Ireland: the Irish School of Ecumenics, Glencree, the Society of Jesus, the Irish Council of Churches, Peace Point, Corrymeela, the Community of the Peace People, the Religious Society of Friends, and the Fellowship of Reconciliation.

In the United States, Fr. Bowman wishes to give special thanks to Dr. Eugene Stockwell, Dr. Paul McCleary, and Mr. J. Richard Butler of the Division of Overseas Ministries of the National Council of Churches of Christ of the U.S.A. and to the Mennonite Central Committee. Both organizations provided resources which permitted the text to be completed. Fr. Bowman also thanks the Chicago Province of the Society of Jesus for assigning him to the National Council of Churches of Christ of the U.S.A. during thirteen years.

Also in the United States, Lynne Shivers wishes to give special thanks to Jo Rowlands, Peter Jones, Marion McNaughton, Jonathan Betz-Zall and Joan Bauer for their support. Special appreciation goes to George Fischer who acted as editorial consultant in the final stages. The typists at various stages of the writing were dedicated and sensitive; we both appreciate their work—Carmelita Roche, Liddy Patterson, and David Brown. Ruth Seeley and Barbara Benton designed the maps, and Barbara also designed the Chronology of Northern Ireland Organizations. We are also grateful to the people who read the manuscript and gave us valuable insights—Dennis Clark, George Fischer, Ruth Seeley, Donald Campion, S.J., and Philip Land, S.J. Stanley Marcus contributed masterful copy editing.

—David Bowman, S.J.
—Lynne Shivers

Contents

*If people say they understand the Northern Ireland
situation you know they have been badly misinformed.*
                            —Belfast saying

Introduction

Northern Ireland has been in the news for many years, yet to most people living outside the province, the conflict seems almost impossible to understand. It is difficult to believe, but almost no books about Northern Ireland have been written expressly for Americans. Northern Irish people know that dozens of books in Northern Ireland have been written about their conflict. The difficulty with these books is that they either assume the reader has some background knowledge of the subject, or make references which simply compound the confusion for American readers. Americans, for example, would assume that "EPA" means "Environmental Protection Agency"; but in Northern Ireland "EPA" means "Emergency Powers Act." On top of that, the background of the EPA and its significance need explanation as well. A well-written book which explains is not enough; the history and context need to be included if the book is to be valuable to people outside the province.

This book is an attempt to present enough information and background about the present Northern Ireland conflict so that Americans in particular can more accurately interpret events there as they develop. Thus, this book presents factual information: history, economics, conflicting views, chronologies, and profiles of organizations. We have deliberately not included a lot of analysis. Other writers have frequently offered their analyses as the only valid ones. We would like not to repeat that mistake. In addition, writers who do not come from Northern Ireland tend to judge Northern Irish events harshly. Rather than being patronizing or judgmental, we prefer not to attempt an explicit analysis.

But this book does include our views, perspectives and values, since no writing is entirely value-free. The most prominent perspective is that we support nonviolent action in its various forms as a means

1

to create social initiatives in Northern Ireland. We deny that violent actions are either necessary or effective. We deny that people claiming to love God and neighbor can morally use violent means in Northern Ireland to whatever goal they intend: a "new Ireland," an "independent Ulster," a "return to Stormont," "law and order," or any other goal.

Violence, the use of force designed to injure, is by definition unjustified. It is unacceptable whether inflicted by army, police, vigilantes, freedom-fighters, free-lancers, psychotics, teenagers (or younger children), or spouses, male or female. Our position is that violence is unjustified in the present situation in Northern Ireland— awful as that situation might be.

What action then, if violence is unwarranted? Chapter 6 describes many groups following a nonviolent strategy. Some day we hope that the whole story of nonviolent action and initiatives in Northern Ireland can be told. People there and elsewhere are still discovering its power. We are still learning the wisdom of Martin Luther King, Jr.'s words, "The choice is between nonviolence and nonexistence."

To summarize: Because the Northern Ireland conflict is first of all complex, this book gives background material and contextual information not readily available elsewhere. Because information needs to precede analysis, this book is heavy on factual information and light on analysis. And because the Northern Ireland conflict is so often characterized as solely violent, this book presents a chapter on nonviolent and reconciliation organizations and initiatives. This is done not to imply that they can bandage all the wounds of the whole society. They cannot. But the nonviolent initiatives are almost completely unknown outside Northern Ireland, and they are an important element.

LANGUAGE

When Americans learn that "Protestants" and "Catholics" in Northern Ireland are shooting, bombing, and harassing one another, they assume that these terms have the meanings we give them in the U.S.A. Yet the terms are used quite differently in Northern Ireland;

they connote not mainly the churches that people attend, but two diverse and sometimes conflicting cultures.

To be a "Catholic" or a "Protestant" (a term that brackets together Anglicans, Presbyterians, Methodists and others) in Northern Ireland is to be baptized into a certain closed way of life. The nearest example for most Americans is the racial grouping in our cities, based on color.

In Northern Ireland, color is not the factor; *history* is. To be "Protestant" or "Catholic" means to accept a view of oneself, one's family, one's neighborhood, one's context within a closed group that gives identity. The distinguishing factor is mainly internal, although name, home location, and job often give clues to one's identity.

Unionists/Protestants, from 1920 onward, completely dominated the political scene of the six counties; this area became "Northern Ireland," a new "Ulster" instead of the nine counties of the ancient province. The result was a permanent two-thirds political majority, sustained by emigration of the minority because of public discrimination in jobs, housing, and civic power, as British government reports have shown (Scarman, Compton, Hunt, Cameron). The extreme elements of the Protestant majority brought down the Faulkner coalition government in May 1974, and have been defying the Westminster government again as they refuse to accept the British wish for some kind of devolved partnership at executive level. They want a continuation of the U.S. style of "democracy" in which the winner takes all; they had it this way from 1921 until 1972, when the British instituted direct rule.

The Catholic community holds to its own version of the history of Northern Ireland. As a one-third minority, it has been too large to be placated by civil rights tokens, but too small to achieve political power at the top level even with British insistence. It has its own faults to go along with its hurts: resentments resulting in refusal to listen or believe; inability to "forgive and forget" in political and civic matters; suspicion verging on hatred of the British army and Parliament and of the Royal Ulster Constabulary (police). In general, it wants a share in top-level political decisions, asserting that "normal democracy" has not existed and cannot exist in Northern Ireland at this time.

Both communities include rich and poor people, urban and farm people, hard-line and reconciling people. Neither belongs exclusively to one political ideology, and many in each community would reject any real church connection. There may be some devout churchgoers who deliberately use violence as members of paramilitary or security organizations. But the major issues are political power, social justice, civil participation, economic opportunity, consensus in psychological terms and love in religious terms.

The almost exclusive use of the religious shorthand terms "Catholic" and "Protestant" inevitably gives Americans the impression that the religious factor is the principal if not the only cause of the violence. This is seriously misleading, since religion is only one of the factors influencing the conflict. The suggestion here is to give a truer account of the complex situation by using other shorthand terms as well. "Sectarian" is a frequently-used term in Northern Ireland and connotes "bad religion" rather than "religion" in general. If only one pair of terms for Northern Ireland must be used constantly, then "majority-minority" seems appropriate.

If Northern Ireland were to become part of the Republic of Ireland, the majority-minority roles which now exist in Northern Ireland would be reversed. The one-million member (sixty-six percent) Protestant majority in the six-county Northern Ireland would become a twenty percent minority in a thirty-two county Ireland. The half million (thirty-three percent) Catholic minority in Northern Ireland would become part of the eighty percent majority in a thirty-two county Ireland. Thus, both communities in Northern Ireland today view themselves as victimized minorities in relation either to Northern Ireland or to a possible united Republic.

Northern Irish people have used other terms to explain the majority-minority split: Insiders/Outsiders; the haves/the have nots; colonials/natives; Scotch-Irish/Gaels; Protestant/Catholic; Unionist/Nationalist; Loyalist/Republican; British/Irish; the Orange/the Green. No common terms have become current, although "Ulster people" and "Northern Irish" seem to gain favor slowly.

These suggestions will help show how inaccurately the simple shorthand "Protestants/Catholics" conveys news. To identify opposing groups in this way always or nearly always does disservice to truth. In this book we shall try to follow our own advice.

CHAPTER SUMMARIES

Chapter 1, "First Impressions," provides firsthand and subjective impressions. We deliberately put this chapter first to remind ourselves and readers that Northern Ireland, like all social conflicts, involves people and has human implications. The Northern Ireland conflict is not simply composed of impersonal forces playing out ideological positions.

Chapter 2, "Sorting out the Power Structure," presents profiles of the most important organizations which have been responsible for creating history there since 1968. We include political parties, paramilitary groups, governmental bodies, and a few organizations that do not fit easily into any of these categories. Commission reports are summarized since they have been landmark decisions and are often referred to. We recognize that readers may find chapter 2 confusing. But readers need this initial information before reading chapter 3.

Chapter 3, "What Issues Divide?," is a delineation of four main groups of issues which divide people in Northern Ireland.

Chapter 4, "Facing Backwards," is essential in a book about Northern Ireland, a conflict which frequently uses historical events to justify present initiatives and analyses.

Chapter 5, "The New Troubles," sets down main events from 1967 through mid-1983.

Chapter 6, "The Search for Alternatives," details the work of over twenty organizations which provide services or take action initiatives with the overall goal of healing the Northern Ireland society. This chapter offers a different picture of Northern Ireland from those we usually receive.

Chapter 7, "The American Connection," discusses the numerous ways in which some American people and institutions are involved in Northern Ireland.

Chapter 8, "Final Questions," is based on actual questions so frequently posed that we realized they were on many people's minds. They also serve to summarize some of the major issues.

Appendix II, "Peace Education: Its Relevance to Northern Ireland," is written by Dr. Joseph Fahey, a professor in peace studies who has for some time addressed himself to the Northern Irish conflict.

The story of Northern Ireland is about the pain of history and how the past can prevent us from living in the present. Northern Ireland is also about rigidity: how brutality and hatred can prevent us from seeing each other as people. But Northern Ireland is also about bravery—how stamina and a commitment to each other have overcome fear and violence.

Anyone who becomes aware of the many forces crisscrossing in Northern Ireland realizes that people there are struggling with complicated and intense issues that no other modern societies have been forced to confront so intensely. High unemployment; housing shortage; separate schools; unusual criminal justice laws; a recent history of brutality and violence leading to over twenty-one hundred deaths; a number of active armies; serious lack of social services; frequent changes in governmental structures: any one of these issues has created serious disruption in other societies. Since 1968, Northern Irish people have experienced them all. Rather than decry these events, we should look to see what Northern Irish people can teach us. If nothing else, they can teach us what our own title speaks to: Northern Ireland means more than the troubles.

And what is meant by "The Troubles"? Any event which has disrupted society in Northern Ireland or the Republic of Ireland since the 1916 Uprising in Dublin, and is related in some way to the political status of Ireland or Northern Ireland vis-á-vis Great Britain. Thus, the term has meant different things to different generations. In 1919-22, "The Troubles" could refer to the Uprising, the war with Britain, and the civil war. From 1922 to 1967, it could mean, among other things, sporadic military activity involving the IRA—gun-running, prison terms, explosions at the border. Since 1967, the term has meant any event which has affected Northern Ireland or the Republic and can be related to the political status of Northern Ireland. "The Troubles" could refer to a bank robbery carried out by a paramilitary organization. It could include a civil rights march if people feared the event were related to a change in political status of the North. The event does not have to be military or violent in nature in order to be considered part of "The Troubles."

We hope that this book can be a bridge of understanding, leading to hope and action and away from despair and inertia. So, in a larger sense, this book is indirectly written for Northern Irish people. Any effort which helps people understand what is happening there and which tries to offer a balanced understanding will, we hope, contribute toward a peaceful resolution in Northern Ireland.

Lynne Shivers
4722 Baltimore Ave.
Philadelphia, PA 19143

David J. Bowman, S.J.
Jesuit House
5554 S. Woodlawn Ave.
Chicago, IL 60637

Two Northern Irish Faces

First Impressions

Most of this book presents information, an objective presentation of events, straightforward analysis, and data. This chapter is different. It attempts to present some of the less objective but real quality of the conflict. This chapter consists of the thoughts and experiences of two people. It is unavoidably personal. Trying to communicate the nature of a war in its fifteenth year is not a matter of balance and objectivity. It is remembering the way children act on a summer beach and seeing how differently they act when they return to their neighborhood, or how a street feels at night, deserted, with only soldiers patrolling, or how miles and miles of boarded-up homes affect people's emotions. In short, this chapter tries to present some of the reality that Northern Irish people know much better than any outsider can ever understand or completely explain. Fr. Bowman's pages are reflections on his experiences. Lynne Shivers's section follows.

REFLECTIONS Fr. David Bowman

"Memory's geese are always swans," was a favorite adage of a favorite Jesuit professor of mine. Even so, I would like to try to remember my experiences in Ireland and Northern Ireland with more objectivity than romanticism. The swans will be there, for the people of that island are marvelous, north and south. But the geese will also appear; otherwise the conflict would be even more inexplicable than it is.

It seems useful to dwell at some length on two "visits": my first experience of conflict on that island, from 1969 to 1973, and the recent years when we tried to help people exhausted by ten years of disappointments. These reflections will be in a different style from Lynne's; I hope they will complement hers.

Since 1969 I have been in Ireland and Northern Ireland thirty-six times, give or take a time or two. In previous visits in 1953 and 1954, while I was doing my doctoral studies in Rome, I did not really think of going to Northern Ireland, even though I spent the summer of 1953 in London, working in the British Museum library. There was very little in the news about Northern Ireland in those days.

But in 1969 a Jesuit friend took me up by train for a one-day visit to Belfast, and the devastation of Bombay Street hit me hard. We walked past the spot outside the Clonard Monastery where a sixteen-year-old boy had been shot to death, and looked at the double row of destroyed houses marking the place where the "civil war" had come to a head. But even then, the complexity of the conflict simply did not come home to me.

In 1971, Father Richard Rousseau, S.J., and I went from a World Council of Churches Faith and Order meeting in Louvain to Dublin and rented a car for three days. We drove to Cavan and at the border near Belturbet we turned back and did not go into the North, when a friendly chap at the Irish checkpoint said, "There's trouble in Enniskillen today, Fathers, and I'd advise you not to go through there. However, you'll be OK unless you have guns in the boot," and he laughed. Needless to say, we had no guns in the trunk of the car, nor did we have any inclination to get in the midst of the newly-resumed troubles. It was mid-August, and the Unionist government had just tried internment as what turned out to be their last gasp.

On August 9, 1971, the British army "lifted" 363 men in Derry and Belfast, imprisoning them without charge and indefinitely, as the law allowed at that time. The result, of course, was deep resentment and resistance on the part of the minority community, from which 361 of the "lifted" men had come. We encountered their spirit in Sligo that Sunday, when a young couple sat down at our table in the crowded restaurant and told us of their hopes and fears. He had just come back from two weeks "fighting the Brits" on his holidays; she, a young mother of two, told us she thought it was simply necessary for him to do so, for the children's sake. We began to understand the conflict a little better.

The Jesuit International Ecumenist Congress was held in Dublin the following week, and we heard four clergy from the various traditions in Northern Ireland speak to the matter of the conflict. Their common statement that "it is not a religious war" became the truest truism of the next few years. They spoke of the inequities suffered by the poor of both sides of the political and religious divide, and of the disastrous effect of the army's trying to do police work without training and without the will for it. I was reminded of the stories heard during my boyhood, when Mary Burke from Ireland helped my mother with the nine children of the Bowman family, and told us of the "Black-and-Tans" of the early 1920s. In 1971, the stories seemed all too familiar, and all too frightening.

Returning to New York, I reported to the governing board of the National Council of Churches, and found to my pleased surprise that there was a great concern for Northern Ireland in many denominations, especially the United Presbyterian Church in the U.S.A., the Presbyterian Church of the U.S., the Episcopalians, the Methodists, and many Baptists, including Dr. R.H. Edwin Espy, general secretary of NCC, U.S.A. He not only allowed, but urged me to continue my interest in Ireland and Northern Ireland, so that gradually my time was more and more spent on this issue. The American churches at the time were simply baffled and bothered by the seemingly senseless and unnecessary conflict in the island of Ireland. Many of the clergy had good friends in Northern Ireland, and wondered why the Christian churches could not prevent or at least lessen the bitterness that obviously separated the two communities there.

That was the real beginning of my deep concern for the people of Northern Ireland. In January of 1972, en route back from a Jesuit meeting in Rome, I met Rev. Donald Campion, S.J., then editor of *America*, and Rev. Wesley Baker, of the United Presbyterian Church in the U.S.A., for a week's insertion into the Irish conflict. In Dublin we visited politicians, trade unionists, church people, newsmen, and had a memorable late-night rendezvous with two of the leaders of the Provisional IRA, Sean MacStiofain and David O'Connell. The latter jokingly told us that they would send word ahead to the North to "the boys" not to harm us, and I must say that we were happy about this assurance. We set out for the North with great anticipation and some trepidation; neither of the others had been there before, and I had been there only once.

We stayed with Archbishop Simms, primate of the Church of Ireland in Armagh, and heard the sound of bombs exploding nearby. We recalled the promise of the Provisional IRA leaders, and assured the archbishop that his palace would remain unharmed. We were grateful to him and his wife, Mercy, for their gracious hospitality, and perhaps above all for the electric blanket with which they supplied us. It was cold and wet in Northern Ireland then, just as it is now.

We stopped in Cookstown where we had an appointment with Bernadette Devlin, who was much in the news at that time. Her sister came to the door, however, and informed us that Bernadette had been called to London the day before and would not be home to see us. We headed for Belfast along the M1 motorway, and had our first sight of carbines pointed at our heads.

It is not a pleasant sight. We were cruising along the four-lane road and were about to pass an army lorry in the back of which were seated perhaps six soldiers. As we came up to them, our driver called attention to the state of readiness of the military, and we saw with some anxiety that six automatic rifles were trained on the four of us. No doubt it was a necessary precaution in those days when army personnel could expect the worst from any passing car, but it still was a disturbing experience to go through for the first time.

With the passage of time, it no longer disturbs. (It only bothers you to think that you are not even disturbed by it any more.) In Belfast we had an unforgettable visit. We stayed for three days with the Redemptorist community in the Clonard Monastery in the heart of the Republican community. Our car, with its southern license plates, seemed safe within the walls of the monastery and parked up against the church.

It was life in a different world, of course. Even though we had been concerned with the conflict during our days in Dublin, we simply could not have imagined the situation in Belfast. The Brian Faulkner Unionist Party was in apparently complete control of the situation; that party had governed the province for the entire fifty-one years of its existence. Serious discrimination in regard to housing, jobs, police-community relations, and justice in the courts of law was all too often the lot of the poor, as was proved by commission after commission sent over later by the British government. The situation was deteriorating rapidly, and even we on such a short visit could see this.

Brian Faulkner, who later risked and lost his political power by accepting the concept of an "Irish dimension" to an all-island settlement, told us on Friday, January 28, that the army had the Provisional IRA well in hand, and was simply engaged in a cleaning-up exercise. Two days later, on Bloody Sunday, fourteen people were killed during a civil rights march in Derry, and the Faulkner government never recovered.

One of the Irish priests at Clonard took us to see people living in the tiny houses of the neighborhood so that we could hear some stories directly from those affected. One man had only recently been given the opportunity to learn to work a buttonhole-making machine. He had never been offered a job before in his life, and he was forty-three years old. His joy at becoming a productive citizen was obvious; his past history of unemployment was due only to the impossibility of finding a job. The parish priest assured us that there were hundreds like him in that parish, and thousands in the city of Belfast in the minority ghettos.

On Saturday, January 29, there was trouble at a civil rights march in Dungannon. We had wanted to observe this, or else the one in Derry on Sunday, but a rather heavy snowfall on Sunday morning prevented our making the one-hundred-mile trip to the west. Instead, we drove back to Dublin, only to hear that evening of the killing of fourteen people in Derry. We seriously considered returning to the North to confront the politicians and church people we had seen, but our Irish friends adamantly opposed this, so that we were left only the emotionally unsatisfactory step of flying home on Monday. With only a week's experience of Ireland and Northern Ireland, we had become convinced of two things: people there are in danger of being immobilized by the latest atrocity, and outsiders may have some supportive role to play if they offer services humbly.

In the plane on the way home, Wes Baker, the Presbyterian, felt even more strongly than Don and I that we had been given a special grace by God which we could not ignore: the grace of that experience, which impelled us to tell Americans what we thought and what we hoped. By the time we reached New York, we had agreed to try to start a group that would be interested in and of service to the Irish, North and South. That group came to be known as "Colleagues from American Churches."

Wes and I reported to the governing board of the National

Council of Churches and challenged the ecumenical organization to "do something" to be of service to people in Northern Ireland. A young Presbyterian seminarian, Jim Annelin, immediately came to us and volunteered his services. This led to a trip by Jim and me at Easter, on which we looked for opportunities for Americans to be of service. We visited Norman Taggart, the part-time secretary of the Irish Council of Churches, who gave us two names: Ray Davey of the Corrymeela Reconciliation Community in Ballycastle, and John Maultside, of St. Joseph's Boys School in the Creggan, Derry. We visited them, asking whether American volunteers would be of any help to them the next summer, and promising to try to find such volunteers on our return to the U.S.A. Ray and John put us on to other people, and we ended with requests for seventeen American volunteers. Our idea was to supply these in mixed pairs, Catholic and Protestant, so that their very presence would be a witness to the loving unity of Christ's church. We came home and recruited the seventeen, including my niece, Kate Hopkins, and her brother Pete, as well as Wes Baker's son, Ernie. They fitted into programs already planned and run by the people of Belfast and Derry; they lived with these people and shared their lives. As usually happens with volunteers in such situations, they all felt later that they had been far more enriched than they had enriched others.

Almost all of our volunteers were pulled out of the North that summer when "Operation Motorman" became imminent to open up the "no-go" areas of Belfast and Derry. Tension became so great that about a thousand people per day were leaving the North for Dublin, practically as refugees.

All our volunteers returned home safely at summer's end except for Kate, who stayed on at Corrymeela. One of the first things that Colleagues did was find the money to keep Kate there for an extra three months. A second good thing done by Colleagues was a visit by two Presbyterian couples, the Shaws and the Pardees, to all the Irish groups who had utilized American volunteers that summer. The Pardees wrote a lengthy evaluation, both of the programs and of the Irish reactions to American participation; this evaluation proved of the greatest use to us in planning future activities of Colleagues. For 1973, we found thirty-three positions for American volunteers; this was the largest single group that we enabled to go over at any one time. During the six subsequent summers, positions were found for about forty more Americans in all. We feel that the major reason for the decline in requests was that young people from Northern Ireland have been volunteering themselves for work of this kind in sufficient numbers to make it much less desirable to have outsiders come. In this sense, we feel that we helped to achieve something very good.

So much for the first part of these "First Impressions." I would like to reflect a bit now on some of the personal aspects of beginning work like this in a province like Northern Ireland. What did it mean for an outsider like myself to try to be of service to people caught in such an unyielding conflict?

First of all, it meant coming to know and love a great many people from both sides of the community. This alone made the years of relatively fruitless concern seem much more than worthwhile. The women and men of Northern Ireland are heroines and heroes, caught in a conflict not of their own making and striving against all odds to humanize and reconcile their surroundings. Not all of them, of course, but the great majority of them are this way. They see a tiny minority of violent people at the extreme ends of the community determined on victory over "the others" at any cost. They are baffled, frustrated, disappointed—but never defeated. They are the "ordinary" people of Northern Ireland.

For a Jesuit priest from outside, however, they were a long time in coming to trust. Outsiders find it difficult to gain the confidence of insiders in any society, and the abnormal conditions of the political and civic circumstances of Northern Ireland only make the process much more difficult. You can well imagine what a quantum leap in faith it must take for a Protestant to come to believe that a Jesuit priest could have Protestant values and sensitivities at heart in the face of the obvious difficulties for Catholics in Northern Ireland. I, of course, was unable to win over some, no matter what I did or said. It was a slow process with all, even those who were fairly well-disposed. Language at times caused real problems, since the same words simply carry different connotations in America and Northern Ireland; more than once I had to explain what I meant by phrases and sentences which seemed threatening or simply false to my listeners or readers.

"What's he visiting there for?" was a reiterated query, and could refer to the Northern Ireland Office in Belfast, the Clonard Monastery, the home of a Presbyterian or a Methodist or a Catholic, or practically anywhere else that I went. For a full year, I did not stay with my Jesuit brethren in the South, since I was accused of "plotting" against the best interests of the people with whom I was working in the North. You learn to live with such accusations, of course, and simply to live through them until trust has been established or re-established. Thanks be to God, mutual confidence was the usual relationship that I had, once friendship had been established.

People wonder about discouragement. Surely everyone who lives and works for reconciliation in the North is bound to be discouraged at times. Listening to one of Mr. Paisley's vitriolic sermons, or visiting unfeeling military chaplains at army bases, or listening to the "little people" give instances when they tried and failed to reach the ministers of the gospel with their hurts and hopes—these were discouraging moments. The failure of neighborhood people to control or reject the violent among them remains a source of keen disappointment to me. The apparent impossibility of crossing political-denominational lines even to pray during the week of prayer for Christian unity was deeply distressing. The hostility encountered by laity trying to change the community dynamics in matters like mixed marriage and segregated schools was sometimes due to misunderstanding, but all too often it represented the unrelenting narrowness of prejudiced people. And constant through all such experiences was my own failure to be sufficiently sensitive to all these people. Discouragement was fairly frequent.

So was danger, and no doubt this had something to do with the discouragement. Car bombs exploding a block away, gunfire going over the roof of the car as you backed it furiously around a corner in the Suffolk area, explosions seemingly going off all around you in the downtown area, just the sight of the barbed wire and the iron fences and the obstructions in the road—all these contribute a negative dimension to visits and life in Northern Ireland. One night we stood in the rain outside the headquarters of the Ulster Defence Association, waiting for their leaders to arrive and fearful that any passing vehicle might open fire on us in the dark. I rarely stayed in a hotel, mainly because friends or "bed and breakfast" places were much nicer to stay in, but also because five of the six hotels in which I ever did stay were bombed at one time or another.

One November evening as we left a Republican home in Andersonstown, we failed to turn down our headlights as we approached an army patrol. At once, sharpshooters materialized at either side of our car, guns trained on us and fingers on the triggers. You may be sure it was the last time we drove with high beams in an area like that. But after awhile you do become used to having guns pointed at you, little as you like it.

Meanwhile, the people live as if the dimension of violence is not there, difficult as it is to disregard it. Actually, the most dangerous moment for me was while driving on the Ballygawley Road near Dungannon in a midnight rain, when the left front wheel went into the muck on a turn and the whole car followed it down into the ditch. When we arrived at the hospital, the nurse on duty said simply: "The Ballygawley Road, isn't it? We get a constant stream from there in this weather." Nursing my bruises, I wished that someone had told us before we hit that almost fatal curve.

Counterbalancing the discouragement and the danger, however, was always the deep appreciation of the people. Their profound faith and bubbling good humor are guaranteed to carry them through all adversity, it seems. The members of the churches belonging to the Irish Council of Churches struck me not so much as bureaucrats, but as devoted servants of our Lord, ready to run risks for the sake of the gospel. David Bleakley, a Church of Ireland layman, combines the fire of a lay preacher with the political wisdom of an ex-politician in serving the Irish Council of Churches as executive secretary. In 1974, some of the most prominent Protestant leaders of the North did what no politician would do, and risked their careers thereby. They met with the Provisional IRA Army Council at a place called Feakle in County Clare (Republic), to tell them what unionists of the North really feel about the violence of the Provisional IRA. Rev. William Arlow became trusted by both extremes of the paramilitary groups, thereby incurring the anger of all the governments concerned, but giving a credibility to the churches that otherwise would have been impossible. Rev. Eric Gallagher and his wife Barbara embodied the wise kindness of the Methodist church as few others in my experience ever have. Archbishop George Simms and now Archbishop John Armstrong, primates of the Church of Ireland, were always strongly supportive and understanding. Cardinal Tomas O Fiaich, a strong Nationalist, is gaining greater influence constantly because people know that he says what he thinks and opposes violence whatever its source. Corrymeela in the North and Glencree in the South stand forth as beacons of reconciliation in what can be stormy nights. And there are always the wee people in the back streets working, praying, and hoping that the day of justice and peace will soon dawn. They know that political change will come only when conditions are right for the violence to cease and for the two communities to come together in honest dialogue. How this may come about may escape them, but that it will happen is their unshakable conviction. The women and men of Northern Ireland deserve the dawning of such a day soon.

I have just now returned from an Irish Council of Churches annual assembly on March 18-19, 1983. The situation seemed to remain the same. But on St. Patrick's Day at his grave in Downpatrick, an ecumenical service marked the occasion—a holiday and a holy day in both North and South. He belongs to *all* in the island; perhaps his example and prayers are our best hope for justice and peace.

NOTES THEN AND NOW   Lynne Shivers

1970   On my first visit to Northern Ireland, I remember all sorts of flags: Union Jack, the Ulster flag, different signs of identity for segments of society. In the 1960s a Catholic raised the Irish tricolor flag, and a riot followed. Ever since, it has been illegal to show that flag in Northern Ireland. Some Protestants have painted their curbs red, white, and blue. Signs of the military are everywhere: sandbags piled up, jeeps and armored cars. It is unnerving to see soldiers with loaded guns downtown; people walk past trying not to show that they notice. A woman explained that her greatest fear is not knowing what governments and organizations are planning next. I learned how some people have enormous resiliency. The real surprise is not why people are depressed, but how they come out of depression and keep on going.

. . . I initially visited Northern Ireland because I was invited by a community organizer working in Belfast. We were both attending a conference in England called to examine whether training methods in nonviolent action developed in the U.S. were limited to use there or if they were also applicable elsewhere. The organizer thought that my experience in training hundreds of marshals in nonviolent techniques might be applicable in Belfast. He explained that Orange

Order paraders coming home after a day of marching would sometimes deliberately walk past Catholic areas. Being tipsy, the marchers would toss bottles and stones, provoking fights. My friend suggested that perhaps block organizers would benefit from discussing the viability of unofficial nonviolent peace-keeping on the neighborhood level.

As it turned out, my visit coincided with an army-imposed curfew. Neighborhood organizers were too busy responding to the crisis to meet with us. But the visit began a permanent relationship with Northern Ireland and its people.

I experienced the potential of Northern Ireland at a Belfast community meeting. A professor spoke about how the conflict is about redefining democracy and how much people will participate in government. People were angry and spoke powerfully. Then I experienced day-to-day reality when the meeting ended abruptly. We heard stones hit the windows. That was not enough to frighten people, but there was no way to tell if it would end with stones. As we left, one woman described how tear gas blew through the neighborhood until four in the morning, and her children had been nauseous.

. . . It occurs to me that things are so bad here that people have long ago given up on piecemeal solutions and are searching for permanent ones. And when they are not found, people become frustrated and angry. If individuals lose the right to make decisions for themselves, they lose their sense of self-worth.

. . . I read in a British newspaper a story about a professor who claims that the Irish people and the American Blacks have an IQ averaging about fifteen points lower than British people or white Americans. (How many times have we heard that line?) The headline was "Irish Aren't as Brainy as the English, Says Prof." Racism and stereotypes sound the same the world over.

1971   The more I read about Northern Ireland the more I ask myself: Is there anything I can constructively do? I have gotten past the point where I think I have answers. During my visit last summer, I kept asking myself, "Why don't they just sit down and talk things out? Why don't they create more jobs? Why don't they pour money in for welfare relief?" Now I see that "they" haven't done these things because "they" can't (or won't?)! Too much fear, too much unemployment, too many people who have emigrated or died. There is thirty percent unemployment in some sections.

. . . Impressions of a walk around Derry at night: The abnormal silence. The roar and echo of the army vehicles. The street after street of charred shells of empty houses, windows out, walls covered with boards or plastic. The discount sales of damaged goods. Signs which announce "Still open for business." How alert I am to notice anything unusual: loud noises, people standing in clusters, someone running. How few people are out at night. Soldiers checking everywhere. Dark shadows. Men against the wall being frisked.

. . . Coming back from the house we were renovating was unnerving. Two soldiers were positioned where they usually weren't; a certain gate of the old city wall was locked, so I had to go around; the frisking was more aggressive than usual. I saw a mother standing in the doorway. She called to her young daughter to come inside. I could clearly hear tension and fear in her voice. Then I knew something important was going on in the city. At supper with other people from the workcamp, I learned what it was: soldiers had been searching houses for arms. A friend said one of the kids in the afternoon told her, "I have to go...the soldiers are at my house."

. . . After the workcamp ended, I stayed in Belfast for a few days to see old friends. One night we stayed up late, talking. We decided to drive them home. The street we wanted to take was closed off, so we drove the longer way around. The residential area we drove through had no street lights; I was told that soldiers shoot them out so the IRA will not have easy targets. All of a sudden in the darkness ahead, I noticed a soldier in the middle of the street with a rifle trained on us, and someone else shouting at us to stop. I saw a second soldier kneeling in the street, also with a pointed rifle, and a third soldier between two houses with another pointed rifle. We stopped and were ordered to get out; they searched the car thoroughly. The first thing they found was a box of powder paints left over from the workcamp. And the first one they opened was gray, and I imagined in my fear that it was the color of gunpowder. We were finally released. As we turned the corner and drove up a hill, we saw a large armored vehicle backing down the hill and turning a corner, right where we were headed! The thing was so huge and was making so much noise that the driver could not possibly hear or see our car. It looked like a mountain coming down on us. We quickly reversed and swerved around. We dropped our friends off and returned home the same way. The same group of soldiers stopped us again, but let us go when they realized our actions verified our earlier story. As we drove off, one soldier called out: "Don't turn on your lights so soon," referring to the danger they had of being shot.

I did not sleep for a long time that night because I heard continuous rifle-fire sounds for forty-five minutes. I learned the next morning that there had been a major battle around the hospital. The soldiers were tense because we were just a mile and a half from the shooting.

. . . I hear more and more about protection rackets and the widespread intimidation they generate all over the North, especially in the cities. In some sections, people are required to pay a certain amount each week to live there—not much, about five cents a week or so. But people are afraid not to pay. I suppose businesses and little shops have to pay more. It is one way the paramilitary groups control their areas. No one knows any details...

1973. . . A friend and I were sorting clothes to give away, and we heard a voice making an announcement through a bullhorn in the street. We could not understand exactly what the man was saying except something . . . something . . . "immediately." We guessed it had to do with a bomb planted somewhere. A few minutes later we heard an enormous BANG! followed by a wall of acrid smoke drifting toward us. Then a fire started in the gas station which had exploded (only a ten-pound bomb, I learned later), then dozens of smaller explosions, perhaps oil cans exploding from the heat of the fire. Then twenty minutes later, another large bang. No injuries, since there was enough advance warning. My friend, who lived through some of the London Blitz in World War II, saw I was still on edge. To calm me, she said, "It's over now, it's all right." And she was right; I realized that until she spoke I kept expecting more explosions.

. . . One Catholic woman told me how she urged a soldier to get out of her garden since a sniper could shoot him from any angle. And the soldier refused to leave, thinking she simply wanted him out of her garden!

We took a bunch of kids to the countryside to play in an old fort. The view was spectacular: mountains to the north, small lakes, small towns, and green, green hills. Coming back, we drove into the Catholic area and right into the back of a riot. The memory of the scene is like a silent movie since I remember no sounds. The first thing I saw was soldiers walking backwards toward us. As we drove on, we saw stones landing all around the car. Then we saw the kids who were throwing the stones, then their parents standing in doorways shouting to the soldiers to leave the area. What I remember most is people's expressions: they were all the same, for soldiers, kids and adults alike: hatred, panic, terror, and grief behind their eyes.

1976. . . Saidie Patterson of Women Together has written, "It will be the women who will overcome in the end, not the politicians nor the soldiers." Intuitively, I know this to be true, but is there anything more substantial than intuition to support this idea? Saidie Patterson wrote this five years after Women Together had begun and nine months before Betty Williams and Mairead Corrigan formed the Community of the Peace People. I think the main reason that women will "overcome" is that they are not caught up in the connection between masculinity and militarism. In a society where so many men are out of work, they feel depressed and useless, and where the paramilitary tradition is so strong, men see no alternative other than taking up guns for what seems to be the survival of their values. Women, on the other hand, while they are influenced by the same forces and traditions, are not expected to pick up guns; they are expected to raise the children and stay home. But the situation has affected them as well.

I think it has taken women longer than men to move out of restricted roles - "Stay at home, this is men's work" - but when they did move, it was movement in different directions. I cannot help but think that when Northern Irish women have moved ahead for social change, their activities have been innovative and dramatic. They acted in unique ways in their own situation. When men acted, they moved in traditional ways: armed military struggle.

This is not precisely true: it is only a general observation. Many men have acted in innovative ways and created alternatives. Here I think especially of Rev. Joe Parker, whose son was killed as a result of a bomb explosion. Rev. Parker founded Witness for Peace which helped many other people find their voices. And some women acted in traditional ways by joining women's branches of the paramilitary groups.

1977. . . Over and over again, Gandhi wrote that the biggest obstacle to social change is fear. This is certainly true in Northern Ireland. People fear government initiatives. What will they do next? Where will the initiatives lead people? Where will they come from? People have had the sense of being victims of forces they cannot see and do not understand. They feel that they are being manipulated and that they are not in control of their lives. Events happen to people, rather than people creating events by acting and changing their lives. People especially fear the British army and paramilitary organizations. It is especially hard to move against the fear when others who have acted have been intimidated, terrorized, or even killed. How can the "other side" be human when they have shot so many of "our side"?

Women Together, the Derry women's peace initiative, and Betty Williams's and Mairead Corrigan's actions electrified people in Northern Ireland. When these actions took place—1970, 1972, and 1976—all the focus was on these activities for a while. They all created hope, they loosened the tangle of contradictions and dilemmas for a while, gave people a vision of how they, too, might act on their situation, and they challenged the usual roles of women and men. Most of all, these initiatives fought the fear.

1977. . . I found in the attic of my house an old trunk filled with books and pictures left behind by former owners. Included were a history of Ireland, an atlas of Ireland, the family Bible, and a two-volume history of the United States, as well as photographs of the owners' homestead in Ireland. I became aware of nostalgia for someone else's heritage. The history of Ireland became vivid for me; I seemed to experience someone else's history. I imagined Irish immigrants mentally weighing books about Ireland in one hand and books about America in the other.

Richard Rose, in his book *Northern Ireland: A Time of Choice,* has written that the essential problem of Northern Ireland is that there is NO SOLUTION. What a devastating statement! Does this mean that the people of Northern Ireland are condemned to conflict and division all their lives? Yet Rose outlines fifteen different ways in which a settlement might take place, and they are important to keep in mind: self-government within the United Kingdom, rule by a Loyalist majority, rule by a broad Unionist coalition, power-sharing within the parliamentary framework, power-sharing by a non-parliamentary representative government, continuing direct rule, integration within Great Britain, an independent Northern Ireland, a unilateral declaration of independence, negotiated independence, unification with the Republic of Ireland, a federal Ireland, British-Irish condominium rule, the transfer of Northern Ireland to the Republic of Ireland, and repartition by local option ballot. All these options have factors for and against them as ways out of the present situation. But they are all better than the last option: civil war. Even though some of these options are far from likely, it is important to remember that they are options, lest we think that the last option is the only one.

1978. . . Someone asked me years ago: if I had a million dollars to use in changing conditions which promote injustice and violence in Northern Ireland, how would I use it? I've never been able to give a satisfactory answer. Surely I would try to do some of the things that the reconciliation groups are doing, especially developing local employment through cooperatives, reopening factories, creating jobs. I would also open the houses presently bricked up and standing empty. This would also provide employment, since jobs could be created by hiring people to take down the cinder blocks and clean out the houses. Some of the million would go toward developing pilot projects of integrated schools and developing curricula for the teaching of history and religion. (I don't think integrated schools would solve everything, but I would like to see a good try at it.)

But how can an outsider know? We can't. It is in the final analysis impossible to act for someone else. But we can find ways to support people in Northern Ireland who continue to struggle and endure. How different Northern Ireland feels in the country than in Belfast and Derry! It is as though there is no war at all: hills and valleys, little houses, lovely gardens, and the enormous sweep of the sky with clouds forever blowing over (unless there is fog or rain). Such a contrast of war and peace cannot be imagined; it is only to be experienced. There are a few signs of war in the country—sheet-metal fences around army posts, an occasional flag, political graffiti. And some gruesome murders have taken place there, but nothing like in the cities.

1980. . . What can we learn from events in Northern Ireland? I do not have a final answer, but many issues come to mind. The consequences of ignoring the causes of violence have been enormous. For two generations, Unionists preferred to ignore discrimination. Mean houses, miserable jobs or no jobs at all, discriminatory electoral laws: all these practices went on and on and guilt and grievances piled up. People got used to the system, and no one felt there was any hope of change. People became accustomed to not seeing what was there to see.

The consequences of monolithic politics have also been enormous. If there had been many political traditions respecting one another, various cultures rubbing against each other, perhaps people would have developed the idea that different traditions have a right to live side by side. People seemed more in love with justifying their ideas through the precedent-setting brutalities of history than dealing with present realities of injustice and cruelty.

But the consequences of fear have been the most critical force of all. People fear the "other side." They believe almost with the force of a commitment that change is impossible, so do not bother trying. Fear of the "other side" brings people to think that they must be tough and ruthless, since small efforts against seemingly monolithic opposition will be in vain. People have feared that small compromises will allow the opposition to win; compromises feel like the beginning of the end. People fear that everyone is against them, and they believe they must defend their values completely alone.

Overriding all this are the consequences of war. People are polite but refuse to be straight and honest because of fear of not knowing where other people stand on important issues. Better not to speak out for fear that others will disagree. And disagreements might mean harassment, your children followed home, intimidation to get out of the neighborhood in forty-eight hours or worse. These are not empty fears since they have happened to people you know in your own neighborhood.

The dreadful consequences of violence: so many lost their homes; some destroyed their own homes so that the "other side" could not move in. The strong sense of local community creates an enormous pressure to conform to others' views. There seems to be no room to move or speak out. I have driven through Belfast and seen mile after mile of houses bricked up (as much from redevelopment as from intimidation) and standing empty while people live in substandard houses a few miles away. No wonder one-fourth of the adult population in Derry was on tranquilizers at one time! No wonder children would wake up crying when they heard fire sirens at night. No wonder the awful graffiti. A wall message in Ballymurphy: "Is there life before death?" Lots of people doubt it.

I have been surprised at the mixture of military strategies, reliance on bombs and bullets and assassinations, with nonviolent strategies: sit-downs, marches, refusal to pay taxes, various forms of boycotts and noncooperation, petitions and pledges, vigils, prayer meetings, official letters being sent, people taking stands in spite of possible violent retaliation.

I have been deeply moved by the enormous courage of all those who have spoken out against the murders and violence and the refusal to accept the divisions any longer. Individuals, especially women, have risked their security and families to stand for what is right and to act against what is wrong. They have acted often as individuals without support. Sometimes groups have taken action, knowing that funds or staff would leave if the action became too risky.

How many of us would be able to act with such courage? Yet some people who have acted often deny courage on their part. It was just something they had to do.

Lynne Shivers

The Orange Order parade in Belfast. Each Orange Order Lodge
has its own banner.

Brad Lyttle

Provies rule. A house bricked up and a reminder to neighbors
of Provisional IRA local power. Londonderry

Two British soldiers in green uniforms pose with a member of the police, the Royal Ulster Constabulary.

British soldiers in Londonderry.

Chapter 2

Sorting Out The Power Structure

To an outsider, the number of political organizations in Northern Ireland is very confusing. For a population of a million and a half, at least a dozen political parties are in the field. Some of them seem constantly changing, or at least changing their names. We need to identify the various groups which have figured most often in Ulster politics and public life and most often shape people's lives.

The main polarization of political ideologies in Northern Ireland is between the Unionist/Loyalist position and the Nationalist/ Republican tradition.

Unionists and Loyalists (the two-thirds political majority in Northern Ireland). All Unionists stand for union with Great Britain and the Crown in the United Kingdom of Great Britain and Northern Ireland (U.K.). They therefore regard the six-county Ulster (in which they live) as an integral part of the U.K., like Scotland and Wales. Another generic name for them is Loyalists, i.e., loyal to the Crown and to "Protestant Ulster," since probably ninety-eight percent of them would identify religiously with a Protestant tradition if with any.

A majority of Loyalists has been adamantly opposed to "power-sharing" or co-responsibility at the executive level. Some of them would favor it at the committee level, but this has so far been unacceptable to the minority politicians.

Nationalists and Republicans (the one-third political minority in Northern Ireland). As distinct from Unionists, Nationalists in general stand for some kind of eventual thirty-two-county Ireland— union not with the United Kingdom but among all the people of the island called Ireland, to make one "nation." They therefore dislike the six-county "Ulster" as a gerrymandered part of the ancient nine-county province of Ulster, and want an eventual "agreed Ireland" of which the North would be an integral part—but by consent, not by force. The form of government would be whatever the nation agrees on. About ninety-eight percent of them would be baptized Roman Catholics.

Republicans is a generic name for those Nationalists who want some kind of republic, although not necessarily the present "Republic of Ireland," extended through the thirty-two counties. Many of them follow a political rather than a military strategy, looking to some federation or association of North and South in which all sections would have devolved self-government.

All brands of the Republican tradition take some of their vision from Wolfe Tone, who was inspired by the ideas of the French Revolution. His analysis was that various Irish religious traditions could unite under the banner of Irish nationalism. He said, "Irishmen [sic] could unite under the common name of Irish—neither Catholic, Protestant, or Dissenter."

Within these two main traditions, or political ideologies, are dozens of political parties, quasi-political organizations, security forces, and paramilitary groups. In a highly polarized conflict, disagreement often leads to splinter groups that form, build, and dissolve as the conflict changes. Northern Ireland is a highly political conflict, and the various stands taken seem incomprehensible unless one is willing to study the differences. It is these differences which fuel the conflict and continue it.

Most political conflicts can be understood within a right-left political specturm. Northern Ireland does not fit into this continuum since qualities of "right-left" can be found in both the Unionist and Republican traditions. Thus, we use the continuum of Unionist and Republican instead of left and right.

We group organizations here according to where they fall along this spectrum. Political parties, quasi-political groups, and paramilitary groups are considered together. At first this may seem confusing, but we have decided it is more useful than arranging all the political parties together across the spectrum, then all the paramilitary groups, and so on. Some organizations often deny that there is any connection between them (e.g., Provisional Sinn Fein and Provisional IRA). But groups in the same tradition obviously have a lot in common, if only their main political goals. Often the link is much closer, even to the degree of overlapping memberships.

And people in Northern Ireland link them, so we should as well. The disclaimers are often for important reasons: some groups are illegal, and if a person is found to be a member s/he could serve a prison term.

A special note about paramilitary groups: these began in Northern Ireland as "citizen armies" to protect their areas and people. They often evolved into military forces, expressing political viewpoints, often connected ideologically with a political party. Some groups have lasted for decades; others have disappeared in a matter of months. Some existing groups are very large, others are small. Some groups include women.

Two elements in common are secrecy and military discipline. Information about them is therefore hard to obtain. Clearly, their control of areas is based largely on fear and intimidation. Their military discipline is rough, often imposed brutally. In the official record of casualties for Northern Ireland, members of paramilitary organizations are listed as "civilians" along with those who did not belong to any paramilitary group. This accounts in part for the high number of civilian casualties.

These groups have continuously changed tactics and politics, so it is necessary to ascertain the latest information on them from current sources. They have not only fought the army, the Royal Ulster Constabulary and their counterparts on the other side. They have regularly engaged in interfactional feuds, which have been fiercer and bloodier than the other armed conflicts.

A final note, pertinent to all the nomenclature of paramilitaries. It is often simply impossible for anyone to figure out who has done a bombing or shooting. Almost all the current international terrorist nomenclature is used from time to time and from year to year. Some of those taking credit for recent violence may well be just one person in a phone booth calling the security number. That person might be a maverick or a psychotic, or simply someone who has worked off a personal feud under the cover of the civic conflict. Code numbers are given to some organized groups, so the security forces will know immediately that it is a legitimate communication. On occasion, however, one group has accused another of lying about responsibility, attributing it to another organization, or claiming responsibility for something done by another. The situation has been and will remain extremely confusing.

MAJORITY ORGANIZATIONS

1. Orange Order
2. Democratic Unionist Party
3. United Ulster Unionist Party
4. Ulster Defence Association
5. Ulster Freedom Fighters
6. Ulster Volunteer Force
7. Ulster Special Constabulary
8. Smaller Loyalist groups
9. Vigilantes
10. Official Unionist Party
11. Ulster Loyalist Democratic Party
12. Ulster Independence Party

1. Orange Order

The Orange Order is the largest single Unionist body. It dates from 1795 and is essentially a social institution with a strong religious and political orientation. It is not a political party. Its influence, however, has been strongly political, and its goal has been to maintain the status quo of complete majority dominance. For many years, membership in the Orange Order was practically necessary for political advancement in the majority party which the Order helped to found, much as trade unions have helped to found Labour parties. About fifteen hundred lodges are scattered throughout Northern Ireland, each with a chaplain, who is often a Protestant minister. An estimated one hundred thousand members (about one-third of the total Protestant adult males in Northern Ireland) take part in Orange parades each year.

It is important to note that Orange Order membership cuts across class barriers. The Order has considerable political influence because of its size, class membership, and structure. The Grand Master of the Order is Presbyterian Rev. Martin Smyth; Grand Master in Belfast is Thomas Passmore. Free Presbyterian ministers (such as Ian Paisley) have not been allowed to be chaplains in the Order. For many, especially in rural areas, the lodge has been the only social club available for the majority, and has served as a focus for neighborhood life.

Lawrence Orr, leading Orange Order member and once a leading Unionist politician, said in 1970, "Without the Orange Order there would have been no Unionist Party and no union. If the Orange Order and the Unionist party were to be separated, the Unionist Party would cease to exist as such."

2. Democratic Unionist Party

The Democratic Unionist Party (DUP), led by Rev. Ian Paisley and Peter Robinson, stands mainly for extreme populism, and regularly gains about one-eighth of the votes and seats in elections. Founded in 1971, the DUP insists that the majority should have their "democratic right" to have the say in running their own country. More than any other party, the DUP is associated with a particular sectarian church, the Free Presbyterian Church, founded by Rev. Paisley, which is in no way associated with the mainline Presbyterian Church in Ireland.

The DUP has staunchly opposed sharing executive political power with any party of the minority in Northern Ireland, parties which they regard as disloyal. The DUP also defends its differences with Official Unionists; for example, the DUP took a firm anti-EEC (European Economic Community) line.

Since the leader of this party is also the founder-moderator of the Free Presbyterian Church (around forty thousand members, with one congregation in the Republic) and habitually wears clerical clothes, it seems useful to speak a bit here about the church as well as the party. Rev. Paisley is a dominating man with a dominating personality, and uses the pulpit of his Martyrs Memorial Church on Ravenhill Road to attack "enemies" of the ultra-evangelical "Protestant Ulster" of which he dreams. He has an honorary degree from Bob Jones University in South Carolina, and regularly visits the U.S. and Canada on fundraising trips, mainly in the Bible Belt and Toronto. His church publishes the weekly *Protestant Telegraph*, a jumble of in-group news, pseudo-history and political demagoguery. Ironically, he insists on separation of church and state. He opposes the ecumenical movement and identifies it with the World

Council of Churches, which he attacks as a step to slavery to Rome. His influence has been considerable in both government and ecclesiastical circles. His reelection to the Westminster parliament in May 1979 and to the European parliament in June 1979 increased his political strength with his constituency. The Democratic Unionist Party won 20% of the vote in the Westminster June 1983 election, while it won 23% of the vote in the Assembly election in October, 1982.

3. United Ulster Unionist Party

The UUUP, led by Ernest Baird, represents hard-line sentiments, tough law-and-order measures, and political positions close to those of Ian Paisley—sometimes even further to the right. The party was formed in 1977; in 1979, it received 5.6 percent of the total vote. Some of its members have occasionally been in favor of a "Third Force" of vigilantes (besides the army and the RUC) to attack the IRA and wipe it out, or at the least to patrol the border of special majority areas. Many of the Ulster Special Constabulary (USC) and of the former B-Specials (see page 51) are oriented toward this party.

4. Ulster Defence Association (UDA)

A paramilitary organization, the UDA was formed in 1970 from a number of Loyalist vigilante groups and local defense associations, mainly in reaction to the Provisional IRA. Its tactics up to 1974 replicated those of the Provos: no-go areas, barricades, "romper rooms" for physical violence against individuals, and killings. The UDA is legal and has been by far the largest of the Loyalist paramilitary groups, once claiming more than fifty thousand members. It formed the heart of the Ulster Workers Council (UWC) which ran the successful strike in May 1974, but failed when it joined Paisley's unsuccessful work stoppage in May 1977. Since then it may have fragmented somewhat, and lost considerable numbers, but guesses are merely guesses. Leaders are Andy Tyrie, Andy Robinson, and Jim Smyth. (See Ulster Loyalist Democratic Party, below.)

5. Ulster Freedom Fighters (UFF)

An illegal group formed a few years ago, the UFF claimed responsibility for a number of assassinations and bombings. Rumor has it that many of its members are dissidents from the UDA, determined to go their own military way without the restrictions placed upon UDA members.

6. Ulster Volunteer Force (UVF)

The UVF was first formed in 1912 as a volunteer army opposed to the Home Rule Bill, which would have established home rule for Ireland within the United Kingdom. It was not an official body and could not officially carry arms. In 1966, the UVF was revived to kill IRA members. The best-known leader, Gusty Spence, was imprisoned for life after he was convicted on a murder charge. The UVF was declared illegal. By 1972, it had a membership of about fifteen hundred and was heavily involved in sectarian assassinations of Catholics. A sensational and costly trial in 1977 resulted in the conviction of twenty-six UVF men, who received a total of seven hundred years' imprisonment, including eight life sentences. The organization, though much smaller, continues.

7. Ulster Special Constabulary (USC)

The USC was originally formed in 1922 when Northern Ireland was created. As late as 1961, only twelve percent of its members were Catholic. There are two different identifications or associations of the USC: (1) the original group, which was a police force (in addition to the RUC) up to 1969; (2) the Ulster Defence Regiment, created in 1970 after the Scarman and Hunt Reports recommended the disbanding of the USC because of its activities during 1968 civil rights agitation.

8. Smaller Loyalist Groups

These include the Red Hand Commandos, the South Orange Volunteers, Tartan Gangs, and whatever others have recently surfaced.

9. Vigilantes

Vigilantes are a common phenomenon in Northern Ireland. Many of them are ad hoc groups formed after a local tragedy or outrage. Some of them are more permanently organized and seem ready to go into action whenever their leadership has decided the moment has come.

10. Official Unionist Party (OUP)

This party, led by James Molyneaux, laid claim in 1974 to the mantle (and offices) of the former Unionist Party (UP) when Brian Faulkner left office. The Unionist Party was the monolithic controlling group in Ulster politics from the time of partition in 1921 until 1972 when "direct rule" began. Its more important leaders were James Craig (Lord Craigavon), 1921-40; Basil Brooke (Lord Brookborough), 1943-62; Terence O'Neill, 1962-69; James Chichester Clarke, 1969-71: and Brian Faulkner, 1971-72, 1974. The monolith began to crack in the late sixties when the civil rights marches appeared. Since then, Unionist parties have formed and reformed, including many described in this section.

The OUP has been by far the biggest and most powerful Unionist party in recent elections—until June 1979. Other prominent leaders are Rev. Martin Smyth, who is also grand master of the Loyal Orange Lodge; Austin Ardill; John Taylor, elected to the European parliament in June 1979, with fifty-five thousand votes, compared to Ian Paisley's 170,000 votes. The Official Unionist Party won 34% of the vote in the Westminster June 1983 electin, while it won 29.7% of the vote in the Assembly October 1982 election.

11. Ulster Loyalist Democratic Party (ULDP)

The ULDP was formed in the summer of 1981 from the New Ulster Political Research Group (NUPRG), which was founded in 1978 by Andy Tyrie, Glen Barr and other Ulster Defence Association (q.v.) men. Glen Barr is no longer with the organization. The NUPRG was neither a political party nor an action group but a research group, a think tank. But the ULDP is a full political party which runs candidates. It advocates a negotiated independent Northern Ireland with a special emphasis on devolution. Devolution is the principle of returning decision-making powers from Great Britain to Northern Ireland levels of government, but the ties with Great Britain would remain.

Tyrie reasons that a political stalemate exists in Northern Ireland which cannot be broken because (1) the majority community is aligned with Great Britain and the minority is aligned with the Republic of Ireland; (2) this polarization is reflected in the sectarian and religious division. So long as this is true in Northern Ireland, politicians will be elected not on the basis of their stands on issues, but because of their religious identity.

Andy Tyrie and John McMichael think that a negotiated independent Northern Ireland is the only solution. They think that Northern Ireland people have more in common with each other than they have differences; they further believe that Northern Ireland people would be viewed as second-class citizens either in a united Ireland or in a United Kingdom federation.

The Ulster Loyalist Democratic Party proposes a U.S-government-type structure with three federal tiers (prime minister, legislature, courts), rather than the British structure in which the head of the majority party in the legislature is the prime minister.

Along with his membership in the ULDP, Tyrie remains chairman of the Ulster Defence Association, the major Unionist paramilitary organization. This may seem incongruous to people outside Northern Ireland, but Tyrie feels it is essential to be part of both organizations. As he put it, the members are trying to strengthen the party's activities and decrease the UDA activities. If

Tyrie were to drop ties with the UDA, his persuasive powers with UDA members would end.

Given the strength and bitterness of the sectarian polarization in Northern Ireland, it seems unlikely that a majority would develop to support a negotiated independent Northern Ireland. But even if this solution is not finally adopted, the ULDP has provided leverage for new ideas to be considered. This is a benefit in itself.

The ULDP is still alive, but it sees less activity than in 1981.

12. Ulster Independence Party

This was formed in 1977. It stands for a negotiated independent Northern Ireland. Not connected with the ULDP, it has a small following.

NON-SECTARIAN ORGANIZATIONS

13. Northern Ireland Labour Party (NILP)

Dates from 1924, but it has never enjoyed the success of the Labour Party in Britain. Its most prominent member has been David Bleakley in the mid-seventies; Brian Garrett is the present leader. The party has some labor-union membership, with policies similar to the British Labour Party. Changing Northern Ireland politics has meant that votes have gone to more polarized political parties. In the 1979 elections, the NILP ran three candidates and they all lost.

14. Alliance Party (AP)

This is one of Northern Ireland's four main political parties and is led by Oliver Napier. It was formed in 1970 largely from the New Ulster Movement and elements from the liberal wing of the old Unionist Party. Napier and others wanted a non-sectarian political party which could bring the two communities together. The Alliance Party has had a good deal of success in trying to reconcile the apparently irreconcilable traditions, but has also met with inevitable antagonism from both sides. It has had Catholic and Protestant membership from its beginning.

Its membership is well-integrated, whereas other parties draw mainly from only one of the communities. The Alliance Party has grown slowly but steadily, gaining strength with its increasing number of elected representatives. Recently it gained one-eighth of the seats in the local elections, but failed to elect anyone to Westminster in 1979. The Alliance Party supported power-sharing until a few years ago, and remains staunchly devoted to reconciliation within the six counties. It stands for a moderate position between the extremes. The Alliance Party won 8% of the vote in the Westminster June 1983 election; it won 9.3% of the vote in the Assembly election in October 1982.

MINORITY ORGANIZATIONS

15. Irish Independence Party
16. Ancient Order of Hibernians
17. Social Democratic and Labour Party
18. Official Irish Republican Army
19. Official Sinn Fein Workers' Party
20. Republican Clubs
21. People's Democracy
22. Provisional Irish Republican Army
23. Provisional Sinn Fein
24. Irish Republican Socialist Party
25. Irish National Liberation Army

Unionist organizations have changed rapidly since 1970, but these changes have been mainly among political parties and organizations. Unionist-related paramilitary groups have remained fairly stable. On the Republican side, however, it is the paramilitary groups which have changed rapidly and continuously since 1970. That history is confusing, but it is essential to understand the changes if we are to understand future political initiatives in Northern Ireland. We interject some historical background before continuing with profiles of organizations.

Changes in the IRA since 1970

The Irish Republican Army is the best-known paramilitary group in Northern Ireland. The original IRA was formed in 1919 at the meeting of the first Dail (the Irish parliament). With roots in the Irish Republican Brotherhood, it was a major fighting force against the British army at first and later against the treaty forces during the Irish civil war of 1922-23. The IRA has surfaced about every decade since then, creating active military campaigns to drive the British government from Northern Ireland.

The split which created the "Officials" and the "Provisionals" occurred in December 1969 at a meeting of the IRA Army Council. A three-to-one vote decided to give token recognition to the three parliaments of Westminster, Dublin, and the Northern Irish Stormont. This went against the traditional abstentionism and physical-force policy of the IRA. When the Sinn Fein (political party counterpart of the IRA) annual convention met in January 1970 in Dublin, a group of members walked out and formed the Provisional Sinn Fein and Provisional IRA. Members who were left made up the Official Sinn Fein and Official IRA.

Both wings claim to be the true heirs to the Republican legacy of the Irish independence struggle. In fact, there has always been a conflict in IRA history between the strategy of working within the electoral system, forming political parties and running candidates on the one hand, and the strategy of military campaigns, refusing to recognize the legitimacy of political offices and parties, on the other. The 1970 split was the most serious of recent splits; but, as we shall see, it was not the last.

Comparison of Provisionals and Officials: Goals and Strategies

The Provisionals, or "Provos," have as their goal the creation of a unified Ireland. More explicitly, they want a "reunited Ireland," since they argue that Ireland was once one country before the border was created in 1922, separating Northern Ireland from the Republic and creating the political entity we now call Northern Ireland. Furthermore, this vision of a new Ireland would be thirty-two counties divided into the four traditional regions of Leinster, Munster, Connacht, and a nine-county Ulster. The capital of this new structure would be moved to Athlone, the center of the island. Their strategy paper, *Eire Nua (New Ireland),* outlines this socialist vision in more detail, though it was repudiated in December 1981.

The Provisional IRA strategy is based on their analysis that it is solely the presence of the British government, in the form of its representatives, the British army, that causes injustice and violence in Northern Ireland. By removing the British army and therefore the British government, the conflict would be halted and the Irish people could work things out for themselves. The military strategy of bombing buildings (for which the British government compensates owners), the Provos theorize, will make the British presence too costly to maintain.

The Provisional IRA has continued the IRA strategy of working mainly outside electoral politics. Prominent leaders have included Ruadhri O Bradaigh, Sean MacStiofain, Martin McGuinness, Seamus Twomey, Joe Cahill, and Gerry Adams. The Provo newspaper, *An Phloblacht,* sells in Northern Ireland. The Provisional IRA is illegal in both North and South; people have received prison terms solely on the basis of being a member of the Provisional IRA. People in the South have been convicted solely on the basis of testimony from a senior police officer.

In summary, there are major issues which distinguish the Provisional IRA from the Official IRA. The Provisionals (1) insist on a military strategy; (2) frequently use the language of a thirty-two county reunited Ireland as their first and main goal; (3) adhere to a one-point analysis stating that the British presence is the sole cause of injustice and violence in Northern Ireland, and that only through removal of the British will there be peace in Northern Ireland.

The Official IRA, or the "Stickies" (from the custom of using gum instead of pins to hold Easter lily labels to coat lapels at Eastertime) has continued an IRA tradition of pursuing basic goals through linkage of many issues, such as housing, unemployment, education, economics, and local political issues. This linkage fosters a radical consciousness, and has led the Officials to espouse a more

Marxist analysis of change. Cathal Goulding, once leader of the Officials, developed this policy of cultivating class politics and class solidarity. At least theoretically, joint action by Catholics and Protestants on issues such as housing works against sectarianism.

The Official IRA called a ceasefire in 1972. Although there have been periods when the Official IRA guns were authorized, the ceasefire has largely been observed, since it is consistent with the organization's general strategy.

In summary: the main points of difference between the Official IRA and the Provisional IRA are that (1) the Officials use a political strategy as opposed to a heavy military-campaign strategy; (2) the Officials frequently use a Marxist analysis which stresses class struggle and class solidarity. The Provos use socialist language, but are against a strong role for the state; (3) Officials link issues and often work at the local community level. The Provos emphasize the national question rather than socio-economic analysis.

We now return to the primary material of this chapter—profiles of organizations.

15. Irish Independence Party

Formed in 1977, this party stood for a British withdrawal and looked forward to an eventual unification with Ireland. Supporters have included Frank McManus and Fergus McAteer. John Turnley, former SDLP member, joined the party; he was killed in 1980. Like the Ulster Independence Party, this party has a small following. Neil Blaney, a prominent politician in the Republic and a member of the European parliament, decided in 1980 not to form an all-Ireland independence party.

16. Ancient Order of Hibernians (AOH)

The AOH is often referred to as the Catholic equivalent of the Orange Order. Two main differences are that the AOH has very little power, and it has stronger connections with Irish-Americans. The present title dates from the 1830s, but the organization itself can be traced from the 1641 Catholic insurrection. The AOH has a network of halls in Northern Ireland where it holds dances and other social events. It decided not to hold parades from 1971 to 1974 because of the level of violence in Northern Ireland. The power of the AOH has declined in recent years; some analysts link this with declining nationalist sentiments, as opposed to increased republican feelings.

17. Social Democratic and Labour Party (SDLP)

The SDLP was formed in 1970 as an alternative and successor to the old Nationalist Party. The latter was more a movement than a political party in that it was a vehicle for anti-partition politics. In its formative years, the SDLP was led by activist young politicians, not all of them Catholic: John Hume, Ivan Cooper, Austin Currie, Paddy Devlin, Gerry Fitt, and others. When internment was begun in 1971, the SDLP sponsored a civil disobedience campaign in protest, asking people to withhold rents and rates (property taxes). At least sixty thousand people took part; some thousands continued the campaign for eighteen months.

In recent years, some of the founders either left the party in disagreement or were asked to leave. Its present leader is John Hume. The SDLP represents moderate to left-wing political views; it shared executive power with the Unionist Party under Brian Faulkner's leadership between January and May 1974. Hume was elected to the European parliament in 1979 with 146,000 votes, second only to Ian Paisley. The SDLP won 17.9% of the vote in the Westminster election in June 1983; it won 18.8% of the vote in the Assembly election in October 1982.

The SDLP has insisted on power-sharing at the executive level in any new government that might be established at Stormont. It demands a practically new police system. Its members are overwhelmingly drawn from the Catholic community, although it insists it is not a sectarian party. It wants eventual reunification with the Republic of Ireland, or at least a close association of all thirty-two counties, to be achieved by political means and with the consent of the political majority of Northern Ireland. The fact that SDLP leaders frequently hold talks with leaders of the Irish Republic government draws criticism from Northern Ireland Unionists. The

SDLP has been second only to the Unionist coalition in winning seats in government, and has been the chief "opposition party" in Stormont, representing the voters in the minority community.

18. Official Irish Republican Army (O-IRA)

As explained above, the O-IRA declared a ceasefire in 1972, and except for brief periods when guns were authorized, that has remained in effect.

19. Official Sinn Fein

The Official Sinn Fein (pronounced shin fane) is the legal wing of the O-IRA and runs candidates in Northern Ireland and the Republic. It had a good showing in the 1979 election. The Official Sinn Fein has also been called the Workers' Party since 1975, and another name is Sinn Fein Gardiner Place. Members are often involved with local political issues, sometimes apparently unrelated to unification of North and South. The president of the Official Sinn Fein is Tomas MacGiolla. The Official Sinn Fein (Workers' Party) won 1.9% in the Westminster election in June 1983, whereas it won 2.7% in the October 1982 Assembly election.

20. Republican Clubs

These are the Northern expression of the Official Sinn Fein Workers' Party. Their American supporters use the same name—Republican Clubs. As implied earlier, members tend to work on housing, development, employment, and other local issues, and to work through other community groups in many urban areas, especially West Belfast. They ran for and won some local elections in the North in 1979.

21. People's Democracy (PD)

The PD was formed in 1968 mainly among Queen's University students in Belfast. Bernadette Devlin (McAliskey), Kevin Boyle, and Michael Farrell were leaders. PD sponsored a number of influential civil rights demonstrations in the late sixties and has had declining strength since. Its members occasionally support issues which the Provisional Sinn Fein supports, especially regarding prisoners, but it has also dealt with feminist issues. People's Democracy prints a newspaper in the Republic.

22. Provisional Irish Republican Army

Although detailed information about events as they occurred is given in chapter 5, the reader might appreciate some information about Provisional activities here. Internment began in August 1971. The British army strategy was to arrest leaders responsible for guerrilla fighting. While this was partly successful, it also backfired, since internment so angered Republicans that many more people joined the Provos! In 1972, fighting developed between Provisionals and Officials; sectarian assassinations also developed, especially in Belfast. This was the frightening dynamic whereby a Catholic would be killed in retaliation for a Protestant killing (or vice versa), solely because they were from the "other side." In 1974, Provos changed their strategy by bombing buildings in England. Especially important were bombings in Birmingham. This led to a public outcry, and Parliament passed the Prevention of Terrorism Act, which made it legal to hold a person without charge for seven days, permitting expulsion to Northern Ireland or to the Republic, and made the IRA illegal in Britain. It also led to the Feakle initiative (see chapter 6, under church activities), when church leaders met with IRA leaders. This meeting, in turn, created a temporary ceasefire. In 1978, the La Mon House restaurant (in County Down in Northern Ireland) was firebombed, and twelve people died. This particular Provo bombing caused an outrage, and the British army took the offensive against the Provisional IRA. On March 1, 1976, Provisional IRA prisoners, especially in the Maze prison, began a protest against the withdrawal of special category status for prisoners convicted of political crimes (see chapter 3). In 1979, the Provisionals took responsibility for the assassination of Lord Mountbatten and, on the same day but at a separate incident, the deaths of eighteen British soldiers in Ireland.

The Provisional IRA War Council is, of course, secret, but probably known to the authorities. It is said to include hawks and doves. There is always speculation as to P-IRA membership. Cells exist in many towns, North and South, although people can be strong Republicans without belonging to either IRA.

23. Provisional Sinn Fein

This is the legal, political-party wing of the Provisional IRA. Although technically it is a separate organization, and members of both deny there is any connection, there is widespread understanding that the organizations are quite close in terms of political analysis, strategy, and even overlapping membership. *Sinn Fein* is Gaelic for "We ourselves" or "Ourselves alone," the rallying cry during the 1916 Irish Uprising. The Provo Sinn Fein claims it is the organization which carries on the original goals of the Uprising. Sinn Fein has not contested elections since it does not recognize the rights of the governments to hold elections. They did not contest the European parliament election in 1979. Its president is Ruadhri O Bradaigh; other leaders are David O'Connell, Gerry Adams, Joe Cahill, and Shaun Brady. The Provisional Sinn Fein is also identified as the Kevin St. Sinn Fein, now located at Parnell Square. The Provisional Sinn Fein won 13.4% of the vote in the Westminster election in June 1983, as opposed to 10.1% of the vote in the Assembly election in October 1982. About 100,000 votes were cast in the 1983 election, and five Sinn Fein men were elected.

24. Irish Republican Socialist Party (IRSP)

The IRSP was formed in 1975, mainly as a breakaway group from the Official Sinn Fein, by people who disagreed with the 1972 ceasefire. A year later, the most prominent member was Bernadette

McAliskey, who denied that the party had a military wing. McAliskey is no longer a leader at this time. For a time, it looked as though the IRSP would run candidates for elections, but the party decided to boycott the electoral process. Seamus Costello, another leader, was killed in 1977; following his death, the IRSP went into decline. But the release of Oscar Breanach from prison may lead to reactivation. The IRSP has been strong enough to control certain sections of Belfast and to occupy its own special category area in the Maze prison.

25. Irish National Liberation Army (INLA)

INLA is the military wing of the IRSP, formed around 1976 from Official IRA members disenchanted with their ceasefire; probably some Provo IRA members joined as well. Its main strength is believed to be in Belfast and Derry. The INLA claimed responsibility for killing Airey Neave, a Conservative Member of Parliament and Northern Ireland spokesman at Westminster in 1979. The British government claims the INLA receives some arms from the Middle East; the INLA would not be unique in this regard.

SECURITY FORCES

Security forces are the organizations recognized by the state to have responsibility for security. Sometimes their actions have been controversial. They have all figured as important forces in Northern Ireland in the recent past. (See chapter 3 for a full discussion of these issues.)

26. British Army
27. Special Air Service
28. Ulster Defence Regiment
29. Royal Ulster Constabulary

26. British Army

The British army had garrisons of about three thousand men in Northern Ireland in the years before 1969, doing ordinary army duty. It was and still is the only army which has a legal right to exist in Northern Ireland, which is an integral part of the United Kingdom. As the civil rights movement grew after 1968, violence increased as majority militants attacked minority marches and even houses. In August 1969, the British army was asked to provide the necessary protection for the minority, which the police were unable (as television sometimes showed) or apparently unwilling to do. The army was asked to increase its numbers so as to protect the minority from this violence. They were initially welcomed by the minority community as their major defense against attacking Loyalists. The IRA had been inactive for some years.

Soon, however, in minority areas, the inadequacy of an army-turned-police-force inevitably appeared. An army is an instrument of offensive and defensive warfare—not of peace-keeping. The army was frequently accused of harassment, especially in raiding minority homes far more often and more brutally than majority homes, for arms and people "on the run." The majority ghettos have resisted soldiers just as forcefully as have the minority when the army has entered their areas to search or to seize.

The presence of the army is one of the most disturbing aspects of Northern Irish life. The fortified camps within the cities, the armed patrols in skirmish order moving about the streets, on country roads, and at entry points to shopping districts, have given the army high visibility, as if the province were truly, as the Nationalists call it, "occupied Ireland." The number of troops has fluctuated, depending on the level of violence; it has gone as high as twenty thousand and in early 1981 seemed to be about twelve thousand. In 1977, the number of British troops during the Queen's visit was temporarily thirty thousand.

Soldiers come to Northern Ireland on rotation for four-month "unaccompanied" stints or eighteen months "accompanied"—i.e., with their families along. Soldiers from Northern Ireland need not accept assignment there. Many of them rotate from the British army in West Germany; the U.S. government is regularly accused by Provo supporters in the U.S. of freeing up these soldiers for duty in Northern Ireland by increasing American NATO forces in Europe.

Many of the British soldiers are in their teens; many are Catholics from mainland backgrounds identical to the Falls or Bogside districts. But quite a few are Scots and some are vehement in their dislike of the Northern Ireland minority. When such rancor is added to the usual army-civilian hostility, the danger of violent interchange increases. Soldiers in flak jackets tend to look on all Northerners as potential assassins, and to be looked on with suspicion by people who have been harassed by them.

Army headquarters are at Lisburn outside Belfast, with smaller bases scattered over the province at key points. "Fort Monagh" and "Fort Apache" tell much of the attitude of local citizenry to the bases, which are surrounded by high iron fences that screen them from view. At intervals, the gates swing open to disgorge military vehicles large and small, for patrols and other routine duty.

There are a number of controversies regarding the British army which are discussed in chapter 3.

27. Special Air Service (SAS)

The SAS is a specialist group of the British army similar to the Green Berets of the U.S. Army. The SAS was introduced into Northern Ireland in 1974, though some sources say 1976, and some groups say the SAS worked there as early as 1973. The SAS is reported to work in plain clothes as well as in uniform and to do the dirty work and use the "dirty tricks" associated with such military elite groups around the world.

28. Ulster Defence Regiment (UDR)

The UDR was formed in 1970 to replace the Ulster Special Constabulary (q.v.). It is a province-wide reserve army or auxiliary for Northern Ireland and is part of the British army. It resembles the American National Guard. It now numbers about eight thousand members. In 1977, a strategy called "Ulsterization" was introduced; this meant that the UDR and the Royal Ulster Constabulary (RUC) would assume security roles that the British army had previously carried out. By 1980, an increasing number of British politicians came to question this strategy. More people began to realize that the UDR is a Protestant organization with few Catholic members. At one time, there was eighteen percent Catholic membership; by 1978, it had dropped to three percent. More serious, however, is the increasing evidence that former B-Specials (q.v.) men became UDR members, either full- or part-time or as reservists. This may account for some members being assassinated. UDR members have been sentenced for crimes, sometimes for murder.

29. Royal Ulster Constabulary (RUC)

The RUC is the province-wide police force numbering seven thousand in 1981, with plans for one thousand more. With political partition in 1921, the Royal Irish Constabulary was also divided. In the north, it became the Royal Ulster Constabulary, with one-third of its membership left open for the minority if they wanted to join. Catholic membership reached a peak at twelve percent and is a much lower percentage now. Until a police force acceptable in both the minority and majority areas is somehow created, there seems little hope for the withdrawal of the army and the return of what could be called normal life.

The RUC Reserve, women and men, full-time and part-time, in 1980 numbered about eight thousand.

PREVIOUSLY ACTIVE GROUPS

30. Unionist Party of Northern Ireland
31. B-Specials
32. Loyalist Association of Workers
33. Vanguard Movement/VUPP

A number of organizations, political parties, and groups were important in the recent past but no longer exist. We include profiles of a few of these groups because of their importance and because readers may see references to them elsewhere.

30. Unionist Party of Northern Ireland (UPNI)

The UPNI was formed by Brian Faulkner when he lost control of the monolithic Unionist Party in 1974 and needed a platform for his idea of power-sharing. Anne Dickson succeeded Faulkner when he died in an accident in 1977. By 1979, the party had become quite small and effectively disbanded in 1982.

31. B-Specials

As reported above, the Ulster Volunteer Force was created in 1912 to resist home rule in Ireland. But it was not an official body, and Unionists pressured for some more official organization. As a result, three auxiliary forces to the police were formed in 1920—"A," "B," and "C" Specials. Their purpose was to help the Royal Ulster Constabulary (RUC) and the anti-IRA campaign then going on. The other auxiliaries were dropped, but the B-Specials had a reputation they never lost, based on a powerful anti-Catholic bias (membership was exclusively Protestant) and slack recruitment procedures and training methods. (The B-Specials were disbanded in 1979; see the forthcoming section on commission reports.)

32. Loyalist Association of Workers (LAW)

LAW was a hard-line pressure group formed around Billy Hull around 1970, and linked to the Vanguard Party as well as the Ulster Workers Council. It seems to have dissolved itself at present.

33. Vanguard Movement

The Vanguard Movement consisted of Unionists disenchanted with the other Unionist parties. Led by William Craig, Vanguard members in 1973 formed the Vanguard Unionist Progressive Party (VUPP) and ran candidates for local offices. The party drew heavily on the working-class people of East Belfast, especially in the Harland and Wolff Shipyards. For some time in 1974 the Ulster Defence Association and the Ulster Workers Council seemed closely connected with the VUPP. The party merged again with the Official Unionist Party in 1978 and so no longer exists as such. Glen Barr was a leading spokesman in it and a loyal supporter of Craig during the turmoil of 1974-77.

COMMISSIONS

Since 1969, the British government has established a number of special commissions and tribunals to investigate various issues relating to Northern Ireland. They have not had the power to make laws, but rather investigated situations and made recommendations. An American parallel would be the Warren Commission, which investigated the assassination of President Kennedy. The British government accepted some recommendations, and laws were passed based on the commissions' work; other recommendations were rejected. It is important to understand these commissions' general recommendations, at least, since they have been milestones in the past decade of Northern Irish history. In this section, we will look at the most important of these commissions, in chronological order. The date in parenthesis is when the findings were made public.

A. Cameron Commission (1969)

The purpose of the Cameron Commission was to investigate the causes and conditions of violence after October 1968, when a civil rights march resulted in a number of injuries. The commission found that several factors led to the violence: a rising sense of grievance among Catholics, especially over housing discrimination; sectarian discrimination in appointment of local government authorities; manipulation of electoral boundaries; failure of the government to investigate complaints; accusations that the Ulster

Special Constabulary was a partisan paramilitary force; resentment of the Special Powers Act; Protestant fears that Unionist domination was threatened. The commission also criticized the RUC.

B. Hunt Report (1969)

The Hunt Report led to far-reaching reforms in Northern Ireland security forces. Especially important was the report's recommendation that the Ulster Special Constabulary be disbanded (it was replaced by the Ulster Defence Regiment). The decision led to Protestant rioting in Belfast, but it was welcomed by civil rights advocates.

C. Compton Report (1971)

The purpose of the Compton Report was to investigate allegations that men arrested at the beginning of internment (August 9, 1971) were brutally treated. The commission found there had been ill treatment, but dismissed charges of brutality. These findings were roundly criticized in Britain and Northern Ireland. As a result, a new inquiry, under Parker, was established, and the case eventually went to the European Court of Human Rights, which did find cases of inhuman and degrading treatment.

D. Parker Committee (1972)

This committee was divided in its findings. Two members held that five methods of interrogation could be justified, given certain future safeguards. The third member found the methods were morally unjustifiable under any circumstances. The prime minister, Edward Heath, announced that the methods would not be used again.

E. Scarman Tribunal (April 1972)

The Scarman Tribunal investigated the riots and shootings which took place in the summer of 1969, just before the British army was called in. The report noted that the RUC was seriously at fault on six occasions. But the report cleared the RUC of charges that it cooperated as a partisan force with Protestant mobs to attack Catholics. The report also stated that the USC was unprepared for riot duty. Finally, the report said in both the Protestant and Catholic communities there were the same fears, the same self-help, and the same distrust of lawful authority.

F. Widgery Report (April 1972)

The purpose of the Widgery Report was to investigate the shootings of fourteen unarmed civilians during the civil rights march in Derry on January 30, 1972, better known as "Bloody Sunday." The report found that the soldiers had been fired upon before they opened fire; but had the army maintained a low-key attitude (instead of arresting hooligans), the event might have passed without fatalities.

G. Diplock Report (1972)

The Diplock Report recommended that non-jury trials be introduced for a wide range of terrorist offenses because of the risks of intimidation against witnesses in an open court. The proposal was adopted.

H. Gardiner Report (1975)

The purpose of the Gardiner Report was to inquire into how to deal with terrorism in Northern Ireland in the context of civil liberties and human rights. Its findings were most important since they established the context for future events. The report held that detention without trial (internment) was a short-term necessity; that political status (or "special category") for convicted prisoners should be ended; and independent means of investigating complaints against the police should be established.

I. Bennett Report (1979)

The Bennett Report investigated interrogation procedures of the RUC and methods of dealing with complaints. The commission was established after an Amnesty International team had looked into ill-treatment complaints of people held at Castlereagh Centre. The committee reported that there was medical evidence that some detainees had received injuries while in custody. Virtually all the committee's recommendations were accepted by the government, including the introduction of closed-circuit TV in interview rooms and the granting of the right of access to a lawyer after forty-eight hours of detention. The report was highly controversial in its assessment of the extent of ill treatment.

A woman's handbag being searched. Searches like this greatly diminished by 1979.

Chapter 3

What Issues Divide?

If the Northern Ireland conflict is not "about religion," then what is it about? In this chapter, we identify four major groups of issues which divide Northern Irish people. Some explanation is in order since the issues are closely related.

CIVIL RIGHTS

The first group of issues, which we label civil rights, includes housing, unemployment, education, and voting rights. These were the main focus of the civil rights movement begun in 1967. Voting rights are no longer an issue, but the first three remain important. Housing, unemployment, and education are the main indicators which sociologists use to measure poverty. Thus, it is not surprising that these issues were the first focus for the civil rights movement; their importance continues. In 1980-81, unemployment became, for many people, a greater concern than the level of violence. Northern Ireland consistently has the highest unemployment of the four sections of the United Kingdom and Northern Ireland (England, Scotland, and Wales are the other three). Membership in paramilitary organizations is no doubt related to the high unemployment rate in both communities.

BRITISH GOVERNMENT POLICIES

The second group of issues concerns British government policies. It includes the British army, troop withdrawal, internment, police and security, criminal justice, the H-Block issue, and the hunger-strike campaign. These became issues after 1969, when the fighting started and people began to be killed. The issues are intensely political. Where a person stands on one issue usually indicates their political position on the others. They arouse so much feeling that intense, emotional campaigns have developed around all of them. In addition to highlighting objective differences, these issues tend to be used to manipulate public opinion on all sides and keep people divided.

VIOLENCE

The third group of issues deals with violence—intimidation, fatalities and injuries, and sectarian assassinations. They are a part of the reality of Northern Ireland that no one wants to talk about or analyze, yet they are a part of Northern Irish life. They help to create a certain unmistakable climate that is noticeable but unarticulated.

GOVERNMENT AUTHORITY

The fourth group concerns government authority—unification of North and South, and the Northern Ireland governmental structure. In one sense, the unification issue should be the first one in the chapter, since historically it is the basis of division in Northern Ireland. Yet, as we see, it is not the only issue—though some people would have us believe that—nor is it necessarily the most important one. And the changes that the Northern Ireland government has seen—almost completely invisible from outside Northern Ireland—

are complex and confusing. Yet they have implications for conflicts involving majority and minority groups coexisting in other societies.

Some observers have identified another group of conflicts in Northern Ireland, sometimes called "church-related" issues: mixed marriages, divorce, and birth control. We have decided not to examine these issues for a few reasons. Some observers question if they are substantial issues, ones which really divide people. Second, these issues do not involve political power, at least not in the way most of the other issues discussed here do. Third, these issues, because they are church-related, would encourage the view that the Northern Ireland conflict is essentially religious. As stated earlier, we reject that analysis. Finally, these issues are very complex; they deserve to be discussed fully or not at all.

How are these sixteen issues related to each other? Unemployment is the highest it has ever been. More people than ever are emigrating to places like Liverpool and London (and Canada and the continent) to find work. Public housing construction is inadequate, and many people live in deteriorating or dilapidated houses. The British army presence, though decreasing, is still very evident. Internment is over, but the issue of a non-sectarian police force remains unresolved. The Emergency Powers Act, a major part of the criminal law, continues to be voted in again and again by the Westminster parliament, despite criticisms. The question of troop withdrawal and the H-Block protests have been highly-charged issues providing opportunities for emotional manipulation. Acts of intimidation, violence, and killing create an atmosphere of tension, hopelessness, and fear.

Taken all together, these are the issues that divide people in Northern Ireland. For each individual, the relative importance of the issues will vary, and so, accordingly, will that person's analysis of the conflict as a whole.

CIVIL RIGHTS

Housing

Housing was one of the first areas in which discrimination against Catholics was identified by the civil rights movement in 1968. In spite of numerous changes which have taken place in Northern Ireland since then, housing remains controversial for various reasons.

Many Northern Ireland houses, especially in cities, were built for factory workers in the eighteen hundreds, when the province experienced an industrial boom. Many were small row houses; a typical row house in Belfast has two rooms downstairs, two rooms upstairs, and an outhouse in back. Before 1969, in the one hundred percent Catholic ward of Cromac in Belfast, for example, at least ninety percent of the houses lacked an indoor toilet, a sink, a fixed bath, or hot water. The worst housing has always been in the inner areas of Belfast and in western rural areas. In the Shankill and Falls areas of Belfast, only ten percent of the houses had all four of these amenities: bath, inside toilet, bathroom sink, and kitchen sink. In general, housing conditions have been poor, much lower than in most other European countries.

Housing became an important civil rights issue because Catholics felt they were victimized by a discriminatory system of housing allocation. Public housing in Northern Ireland is rented by the government, and two-thirds of postwar housing is in this category. Thus, if a city council were controlled by Unionists, they might decide not to allocate houses to Catholics on the grounds that the Unionist balance of power might be upset. In a society where housing is scarce to begin with, people could remain on the waiting list for years.

The initial spark of the civil rights movement occurred in 1968 when Austin Currie, M.P., was unable to get housing for a Catholic family; the local council planned to rent it to the Protestant secretary of a Unionist politician. The Cameron Commission identified "unfair methods of allocation" in housing as one source of grievance which led to demonstrations and disorders in 1968-69.

As a result of identifying housing discrimination, a new centralized Northern Ireland Housing Executive was created in 1972.

This body has the sole responsibility for building and allocating all publicly owned houses. In other words, its goals are to increase the number of houses being built and end the old corrupt sectarian system of housing allocation. The latter has, in general, been achieved. The former is more difficult.

While the Housing Executive eased some problems, it did not eliminate all housing difficulties. Because of fear of the other community, people tend to want to live with people of their own community. When large-scale rioting took place in Belfast in 1970, thousands of people fled their homes because of intimidation and fear. The general trend since 1970 has been for people to move from mixed areas to areas where one community is concentrated.

Houses have not been built as fast as they are needed, because of the generally depressed economy. Building costs are high, and small firms have little chance to survive. From January to November 1977, 7,104 new dwellings were completed by the Housing Executive, and 2,593 were built by private enterprise. Squatters often move into houses illegally because of overcrowding. Rent and rate strikes have been called from time to time by both communities to protest particular grievances. High-rise apartment houses are often built to replace row houses, and many people find this housing style unpleasant since it makes the familiar "village community" lifestyle almost impossible. In addition, new housing developments built since World War II have overlooked access to shopping centers. For example, when a food store was burned down by vandals in a housing development in Belfast in August 1980, hundreds of families found themselves miles away from any alternative store.

It is no surprise that housing remains one of the root causes of social dissatisfaction and unrest.

Unemployment

For many people in Northern Ireland in the second half of 1980, unemployment and the economy became more important than the level of violence. From June through November 1980, unemployment for men had risen from 14.9 percent to 18.9 percent, and for women, from 9.6 percent in June to 11.8 percent in November; this was a total of 15.9 percent or 91,686 people unemployed. The main industries of Northern Ireland have been hit hard: shipbuilding, construction, linen, and engineering.

But we also need to inquire about discrimination in employment. Irish labor law is like that of Great Britain, with protection of workers and trade unions. A Sex Discrimination (N.I.) Order came into effect in 1976 as did the Fair Employment (N.I.) Act; discrimination on grounds of sex, religion, or politics was outlawed.

In 1978, the Fair Employment Agency was established under the Fair Employment Act. The rate of unemployment of minority workers had been two and a half times that of the majority, and jobs held have in general been the lower-paying ones, both in types of jobs and in job level within each category. Minority workers tend to be unskilled, in contrast to workers from the majority.

The point must not be drawn too fine. Many jobs, such as in the shipyards, are passed from father to son or to extended family, much as in many U.S. trades. The discrimination at times works the other way where the minority is in control, e.g., in the docks in Derry in the past. But minority domination exists only in isolated industries. Many majority workers never acknowledged the "institutional discrimination" any more than U.S. whites for years were conscious of the "institutional racism" around them. Familiarity can breed mere ignorance, not always contempt. In the early seventies a Northern Irish labor union leader, invited to the U.S. to see our union system, became unpopular when he told his hosts that they were doing to U.S. minorities exactly what the majority in Northern Ireland had been doing to their Catholic neighbors. Their reaction was identical to that of the Northern Irish majority when the Fair Employment Agency report came out.

Most Americans know how discrimination in jobs can be practiced legally. An employer can easily tell to which community an applicant belongs. The name (Murphy or Graham) or address (Falls or Shankill) may be enough; the school is almost always a sure clue, due to *de facto* segregated housing combined with neighborhood schools (St. Brendan's or Carson School). Employers have no right to ask religious preference, but they do have the right to know job competence, so they can rightly inquire about schooling. But public opinion is changing. A minority woman in Derry recently applied for a library job which she did not really expect to get. To her surprise, she was hired.

An obvious need is more jobs. In recent years, the Northern Ireland Office has intensely solicited American businesses to expand facilities there or establish new ones. Church leaders of all traditions have voiced the same plea: provide our people with jobs, so that human dignity and family life can exist once again. The U.S. government has promised financial help once the troubles end; Terry Carlin of the Irish Council of Trade Unions (ICTU) responds that the jobs are needed now and would help bring civil strife to an end. American industrialists may fear that their factories will be targets of terrorist bomb attacks. The fact is that the Provisional IRA strategy all along has been to weaken the British economy. Thus, American and other foreign industries are not usually targets, though a few have been. Yet the fear remains and provides uncertainty to such an investment.

Since the economic state of Northern Ireland is closely tied to the employment situation, the following information is important. The Northern Ireland government has two sources of revenue. The attributed share of U.K. taxes in 1976-77 was 1.24 billion pounds ($2.207 billion) plus 702 million pounds ($1.25 billion) as "grant-in-aid." Regional and local revenues came to 164 million pounds ($287 million). Public expenditure per person was greater than anywhere in the U.K., and it tripled between 1969 and 1975.

Northern Ireland periodically receives grants to upgrade industry from the Common Market European Regional Development Fund. The province received five million pounds ($10 million) in June 1979, increasing the total from the fund to the U.K. as a whole from June 1975 to twenty-seven million pounds ($57.24 million); the Republic received sixteen million pounds ($33.92 million). In September 1979, Northern Ireland received 13.6 million pounds ($28.84 million) to develop Aldergrove Airport, outside Belfast. Another European Economic Community (EEC—known in the U.S. as the "Common Market") grant of five million pounds to Northern Ireland was awarded in July 1980, and eleven million pounds ($25.63 million) was given to the Republic. In August 1980, the British government allocated an extra forty-eight million pounds ($111.84 million) to Northern Ireland in addition to redirecting fifty million pounds ($116.5 million) from Northern Ireland spending programs. (A further ten million pounds [$23.3 million] was available for security purposes as well.)

The IRA declared war on the "British economy" as one way to achieve their "Brits Out" goal. Up to 1971, the cost in damage was reckoned at 268 million pounds ($549.4 million). A typical attack was the fire-bombing of sixteen stores in Derry on December 4, 1976, with the loss of Christmas supplies and one hundred jobs. The Provo headline: "British Economy Suffers Blow."

A recent development has been a co-op movement among the paramilitaries of each community. As usual, evaluation of this remains ambivalent. Co-ops are valuable for giving employment and for enabling a larger middle-management group to emerge from the working class. But caution is still in order: profits from these may finance paramilitary activities, and competition may be eliminated in gangster-type ways. Protection money has been openly collected from shopkeepers and taxi-drivers by each side's paramilitaries. Entering legitimate businesses may or may not provide financial security.

Whether or not the British will continue indefinitely to subsidize social services in Northern Ireland and pay the damages for destruction remains to be seen. Most signs say yes, but the economic realities may supervene. Imports to Northern Ireland regularly exceed exports by about thirty-five percent. Emigration takes eight to ten thousand each year, many of them young and skilled. Not many of these people go to the Republic; most go to another area of the U.K., where the social services are comparable. The emigration may reduce unemployment temporarily; it bodes ill for the economic future of the province, however.

Education

Public education apart from the universities is administered by the Northern Ireland Department of Education, through five Education and Library Boards (ELB). Education is compulsory from age five to age sixteen. All state schools are wholly financed by public funds. Classroom size averages twenty-five. One fourth of the teachers are men. Only four "independent" schools receive *no* public funds.

The second large school system is "voluntary," almost entirely Roman Catholic. Primary schools are grant-aided for salaries, equipment, and most of the building costs, as in other parts of the U.K. The managing boards are approved by the Department of Education, ordinarily by the local ELB, and in effect are controlled by representatives of the local parish. No tuition is charged at any primary school; books, stationery, and writing materials are free. This is, of course, a quite different situation from that in the U.S. The Northern Irish pay just once for primary education. Religious education is in the curriculum of all schools, with local clergy usually teaching their own traditions. Seventy thousand of 210,000 children in primary schools receive transportation or assistance in transportation each day.

Secondary education comprises ages eleven to sixteen or eighteen. The "eleven-plus" exam is a test given to schoolchildren shortly after their eleventh birthday. It determines students' general vocational aptitude and what sort of courses they should take through the rest of their school years. But more than that, the eleven-plus test reinforces class divisions when people are quite young. The eleven-plus was discontinued in Great Britain in the mid-seventies and in Northern Ireland in 1977. But about a year later, the test was reinstated in Northern Ireland.

Secondary schools are of three kinds: grammar (college-prep), intermediate (general courses), and technical (vocational). In 1976, the twenty-two public grammar schools enrolled 13,500 pupils; the fifty-eight voluntary grammar schools (including Protestant schools) enrolled 41,500. Students who attend grammar schools pay fees, but most students hold ELB scholarships.

In 1976, there were about twenty-five thousand "school-leavers" who finished secondary education, of whom fifteen thousand obtained the equivalent of a diploma. About ten thousand of these intended to do "further education"—two thousand in universities, six hundred in teachers' colleges, the rest as full- or part-time students in other institutions. These statistics are important. They indicate that thousands of youths go into a job-market situation with high unemployment; many are inevitably exposed to solicitation by paramilitaries. Some would join just because "there's nothing else to do."

Attendance figures for total compulsory schooling show an upward trend, but primary schools show a slight decrease. The one-third minority still produces about half the children in Northern

Ireland schools. Some demographers estimate that if emigration would not affect the situation, the present minority would become a voting majority in about twenty years. This would, of course, have serious political consequences that might better be addressed now than then. To put the point to it, the present majority is in a position of strength and can drive its best bargain now. But as long as unemployment is so high, people will be forced to emigrate.

Universities are the first and just about the only place where integrated education occurs. Further education is provided by twenty-seven technical colleges for thirty-eight thousand full- or part-time students, by three teachers' colleges for twenty-six hundred, by the Workers' Educational Association, Queens and the New University for ninety-seven hundred in non-university courses, and by these two along with Ulster College (Polytechnic) for fifteen thousand in university programs. There is also an Open University with nine branches in Northern Ireland, reaching seventeen hundred students for undergraduate, postgraduate, and post-experience students. Magee University in Derry offers adult education programs.

Total public expenditures for ELB in 1976-77 was 259 million pounds ($453.25 million), an increase of thirty-five million pounds ($63.35 million) over 1975-76. This includes one hundred public libraries and two reference libraries. Average expenditure per person was 168 pounds ($299.04).

So much for facts. Another fact is that neighborhood schools in segregated neighborhoods are segregated schools. People in the U.S. have ample experience of the difficulties of trying to "balance" such schools; we have yet to succeed on a national level. Politics get mixed in, sectarianism influences education, and strictly educational matters can become hopelessly confused. Each community in Northern Ireland has at times looked on the schools as a main means of political power. Education may seem to be a peripheral issue, but it is real.

Even in mixed areas in Northern Ireland, the minority community has opted in general for voluntary rather than public schools. To outsiders, this often seems a guarantee of preserving the two conflicting communities, since the children and young people remain ignorant of "the others" until their cultural assumptions and evaluations are set.

To the minority insiders, this is by no means evident. Vatican II encouraged people of different religious traditions to be educated together. But Catholic leaders see their schools as a major way of preserving their traditions, including their Roman Catholic tradition, and they want their culture to be transmitted integrally. They doubt that this can be done otherwise in Northern Ireland in its present state. Not only bishops and priests, nuns and brothers, but also many Roman Catholic parents seem to feel this way.

Surveys are inconclusive so far. The people may be getting ahead of their leaders in this matter; some polls indicate this. The All Children Together (ACT) movement has urged mixing of schoolchildren. Parents at times have confronted clergy on the matter. In early 1978, there were signs of better rapport in areas where emotions have run high.

In May 1978, the Education Act was passed. It aimed to create a third, integrated sector in the Northern Ireland educational system. Two years later, no integrated schools had been started, nor were pilot schemes begun.

A poll published by *Fortnight* magazine in October-November 1980 found substantial support in both communities for experiments in this area. About sixty percent in both communities said mixed primary and secondary schools should be provided as one option in each area. Another question asked if parents would send their children to an integrated school. About one-third said yes (in both communities), a third gave no answer, and a third said no.

Advocates of the separate system accept that this division in some ways distinguishes the products of their schools, but they deny that it makes them uncooperative or antagonistic. They fear that mixing the children in schools would lead to the loss of a legitimate Northern Ireland tradition and would be a serious violation of religious and civic liberty. For many, the dilemma is this: integrate the schools at the expense of freedom of choice, or keep them segregated at the expense of civic peace.

Educational psychologists would not agree that integrated schools almost automatically result in integrated minds. The evidence would tend otherwise: prejudices learned at home are rarely exorcised by schooling when they continue to be reinforced at home.

Edward O'Donnell, in his book *Northern Irish Stereotypes,* discovered that two-thirds of the words used of "the others" by the two groups in Northern Ireland came from the parents and their "tradition"; one-third came from teachers, mass media and paramilitaries put together. Given this phenomenon, the schools cannot be expected to integrate minds and hearts if the home remains a source of bitterness and distrust. Integrating the homes, both in locale and in attitudes, seems to be a primary concern for churches, civic groups and government. The late archbishop of Armagh, Cardinal Conway, said that segregated housing was more basic to community divisions than segregated schools.

And yet . . . and yet. Surely some experiments could be tried in mixed areas or even in buildings on the borderlines of the two communities—only after careful preparation and with respect for the local people involved. Surely closer cooperation and contact between public and voluntary schools should have a high priority immediately.

The *Violence in Ireland* report suggests teacher exchanges, especially in sensitive areas of the curriculum like civics, history of state and churches, Irish culture and language. Common athletic contests could replace the segregated games now played in schools. Debates, dramatics, and joint fieldwork could bring youngsters together; nursery schools could do the same for young mothers. Religion must be taught ecumenically, with respect for other traditions; a good way to ensure this would be to invite representatives of other traditions to come and talk in religion classes.

The state can do much to help people overcome fear stemming mainly from ignorance. So can the churches and many civic organizations which contribute to education, whether they are involved directly in the schools or not. Feelings on both sides must be understood; dialogue must express genuine respect. Joint committees in adjoining neighborhoods might begin to form, so that schools will more and more be havens of reconciliation rather than of separateness.

Voting Rights

Voting rights are no longer a problem, but they were before 1968. In order to provide a context, we should understand what the earlier situation was. Before 1968:

(1) Voters had to be owners or tenants of a house; in this category, only two people in a house could vote.

(2) An owner had to have property worth ten pounds ($24) or over.

(3) Companies were entitled to appoint up to six votes for every ten pounds value of the company.

(4) In addition, voting districts were often dramatically gerrymandered to enable Unionist votes to overpower the minority community.

These laws favored the richer sections of the district. One example: the 1961 census of Derry showed a population of 36,073 Catholics and 17,689 Protestants. But the voting population consisted of 14,429 Catholics and 8,781 Protestants. In other words, forty percent of the Catholics were entitled to vote, and fifty percent of the Protestants.

The civil rights movement of 1968 demanded a vote for every person, an end to gerrymandered districts, and a return to proportional representation in local elections. All these demands were granted in new electoral laws of 1968, 1969, and 1970, and sectarian voting laws no longer exist.

To vote in local elections, an individual must be a British subject, at least eighteen years old, with no legal incapacity, having been born in Northern Ireland or resided in the U.K. for seven years.

For U.K. parliamentary voting, requirements are the same except for one addition: a registering voter must be a British subject or a citizen of the Irish Republic who is resident at an address in the Northern Ireland constituency on the qualifying date and has resided there or somewhere else in Northern Ireland for three months ending on the qualifying date.

The twenty-six districts for local elections were established in 1971. Over a million people voted that year—about forty percent more than in the previous local election.

The twelve parliamentary constituencies also totaled an electorate of over a million in 1976. The British government has accepted an increase in Northern Ireland M.P.s at Westminster; but this agreement has not yet been implemented. The SDLP was the only party to oppose this change, on the grounds that it would make a political solution even more impossible. In any case, the SDLP joined the Alliance and the Liberal parties in recommending that Westminster elections also be determined by proportional representation.

BRITISH GOVERNMENT POLICIES

British Army

Many bitter and deeply-felt controversies have developed regarding the British army in Northern Ireland. This section attempts to explain the conflicts briefly by stating the issues, major views, and relevant background. The major conflicts center on: (1) accusations of prejudicial behavior and brutality; (2) complicity with the RUC and UDA; (3) the role of the British army; (4) behavior of British army chaplains; (5) use of technology and computers; (6) the basis of authority. The major issues of internment and withdrawal are discussed in separate sections in this chapter, immediately following.

Prejudicial Behavior and Brutality

Untrained to do police work, the army inevitably offended Northern Ireland people of both sides, but especially in minority areas. In the first years of the army presence, British troops raided Catholic houses, ripping up floorboards in search of arms, breaking furniture and religious objects, and frightening residents. The victims of such actions often were not paid damages. Charges of discrimination increased when it became apparent that similar raids did not occur as frequently in Protestant areas. Yet a study indicated that there were probably more illegal arms in Protestant areas, if for no other reason than that there were (and are) twice as many Protestants as Catholics. When troops began to raid Protestant homes and intern Protestant men and women as well, both communities came to see the army as their enemy. When the British army admitted that the Special Air Service (SAS) worked at times in plain clothes, the enmity increased.

The Provisional IRA has stated that it has been at war with the British army since 1970. Paramilitary groups from minority areas are very evident, but there are a number of paramilitary groups from majority areas as well; and harsh fighting has taken place in regions of both communities.

Collaboration with the RUC and UDA

Members of the province-wide police force, the Royal Ulster Constabulary (RUC) and the province-wide army reserve, the Ulster Defence Regiment (UDR), have always worked closely with the army, since they are all concerned with security. But since the RUC has always had only a small number of Catholic members, many Northerners question the capacity of the British army to be impartial. Some members of the minority fear that the UDR contains some men who were once part of the highly prejudiced B-Specials and the Ulster Special Constabulary. Thus, the British army working with the UDR has caused greater alarm, and fear of prejudicial behavior.

Fears increased during the mid-seventies when it seemed as though there was a special close relationship between the British army and the Ulster Defence Association, one of the the Unionist paramilitary groups. From the minority viewpoint, what greater proof was needed to come to the conclusion that the army was prejudiced?

Two examples of brutality stand out in the history of the recent troubles. When internment was introduced in August 1971, some arrested men charged the British army with brutality. The Dublin government pursued the case at the European Court of Human Rights in Strasbourg, whose final decision was that the army used "cruel and degrading" treatment, which the U.K. government said had stopped after 1971 and would not be used again. Frequently, men released from police stations or prison have accused security forces of continued brutality. Amnesty International and the churches have considered these allegations serious enough to justify requests for special investigations of arrest and interrogation procedures.

A second example of brutality occurred during the civil rights march in Derry in January 1972, when British soldiers killed fourteen unarmed demonstrators (see chapter 5).

Role of the British Army

In an urban guerrilla-war situation, when at least one force does not wear uniforms and relies on the support of its community, all members of that community are suspect in the eyes of the army. British soldiers, fearing for their lives, tend to suspect all Northerners as potential assassins. When some army divisions consist mostly of Scotsmen and are placed in Catholic areas, fear increases because of the traditional Scottish Protestant-Irish Catholic animosity.

Michael Harbottle, a retired brigadier-general in the British army and ex-chief of staff of the United Nations peacekeeping force in Cyprus, has criticized the way the army has acted in Northern Ireland. The army could not act as an impartial third party since that role depends on trust from the population. The British army, for obvious reasons, is not seen as impartial. In addition, the training soldiers have received has been inappropriate for the roles the army could have taken.

A third-party peacekeeping force has many possible roles; the military function is not even its most important one. A peacekeeping force usually carries only sidearms and uses them only in self-defense. This has not been true of the British army in Ulster. More essential are the roles of negotiating ceasefires; interposing between two conflicting parties; maintaining communication among conflicting parties; and fostering reconciliation and community development with an eye to the structural causes of the dispute. The British army has seen its role as protecting British interests, and thus it could never have been an impartial third party from the beginning.

Behavior of British Army Chaplains

In the mid-1970s, some people in Northern Ireland charged the army with using army chaplains (or men posing as chaplains) to gather information about members of the Provisional IRA. This charge created special bitterness since it suggested that people had been manipulated by deception and misuse of the image of a priest. Army chaplains whom we have visited have been diverse types. They see their jobs as primarily to serve the soldiers and their families without much interest in military activity per se. They do not seem to visit local clergy much, or to care what Northern Ireland people think of their men. They do not accompany troops on their "sweeps," so they probably remain ignorant of the mutual harassment that goes on. For the record, we have met chaplains who are magnificent examples of Christian concern—for everyone, not just their own soldiers—but these seem to be rare.

Use of Technology and Computers

Some observers have noted that the army has introduced computers and other forms of technology to aid its work in Northern Ireland. Army officials readily admit that computers are used. There are some indications that the army hopes to have a complete record of everyone who lives in at least some sections of Belfast and Derry.

In August 1980, in some sections of Belfast, the army installed closed-circuit television cameras to monitor certain streets. Technology like this can, apparently, allow the army to decrease its foot patrols while maintaining surveillance and control and to reduce its troop level while still maintaining power. To have army personnel patrol your neighborhood is bad enough, but at least you know when they are there. Television cameras record all activity, offensive or not. They are a complete denial of privacy and a closer step toward outside control of neighborhoods.

Authorities also tap phone calls made between Northern Ireland and England.

Basis of Authority

To many noncombatants, it has been an open question for years whether the real authority in Northern Ireland rests with Stormont or in Lisburn with the army headquarters. Tension between the authority of the army and the authority of elected officials is one of the enduring sources of conflict in Northern Ireland. Since the army has little contact with civilians other than the RUC and the UDR, its public relations efforts seem at best self-serving and at worst downright deceptive. People come to look on its handouts as no more accurate than those of the Republican Information Service. In a protracted struggle such as the one in Northern Ireland, propaganda plays an important part. There is a strong tendency for news to be managed by all sides; each sector tries to convince people of its rightness or of the brutality of opposing forces.

Troop Withdrawal

The issue of withdrawing British troops has been argued endlessly. Is it possible? Is it necessary? Even among advocates, there are different positions:

(1) An immediate troop withdrawal, advocated mainly by Irish-Americans.

(2) Setting a date for a phased troop withdrawal. This is the position of the Provisional IRA, since they see the army as the main force which sustains the Northern Ireland-Great Britain political union.

(3) Withdrawal to barracks and cessation of frequent neighborhood patrols, which only encourage retaliation. Troops would presumably continue to carry out security searches of shoppers and vehicles when needed, monitor arms shipments and the production of explosives, defuse and dispose of bombs, and help, when necessary, in the evacuation of civilians.

Three perspectives on the troop withdrawal issue need to be explained. The issue of removing troops has always been used for political leverage (some might say propaganda) by a number of groups. The British government has bargained, "We'll remove troops if the level of violence goes down." Thus, the government forces the minority community to pressure the Provisional IRA and forces the majority community to pressure its paramilitary groups to reduce their activity.

The Republican analysis has always maintained that the British army presence is the sole source of violence in Northern Ireland. Remove the British army, they say, and violence would end. The issue of troop withdrawal has become a political litmus test: if you want troops out, you are assumed by many to be a Republican sympathizer. Some peace groups have taken a troop withdrawal stance in spite of this.

The issue of the troop presence is deeply connected with the issue of policing and security. The minority community does not trust either the police or the army reserve (since few Catholic men volunteer for either the RUC or the UDR). There is no sure alternative for the security work that the army does, and does poorly since their training is inappropriate.

Rumors and lack of information about policies covering troop activity constantly color people's feelings about soldiers. The army may change its strategy in one area; the strategy is not announced, since the UDA or IRA would develop a counter-strategy. But the people assume the old strategy is still in effect and act accordingly. An example of the army's dilemma may clarify issues. Armored cars were used to transport and defend soldiers when the army was more visible on the streets. Armored cars drove quickly through areas where the IRA, for example, was strong, since soldiers assumed they were always targets. Local children played in the streets, since they usually have no playgrounds. Parents were terrified that their children would be injured. Thus, the spiral of fear and hatred tightened.

A growing number of groups has increasingly favored the phased withdrawal of the army. In spite of this growing consensus, plans have not been implemented. The army is less active; in a de facto way in some areas, some troops have been withdrawn to barracks. Since 1978, troops have been withdrawn from Northern Ireland; the number of soldiers stationed there has gone down. In June 1980, the number of soldiers was 11,500. Two army barracks were closed down in Belfast in August 1980. A number of pedestrian and vehicle checkpoints have been disbanded in Belfast and Derry. In general, the army is less visible now than a few years ago: this lowered visibility has created a slight easing of tensions.

In the late 1970s, the army adopted a strategy of "Ulsterization," which meant that the Royal Ulster Constabulary (police force) and the Ulster Defence Regiment would play more active security roles and the organizations would hire more people. Consequently, the British army could reduce its activities and size. But the inherent contradictions of the RUC and UDR—especially whether or not both organizations are fair and impartial—weakened that strategy. The general Northern Ireland population has always been undecided about how much to trust their security forces.

Reasons Supporting Troop Withdrawal

The first reason supporting withdrawal of troops is the enormous cost of maintaining the army. Reliable figures are hard to find; one figure is that it costs the British government one billion pounds ($2.05 billion) a year to support the army apart from the cost of economic support (payment for damages, etc.). In May 1979, Northern Ireland Minister Hugh Rossi said it costs 76.6 million pounds ($162.5 million) a year to maintain the army in Ulster. Given the worsening economic conditions in Britain, this financial reason is persuasive.

A second reason supporting troop withdrawal is based on public opinion. A poll taken in 1979 in Northern Ireland revealed that sixty-six percent of Catholics and fifteen percent of Protestants agreed with the statement, "The British government should announce its intention to withdraw from Northern Ireland at a fixed date in the future."

In the spring of 1978, a poll of the British people revealed that fifty-three percent thought that the government should declare its intention to withdraw "whether the Northern majority has or has not indicated its consent." And in October 1979, a poll in the Republic found that seventy percent thought that there should be a unilateral British withdrawal.

The longer the army remains, the more individuals and organizations call for some sort of withdrawal plan. The *Daily Mirror,* a London daily newspaper, in 1980 called for withdrawal. Other individuals and groups have added their voices as well; four British peers, seventeen M.P.s, numerous British trade councils, labor union leaders, a few church leaders, some ex-soldiers, and prominent individuals, including Americans Paul O'Dwyer and Philip Berrigan, and Tony Smythe, executive director of the British Council for Civil Liberties, similar to the American Civil Liberties Union.

Reasons Opposing Troop Withdrawal

One important hesitation about withdrawing troops is that people fear that sectarian reprisals will increase and create such political upheavals that a full-scale civil war could result. Many minority families express great hatred for the soldiers, yet they are unwilling to call for removing them because they fear even more what might happen without them. One can argue that a continuation of the military occupation legitimizes and encourages action by paramilitary groups, thus perpetuating the war situation. One can argue just as easily that a troop withdrawal might escalate the fighting.

How one stands on troop withdrawal depends on one's analysis of the Northern Ireland conflict. Even if one sees the conflict as essentially a religious one—which we do not—one might foresee civil war following a troop departure. If one sees the conflict as essentially political, i.e., based on fundamental differences about political control and political structures, with each community having different cultures and identities, then it is at least theoretically possible (even though some see it as unlikely) that troops could be withdrawn without a civil war resulting. This argument does not take into account the tremendous levels of fear and bitterness which prevent people from seeing their future clearly.

Another issue: if the British army, the UDA, and the IRA were the only active military organizations, some sort of settlement might be possible. But there are a number of other paramilitary groups, many of them secret, some of them formed because people thought the larger paramilitary groups on both sides were not militant enough!

On the one hand, you could say that in light of all the paramilitary armies, the polarization is just about complete. On the other hand, the number of community organizations (see chapter 6) which keep communication open between the communities has greatly increased. Many Protestants say they don't hate Catholics— but they fear the IRA; many Catholics say they don't hate Protestants, but they fear the UDA.

Increasingly, a Northern Ireland identity has developed. This common identity is a potentially powerful force in the long run, yet a number of people who accept a Northern Ireland cultural identity do not support an independent Northern Ireland as a *political* unit.

It would be simpler if the troop withdrawal issue could be considered by itself. Unfortunately, this is not possible. The British army represents the British government. Troops cannot be considered apart from the politics, and troops are also a part of the security and police issue. In other words, if final agreement were reached about the political identity of the North, and if there were a police force acceptable to both communities, then there would develop some agreement about withdrawing troops in a definitive way. But neither condition exists, and neither one appears likely in the near future.

Internment

Internment without trial began on August 9, 1971, and was officially ended at the end of 1975. Just before direct rule was established in March 1972, the number of detainees and internees reached a peak of 924. W.D. Flackes, in his book, *Northern Ireland: A Political Directory, 1968-79,* writes that "in March 1973, of the more than eight hundred persons released from internment or detention since direct rule, only ten had been subsequently charged with offences." Although internment is no longer operable, many conflicts and issues around it caused major controversies in the North and should be examined. The government said internment was intended to decrease the level of violence. Yet internment triggered a great deal of violence by provoking anger. In addition, many people in the minority community were further alienated from the Stormont system of Northern Ireland government.

Internment was legalized through a provision of the Special Powers Act (see the Criminal Law section in this chapter). Initially, almost all 350 people arrested and interned without trial were Catholics. Many had Republican sympathies or were members of People's Democracy (see chapter 2). The fact that many more people who were arrested were Catholic caused a great deal of resentment, since the procedure was seen to be prejudiced mainly against them. Later on, Protestant extremists were also interned, but the damage had been done.

Another source of bitterness and anger resulted from reports that brutal methods of interrogation had been used by British soldiers. The Compton Inquiry of 1971 reported that there had not been any torture or brutality, but the British army had carried out actions that "constitute ill-treatment." The Irish government took the case of troop brutality to the European Court of Human Rights.

After some years of investigation, the court reported that the British army had been found guilty of brutal treatment during the early days of internment.

A special category of prisoner was created through arrests under the Special Powers Act. These internees were permitted to wear their own clothing, were allowed a greater number of visitors, did not have to work, and were given other considerations. Although internment officially ended at the close of 1975, people continued to be arrested for various offenses related to the political turmoil. But arrest and trial procedures were established by a special tribunal and became known as the Diplock procedures. (The inquiries and various commission reports are summarized at the end of chapter 2. Other issues referred to briefly here are discussed at greater length later on in this chapter.)

Police and Security

The controversies relating to the police and security are deeply tied in with the other issues detailed in this chapter. The Royal Ulster Constabulary is the police force for all of Northern Ireland; there are no autonomous local police forces as in the U.S. In April 1979, there were 6,512 members of the RUC; the RUC Reserve had 4,594 members. When Northern Ireland was created as a political entity in 1922, the Ulster Special Constabulary was created as a militia to support the RUC. Originally, there were three sub-categories in the USC: the A-Specials, the B-Specials, and the C-Specials. Eventually, only the B-Specials were retained; the USC then became synonymous with the B-Specials. The latter were made up of hard-line Unionists and had the reputation among Catholics as being particularly oppressive. The Special Powers Act was the legal basis of the B-Specials, and this law has been the envy of the South African government in that it allows sweeping and repressive actions. An investigation of the incident at Burntollet Bridge in 1969 revealed that half of the attackers were B-Special men out of uniform. None of them were subsequently disciplined. After B-Special personnel were found to have taken part in the attack on Catholic areas in August 1969, the B-Specials were disbanded. This was a serious blow to many in the Unionist community.

Since 1969, the main goal of the Northern Ireland government with respect to the RUC has been to make the police force acceptable to the minority community. If this analysis is correct, then the various programs and initiatives developed around the RUC are understandable. Opinions differ about how acceptable the police force is and if members are innocent of prejudicial actions. Thus, the RUC remains a controversial issue.

A second basis of disagreement about the RUC is the issue of "Ulsterization," the transfer of security responsibilities from the army to the RUC, discussed earlier in the "Troop Withdrawal" section of this chapter.

Since 1969, numerous investigations have asked to what extent police discriminate against Catholics, to what degree RUC members as individuals have acted brutally on the job, what kinds of complaints have been made against police, and how the complaints have been handled. The RUC was originally designed in 1922 to include not less than a one-third proportion of minority members, but the number of Catholics has never risen above twelve percent. A procedure has been developed for handling complaints against the RUC, but it has yet to be generally accepted.

Criminal Law

The laws which are part of the Northern Ireland criminal justice system have been and remain controversial. This is a complicated issue because the laws involved have developed in response to unusual situations. The issue appears especially complicated to people outside Northern Ireland because we are wholly unfamiliar with the prevailing legal system. Finally, these laws are tied in with other controversies: the military, policing, and the H-Block protest.

The Emergency Powers Act (EPA) was initially made law by the Westminster parliament in 1973, replacing the fifty-year-old Special Powers Act. Thus, the EPA, initially intended to be temporary (it was at first called the Temporary Provisions Act), has become the basis of the present criminal justice system in Northern Ireland. The EPA has been renewed more than nine times.

Issues

It may be helpful first to set out some important background information in capsule form; we'll follow with a brief discussion of the issues.

1. The Special Powers Act, enacted in 1922, was regarded by many as an instrument to be used by the Unionist government to keep the minority in its place. Since the EPA replaced it, and since the percentage of the minority community in the RUC continues to be low, many minority people feel that the EPA is also discriminatory.

2. The EPA covers wide areas of police-suspect interaction: stopping and questioning, search and seizure, dispersal of assemblies, accusatory and pre-trial procedures, trials, and appeals.

3. One major concern over the EPA is the serious and (apparently) permanent curtailment of civil liberties. This might be accepted on a temporary basis by many people if it were clear that the special laws were effective. But a second level of concern is based on the analysis that the laws have not done what they were intended to do—namely, reduce and control the level of violence in Northern Ireland.

4. More seriously, some Northern Ireland people have concluded that the EPA has, in fact, been counterproductive; it has created a backlash which has increased the level of violence.

5. It is extremely difficult to criticize the EPA, since many people jump to the conclusion that any critics are supporters of the Provisional IRA, the organization foremost in British legislators' minds when the bill was enacted.

6. Critics of the EPA state that, however justified that law might have been initially, the number of years it has been enforced has tended to normalize exceptional powers. Amnesty International reported over three thousand complaints (1971-78) of physical maltreatment by the RUC. Similar important complaints have been made concerning the British army. For example, in a given period, only thirty percent of detainees held between four hours and seven days have been charged. There have been daily searches, on the streets and in the homes.

7. A major element of the EPA is that the burden of proof to determine guilt or innocence is shifted from the prosecutor (defendant is innocent until proven guilty) to the defendant (guilty until proven innocent) in a number of circumstances. One example concerns the presence of a gun in a house. Under the EPA, the person charged is assumed to have knowledge and possession of the gun unles s/he can prove s/he did not know about it.

8. Considerable confusion exists as to the legal definition of "torture, inhuman or degrading punishment." The Diplock and Gardiner government reports, as well as the European Court of Human Rights and Amnesty International, have all attempted to clarify this issue.

9. Jury trial has been suspended in Northern Ireland since 1975. Three main reasons were given: to prevent witnesses from being intimidated, to save time, and to prevent what has been called "perverse acquittals." An increasing number of critics has come to question the validity of this reasoning and calls for the return of jury trials, at least in some situations.

Discussion

There are other important issues involved with the EPA, and they are all complicated. But this brief examination perhaps is enough to show how deep and serious the problems are. Since the law touches on very basic social realities, people have strong feelings about it. Yet some groups and individuals have tried recently to engage in a reasoned examination of the issues.

It seems to us that various strategies, based on differing analyses of the special courts and the EPA, have been attempted in order to deal with the state of emergency in Northern Ireland. Yet none have been successful; most people in Northern Ireland agree with that. The government has responsibility for maintaining order, yet there is evidence to suggest that the law has been counter-productive. Some critics have suggested that certain parts of the EPA should be changed slightly in order to move, little by little, toward a more normal law. Yet, when the EPA was renewed in the Westminster parliament in July 1980, only about twenty M.P.'s voted for changes. The law was renewed as it had previously stood.

As we have seen with other controversies, this issue is tied to many strong feelings of fear and hatred, confusion and bitterness. It is also related directly to the relative amount of power different parties in Northern Ireland have, or feel they have. It is always difficult for a party in a deep struggle to relinquish power, or to appear to do so. In the final analysis, it is important to realize that the criminal law in Northern Ireland is the basis of a lot of strong feelings, but the issue is rarely discussed in detail, point by point.

H-Block Issue

The H-Block protest was one in a series of highly-charged emotional issues in Northern Ireland.

The H-Block is a part of the Maze (Long Kesh) prison, the largest of the Northern Ireland prisons, near Belfast. The H-Block is so called because of the shape of the area of the prison where certain inmates are housed. On September 15, 1976, Ciaran Nugent refused to wear prison clothing and wore only a blanket or underwear. After that, between fifty and two hundred prisoners, most of them Republicans, and most of them men who identify with the Provisionals, joined the protest. From time to time, prisoners identified with other Republican groups, or with Unionist groups, also took part. In addition, in February 1980, women prisoners at the Armagh prison joined the blanket protest.

The H-Block campaign was closely related to the criminal justice issues. Some prisoners felt that the laws which were used to convict them were not normal laws because they restricted civil rights. For this reason, these prisoners protested their status as criminals. They wished to be considered "political prisoners" since they argued that the laws under which they were convicted were unusual laws, created for the special circumstances of Northern Ireland.

But the reasoning was more complex than that. Many people observed that support for the Provisional IRA campaign was weakening before the protest began. They argued that one of the main goals of the protest was to maintain support for the Provisional campaign to remove the British army (hence, also, the British influence) from Northern Ireland. The protest was part of this larger campaign. By developing highly emotional support for the

Republican prisoners and advocating the category of "political prisoner," the Republican cause would increase in legitimacy, and the British government would be put under increasing pressure to negotiate a final settlement.

It is important to know that in previous IRA campaigns, Republican prisoners had occasionally used the tactic of noncooperation with prison rules on roughly the same grounds. In fact, in the 1940s, Republican prisoners in the Republic and Northern Ireland used a noncooperation struggle to develop support for their cause.

The H-Block campaign involved more than Republican prisoners and the British government, however. A Relatives Action Committee sponsored marches and other protests with sympathetic organizations. Mothers and sisters of prisoners draped themselves in nothing but blankets and sat in the open air, sometimes in inclement weather. In addition, prominent figures have spoken out about the protest, sometimes criticizing the protesters, sometimes criticizing the government. Cardinal O Fiaich was one of these leaders; in 1978, while he was still archbishop, he visited the prison and stated that the prisoners were different from ordinary criminals. However, he did not call for reintroducing the special category status. Presbyterian Church leaders in Northern Ireland severely criticized the archbishop's statement, although he had previously spoken out strongly against the Provisional IRA campaign.

The H-Block protest began with prisoners refusing to wear prison uniforms, but their noncooperation escalated. In March 1978, prisoners refused to wash and shower, or clean out their cells. Guards' response was to refuse to bring around buckets to the cells, and human waste overflowed. Some prisoners took this a step further by spreading the waste on their walls, and the H-Block protest became known as the "dirty protest."

The British government maintained that the condition of the prisoners was self-imposed, and took no responsibility for it. The government refused to consider the possibility of granting a "political prisoner" status.

Prison officials maintained that there was no systematic brutality toward prisoners. Yet prisoners claimed that amenities available to other inmates were being denied to them because of their protest. For example, radios were not allowed, letters were limited, as were visits, and exercise was not permitted unless a prisoner agreed to wear clothing.

As if this were not enough, after 1976 numerous prison officials were assassinated.

In May 1979, Ciaran Nugent had served his term, and three months later he took part in a U.S. speaking tour to educate supporters about the campaign. In August 1979, about four hundred prisoners were "on the blanket." In January 1980, Irish Northern Aid held a testimonial dinner in New York City. Fr. Piaras O'Duill, chairman of the National H-Block Committee, was the main speaker. It is clear that emotional support for the campaign ran high among some Irish-Americans. In June 1979, Fr. Denis Faul and Raymond Murray published a book entitled *H Blocks: British Jail for Political Prisoners*. In August 1980, the British government announced that it would allow "compassionate leave" for prisoners. This was the first of a number of allowances that people saw later as concessions. Critics saw the main issues as yet undealt with. Late that month, Daniel and Philip Berrigan and four other Americans visited Northern Ireland in an attempt to "ease the plight" of the H-Block protesters. Not permitted inside, the group mounted a vigil outside the Maze for a day.

On October 27, 1980, seven Republican prisoners in the H-Block began a "fast to the death" in order to achieve "political status" for the prisoners. This escalated the campaign, since the tradition of hunger-striking is a prominent tactic in IRA history. Republican prisoners have occasionally starved themselves to death or have come close to it.

The men stated that if one of them should die, another prisoner would take his place. For the next eight weeks, tension grew in Northern Ireland, the Republic, Great Britain, and within the Irish-American community in the U.S. Government and church officials, prominent civil leaders, and well-known organizations made statements calling for various actions. Demonstrations, especially in support of the strikers, were scheduled with growing frequency— usually in Northern Ireland, but also in Great Britain, the Republic, and the U.S. By mid-November, shopkeepers in Belfast and Derry complained of being intimidated into displaying H-Block posters. On November 28, three Republican women in the Armagh jail joined the hunger strike. However, the seven original hunger strikers—who fasted for fifty-three days—as well as thirty-three other prisoners who joined them, ended their action on December 18. The Provisional IRA and its supporters claimed victory, since the prisoners won the right to wear civilian clothes and to refuse prison work. But the British government also claimed victory, since it did not grant special treatment to political prisoners.

It should be clear that the main element in the H-Block campaign was its high emotional charge, one which both the prisoners and the British government used for their own propaganda purposes. In 1980, a number of individuals and organizations attempted to suggest compromises designed to lower the heat of the issue. One suggestion was to grant "emergency status" to the prisoners involved, since the law under which they were convicted was itself an emergency law. The new status would recognize that the protesting prisoners were not "ordinary criminals." Another position was to focus on human rights issues. This was based on the argument that prison officials were depriving the protesting prisoners of what many people consider "rights" rather than "privileges."

Thus, the H-Block issue raised fundamental questions: How does one define rights as opposed to privileges? Can one remove human rights issues from the political questions involved? Is it possible in the Northern Ireland context to declare a new prisoner status without falling into the propaganda war? These larger issues proved to be just as intractable as the protest itself.

Hunger Strike Campaign, 1981

The hunger strike campaign in 1981 was a continuation of the fifty-three-day campaign which ended in December 1980. The later strike began on March 1 when a Republican prisoner, Bobby Sands, refused food in the Maze prison. Between May 5 and August 20, ten Republican prisoners starved themselves to death. The campaign was officially called off on October 3.

Prisoners demanded the following rights: (1) to wear their own clothes; (2) to have free access to other prisoners; (3) to be excused from prison work; (4) to organize educational and recreational programs of their own, to send and receive weekly letters and parcels, and to have weekly visits; (5) to have full parole rights restored (which might be lost because of the hunger strike).

As is frequently true of Northern Ireland issues, the hunger strike campaign was complicated by many factors of influence and interpretation. One complication developed around a special election held on April 9 for the Fermanagh-South Tyrone seat in the Westminster Parliament. The election was held following the death of the incumbent M.P., Frank Maguire. Bobby Sands, a Republican prisoner in the Maze, ran for the seat. This was unusual, since the typical and historic strategy of the Republican movement had been to deny the value of electoral politics and the government itself, and therefore not to run for office. The other candidate was Harry West of the Official Unionist Party. He had claimed that the past thirteen years' troubles had been caused solely by the civil rights movement. There was speculation as to whether or not Austin Currie or Noel Maguire (brother of the dead M.P.) of the Social Democratic and Labour Party (SDLP) would run. At the last minute, Noel withdrew. The SDLP did not register anyone to run, and they were severely criticized for this. Sands won by 1,446 votes out of about sixty thousand votes cast.

The election was important because it clearly pitted the two poles of Northern Ireland politics against each other. Some observers noted that many votes were cast not so much *for* a particular candidate as they were cast strongly *against* the other candidate. The propaganda value of having a Republican prisoner win a seat in the London parliament should be obvious. By the day of the election, Sands had been on his hunger strike for forty days.

From the time of Sands's victory in April through early October, Catholic neighborhoods, especially in Belfast, were in considerable agitation. Each time a prisoner joined the hunger strike campaign or neared death or died, demonstrations, parades, and funeral marches took place. At first they were massive, attracting tens of thousands of participants. Numerous public officials took action, either making statements as to their positions or offering solutions. Fears of confrontation with the Unionist community were high, but there were no major battles with the Ulster Defence Association (UDA). There were, however, numerous serious clashes between Catholics and police or army. Many people were killed, and street demonstrations sometimes led to vehicles being seized and burned.

The 1981 hunger strike campaign brought worldwide attention to Northern Ireland to an extent not seen since 1972. Campaigns were launched in many countries to pressure the British government into yielding to the prisoners' demands. Nowhere were these campaigns stronger than in the United States.

The British government maintained that the hunger strike campaign was meant to achieve "political status" for Republican prisoners. Thus, granting the five demands appeared to move toward official recognition of the Provisional Sinn Fein/IRA as an organization to be recognized at a bargaining table. Many other voices encouraged granting the demands because the Northern Ireland criminal justice system was far from "normal" jurisprudence.

The hunger strike campaign was called off when families of prisoners, influenced by Catholic clergy, announced that their men would be fed after they fell into comas. Calling off the campaign was clearly a propaganda defeat for the Provos, although as usual they at first claimed it was a victory.

Three days after the campaign ended, the British government announced some changes in the prison regime. It was too late to save ten lives.

The hunger strike campaign attracted global attention for several reasons. The prisoners' fasts translated issues into personal lives that the general public could understand more readily. Allies and opponents, as well as distant, uninvolved observers, could understand the drama of life and death. From far away, the issues looked simple. Up close, they seemed to be far more complicated. Some members of the minority felt the prisoners on hunger strike were carrying on an honored tradition of self-sacrifice. Members of the Protestant community saw the prisoners as murderers. Trust and understanding which crossed sectarian division had been building up over years of hard work. How much has the increased polarization destroyed that goodwill? This is one question that people of Northern Ireland asked themselves in the months following the end of the hunger strikes.

VIOLENCE

Intimidation

Fear is one of the strongest means with which to control a population. All paramilitary groups use it. Intimidation comes in various forms in Northern Ireland: warnings painted on walls, people followed home, anonymous phone calls, paint thrown on front doors, murder. Two particular forms of intimidation and punishment are well-publicized: tarring and feathering, and knee-capping. Tarring and feathering has most often been used against women who have been suspected of dating British soldiers or who were thought to have given out information. Its brutality is part of the message to other women: date soldiers and you'll get this, too. The Provisional IRA punishment of knee-capping has been used against men who were found to loot or steal in Catholic neighborhoods, or against IRA men who wanted to leave the organization. Knee-capping does not necessarily or usually result in death, but the victim can be crippled for life. The need to use canes to walk probably means that the person is a constant reminder to others not to do the same. Similar forms of brutal intimidation are carried out by Unionist paramilitary groups.

Rumors are a major instrument of fear and control, regardless of whether the rumor has any basis in fact. It is well-known that in some areas paramilitary groups demand fee money, or protection money, from families and shopkeepers. If people refuse to pay the small weekly amount, some escalating form of intimidation might result. Enough people have been killed since 1969 that it is almost impossible not to take such demands seriously.

Fatalities and Injuries

From July 14, 1969 to April 15, 1977, an estimated 1,750 people died in Northern Ireland as a result of politically motivated activities. A study indicates that sixty percent of these fatalities were suffered by people who were not members of the conflicting parties.

Identification of victims by any classification is extremely difficult, but one study presents these conclusions:

Victims who were members of security forces (British army) 444
Victims who are classified as Republican subversives   166
Victims who are classified as Loyalist subversives   42
Victims who are classified as civilian non-combatants   1,052
Victims who cannot be classified   44

A few comments are in order at this point. The sixty percent figure—people who are "not members of the conflicting parties"—may not mean only non-combatants; a number of people have been killed who were not known by family members or friends to have strong partisan views.

In a conflict like Northern Ireland, it is not surprising that a British army officer was once quoted as saying, when asked about innocent bystanders, "There are no innocent bystanders." From a military viewpoint, we may understand that statement; from any other perspective, it is unacceptable. There have been, of course, a great many innocent bystanders.

A chart of statistics of the fatalities recorded since 1969 is included in the appendix on page 204.

Sectarian Assassinations

Since 1975, numerous sectarian assassinations have taken place for no other motive than that the victim was either Catholic or Protestant. Since anyone, however uninvolved they are, might be shot in cold blood, such assassinations instill widespread fear. One well-known example occurred in January 1976. On one day, masked gunmen killed five Catholic men. The following day, ten Protestant men were machine-gunned to death in retaliation. The one Catholic on the bus was spared.

The number of sectarian assassinations apparently diminished after 1976, but they continue up to the present time.

Motives vary: revenge, desire to eliminate unwanted elements, psychotic hatred, resentment of alleged treachery or informing. For whatever reasons, individual murders and full-scale feuds have been among the most brutal aspects of the Northern Ireland conflict, and the most difficult for outsiders to understand. Such sectarian murders come out of a climate in which violence and military force are seen as acceptable means of dealing with conflicts; in turn, sectarian assassinations increase the acceptance of such violence.

GOVERNMENT AUTHORITY

Unification of North and South

A united Ireland is not a recent demand made solely by the IRA; it has been a central and divisive issue for years. It is a distant goal many Irish people have dreamed about at least since 1641 and the time of the United Irishmen. The Act of Union in 1800 dissolved the Irish parliament, and governmental decisions affecting Ireland were transferred to Westminster. The 1920 Anglo-Irish Treaty which determined independence for Ireland ultimately did not include the North since the million-strong Unionist majority rejected Irish independence. These people were the descendants of Scottish and English settlers, most of whom had come to live in the North and established plantations during the 1600s during the "Plantation" period. Traditionally, Ireland had been divided into four sections, or "kingdoms," which later became the provinces of Ulster, Leinster, Munster, and Connacht. The Boundary Commission set up in 1921 to determine the precise border did not include the traditional nine counties of Ulster, since this would have given Protestants a political majority of fifty-four percent. So Unionists settled for six counties: Down, Armagh, Antrim, Fermanagh, Londonderry, and Tyrone. The nationalist point of view (which always had a single Irish nation as its goal) has always seen the decision of the Boundary Commission as unfinished business: they want to "complete the revolution" by "uniting" North with South.

Unionists, on the other hand, have insisted, since the North was created, on the continuation of political union with Great Britain. The United Kingdom is defined as Great Britain (England, Scotland and Wales) and Northern Ireland. The latter is the only part of the U.K. that has a provincial government, complete with parliament. Independence movements developed briefly in Scotland,

and to a lesser degree in Wales, in the 1970s, calling for independence from Great Britain.

The constitution of the Republic of Ireland, sections 2 and 3, claims jurisdiction over the entire island. These clauses always act as a subtle weight upon Northern Unionists, since as long as they remain, there is always the implication that some day the North might be united with the South.

It might appear from a distance that all Catholics want to see eventual unification, and all Protestants want to maintain political union with Great Britain. But this is not so; a number of Catholics favor the status quo, and a smaller percentage of Protestants favors unification with the Republic. This is where the "Protestant-Catholic" terminology breaks down. The terms *Nationalist* and *Unionist* are more accurate, since they refer more exactly to how people feel about this issue.

The Sunningdale Agreement in 1973 stated that if a majority of voters in Northern Ireland wished the North to be part of the Irish Republic after a border poll (a test of opinion on the legitimacy of Northern Ireland's existence), then Great Britain would not oppose it. This is where things now stand legally. The border poll resulted in fifty-seven percent of the electorate in the North voting to remain in the United Kingdom.

Northerners give a variety of reasons for opposing unification. Some of them are sensible; some are based on shibboleths. Particular issues are higher welfare benefits in the North, a higher living standard, better employment opportunities, and more money spent on education and health. But Richard Rose in his book, *Governing Without Consensus,* writes, "For every three Protestants who think abolishing the border would be harmful, two think it would make no difference." Many Southerners express a good deal of ignorance about conditions in the North, know little about grievances on both sides, assume that unification will eventually take place, and wish the fighting would go away—at least not come South. Various detailed scenarios and strategies for unification have been considered, but, of course, they remain as discussion topics.

A reason often given by Unionists for opposing unification with the South is the lower standard of living there. Most economists hold that over some years, Ireland's membership in the European Economic Community will bring Ireland's gross national product

(GNP) closer to that of other European countries. Thus, EEC influences tend to reduce differences between North and South.

Overseas investments are desperately needed to provide jobs. On the other hand, a large portion of the profits made from these enterprises leaves the North. Of the total investment in the North, the United Kingdom ranks first, the U.S. second, and West Germany third.

The fundraising of support groups for the IRA in the U.S. is well-known, and often decried. What is less known is that similar groups in Canada and in Great Britain raise money for Unionist paramilitary groups in much the same way (see chapter 7).

Structure of Northern Ireland Government

The terms discussed here—direct rule, proportional representation, power-sharing, and devolution—represent different perspectives on and strategies to deal with conflicts. These terms and the developments they represent are so basic to an understanding of Northern Ireland that a discussion of them is essential.

Direct Rule

Before March 1972, Northern Ireland had been an integral part of the United Kingdom (with England, Scotland, and Wales) since 1922. Northern Ireland was different from the other three sections in that it had a separate provincial parliament by the name of Stormont, which passed laws pertaining only to the province.

The profound changes which took place from 1968 to 1972, however, were so far-reaching that the British government felt in 1972 that Stormont was no longer capable of administering.

Bloody Sunday (the event in Derry at which the British army shot and killed fourteen unarmed civilians) occurred on January 30, 1972. A few days later, the British embassy in Dublin was destroyed by fire. For these and various other reasons, direct rule was imposed March 24, 1972, and it remains in effect today; i.e., the province is ruled directly by the Westminster parliament. This means that there has not been an effective provincial government since then (with the exception of the 1973/74 Assembly). The British prime minister chooses a secretary of state for Northern Ireland, who in turn chooses cabinet ministers for finance, civil service, commerce, education, etc.

Initially, direct rule was widely favored by the minority community in Northern Ireland, since it meant that the Unionist Party could no longer maintain its monolithic hold on government power. Perhaps a faint analogy might be drawn with the U.S. civil rights struggle in the 1960s by reminding readers of the U.S. federal intervention from time to time. Of course, the style and duration of intervention were quite different.

A serious drawback to direct rule eventually was recognized: most members of the Westminster parliament knew little of the Northern Ireland situation (some observers comment that some care less). Thus, bills relating to Northern Ireland would receive less attention than their importance would seem to deserve.

Direct rule relates to the governing of Northern Ireland as a whole. The structure of local government was not affected by direct rule, but it has undergone structural change as well. The old local government structures—which all too often could be and were controlled by gerrymandering and power politics—were dismantled. They were replaced by twenty-six district councils with limited powers, and area boards; the latter cover health, education, libraries, and the like.

Proportional Representation (PR)

Proportional representation is a method of counting votes to ensure fairness in an election; it attempts to guarantee that minority parties will be represented according to their popular vote. PR has been used in Northern Ireland since May 1973, the first time in recent history since the 1920s. It has been used in all elections since, with the exception of those for the Westminster parliament. When a candidate has won enough votes to be elected, for example, to the Assembly, the extra votes are transferred to other candidates with similar political positions. The votes are counted again until the full number of seats is filled. In the twelve regions in the 1973 Assembly vote, the least number of counts in a region was seven; the largest was eighteen—that is, votes were counted and transferred eighteen times to elect six people from East Belfast to the Assembly.

Power-Sharing

Power-sharing is the concept that Unionists and Nationalists should share decision-making power at important levels of the Northern Ireland government. A year after direct rule was imposed, the British Government, under Prime Minister Edward Heath, proposed forming an Assembly. Brian Faulkner as Prime Minister of Northern Ireland worked out an executive committee to govern which included Unionists, SDLP and Alliance Party members. This executive was the most developed expression of the concept of power-sharing in Northern Ireland. It collapsed after only three months under the weight and power of the Loyalist general strike in May 1974.

After that, power-sharing as a political theme became, in some ways, jargon which indicated if a candidate were willing to "give a little" or not give at all. For some years, the SDLP and Alliance and progressive Unionist parties stood on record as supporting the idea. But in recent years, it has come to be seen as a worn-out slogan. Today, not even the Alliance Party is on record as including power-sharing in its party platform.

Devolution

As the 1970s progressed, some Northern Ireland and British political leaders addressed themselves to the inherent political instability of the Northern Ireland government by calling for devolution, i.e., the eventual reinstatement of Northern Ireland provincial government and the end of direct rule. Since 1977, some of the proposed elements of a devolved government have included an Assembly elected under PR which would have real responsibility. The talks initiated with representatives from some major Northern Ireland political parties by Secretary of State for Northern Ireland Humphrey Atkins, 1979-80, can be seen as an attempt to move toward a devolved government.

Rolling Devolution

James Prior, who succeeded Atkins as Secretary of State for Northern Ireland, introduced the concept of "rolling devolution" in the spring of 1982. When the election for a reconstructed Stormont government took place in October 1982, the elected officials did not have any political power to begin with. They were empowered to make recommendations, not to write bills. Majority was defined as seventy percent, in order to ensure that representatives of both communities would work together. As officials prove that they can cooperate, the British Government will grant more political power to the Stormont government.

These are the issues which have divided Northern Ireland people. Some have existed since 1968. Some have been around much longer than that, and a few issues have been controversies only for a few years. Some have faded in importance; others have grown. In spite of the passion and heat which these issues have engendered, we agree with the authors of the book *Violence in Ireland: A Report to the Churches* when they wrote, "... whatever historical explanations there may be for attitudes taken up by various groups in Ireland, and without prejudice to any legitimate political aim, there is absolutely no justification for the campaigns of violence that have characterized the situation in recent years." No issues can justify the deaths of over two thousand people, victims of politically-motivated violence since 1968.

Chapter 4
Facing Backwards

History often seems irrelevant to modern readers, but history is hardly irrelevant when it comes to Northern Ireland. The idea appears in writings old and new: in Ireland there is no future—only the past, recurring again and again. For Ulster people today, events in the seventeenth century are much more significant than most recent world or even United Kingdom events.

Images from history are familiar sights in Northern Ireland, yet two largely contrasting views of that history exist: an "Irish" version and a "British" version.

A wall painting in a Protestant area depicts William of Orange, victor at the Boyne (in 1690), on a white horse, proclaiming Protestant control and power in Northern Ireland. A stone's throw away is a wall painting of James Connolly, one of the small band who declared an Irish republic in 1916 when they hoisted an Irish tricolor above the General Post Office in Dublin.

A book of this size cannot begin to present even a modest history of the island, yet interested readers must be acquainted with at least the major references to historical events which still figure prominently there. So this very brief historical survey up to 1967 is included, trying to strike a balance of the versions. We urge reading more Irish history written from the diverse points of view (see bibliography).

Ancient Times to 1500: England Becomes Involved with Ireland

There may have been inhabitants on the island who came over a landbridge that connected Ireland with England and Europe, between 15,000 B.C. and 6000 B.C. However, the best evidence indicates that the first inhabitants were mesolithic-age seafarers who came from Scandinavia to Britain, then from Scotland to Antrim, reaching Lough Neagh about 6000 B.C. They were hunters. The farmers came next, in neolithic times, traveling from the Mideast along the Mediterranean and reaching Ireland about 3000 B.C. Passage-graves such as those at Newgrange in County Meath are relics of these people. Miners and metal workers, again from the Middle East, came around 3000 B.C., so that by 1200 B.C. a new style of warfare appeared: swords and shields, helmets and gorgets. Their bronze weapons gave way to the iron wielded by Celtic tribes from central Europe who were established in Ireland by about A.D. 150.

These Gauls or "Celts," as the Greeks called them, were groups linked by a common language and some customs. Ironically enough, in view of the modern problem of identity in Northern Ireland, one movement of Celts came to western Ireland (Connaught) from the continent, and the other came from northern Britain to northeast Ireland (Ulster!). Previous inhabitants have left little behind; the Celts dominated the island for more than a thousand years, and are still there.

By St. Patrick's time in the fifth century A.D., practically all the earlier inhabitants had become Celticized, with a common language and culture. Saint Patrick, born in Britain, was the founder of organized Christianity in Ireland, establishing a major church center in Armagh in A.D. 444. He died in 491; his grave in Downpatrick is marked by a huge boulder. Irish monasteries which he encouraged were not only foci of religious faith, but also centers of great culture, learning, and art, doing for the farmer then what towns would later do.

The "Dark Ages" of Europe were in Ireland a time of great culture, building upon the forms found in the legends, the jewelry and the religious objects of previous centuries. Poets and Brehons (law-wise people) were honored. Columcille and Columbanus spread the gospel and civilization back across Scotland and the continent between A.D. 500 and 700. They were predecessors of so many other "Scots" who have moved to and from between Ulster and Scotland. The *Book of Kells* in the library of Trinity College, Dublin, and other medieval manuscripts testify to the wondrous early Irish art. Many of them toured the U.S.A. in 1977-78, as "Treasures of Early Irish Art," and were seen by thousands in this country.

For about two hundred years, A.D. 795-963, pagan Viking raiders plundered Ireland as they did the rest of Europe, sacking monastic centers more than once. Irish round towers are a memorial to these times; when a raid was anticipated, people found refuge in them. One of the first Norse fortified settlements was built in A.D. 841 on the river Liffey, where Dublin now stands.

The "Kings" of Tara and Cashel were overlords in their areas, but the island had no real political unity at the time. King Brian Boru (965-1014) was to Ireland what Charlemagne was to France and King Arthur was to Britain. He emerged as the first secular Irish hero by defeating first the kings of Leinster and Tara, then the Norse at Clontarf near Dublin in 1014. The Vikings became Christians, and left a legacy of towns along the eastern coast—a legacy that has influenced Irish life ever since.

At last Ireland was "united," but very imperfectly; rival kings soon fought over the high-kingship, and among themselves. One of them, the Leinster king Dermot MacMurrough had long before asked the Angevin king of England, Henry II, for aid against the other Gaelic kings. In 1155, Henry had obtained a papal bull, *Laudabiliter,* from Adrian IV, the only English pope in history, commissioning Henry to invade Ireland and reform it. (His great-grandfather, William of Normandy, had been authorized by the pope of a century earlier to conquer and "reform" Anglo-Saxon England.) Henry himself came to visit in 1171, largely to make sure the Normans would not set up a separate kingdom of their own. The Gaelic chiefs accepted him as a constraint on the Normans.

These invaders brought much more than war to the island, although their control was soon limited to "The Pale," the area around Dublin (hence the phrase, "beyond the Pale," meaning outside civilized territory). Coinage, a centralized though weak administration from Dublin Castle, the jury system, inland towns—all stem from this invasion. The leaders outside the Pale intermarried with the Gaels, as had all previous invaders, and took up Gaelic customs and language. Liberties established by the Magna Carta in England in 1215 were extended to Norman Ireland; a parliament was established in Dublin in 1297.

But the Normans never came in sufficient numbers to complete the forming of a "new nation" with the Gaels. Only two English kings even visited the island in the next three hundred years: John and Richard II. A Gaelic revival set in, and gradually the Anglo-Normans were absorbed.

The English made an attempt to prevent the Anglo-Normans from merging with the Gaels, and in 1366 the Statutes of Kilkenny tried to eliminate the Irish language and Irish laws and customs from the Pale. The attempt was notably unsuccessful. Richard II came in 1399 to try to stop the merging of the Anglo-Irish and the Gaels, but had to hurry back home, where he lost his crown to the house of Lancaster. Wars on the continent absorbed more and more of the interest of the English, who increasingly grew apart from the Irish, long before the Reformation.

1500-1685: British Protestantism Comes to Ireland

The English monarchy became concerned about Ireland in the late fifteenth century when the Irish (Norman-Pale) parliament sided with a rival claimant to Henry VII's title to the throne. The Tudor monarchs became intent on making sure Ireland would not foster any rivals to their rule. Their only ultimate guarantee was to replace the authority of the Norman feudal rulers and the Gaelic chieftains with English royal servants.

The process of "Anglicizing" Ireland was further complicated by the Reformation, since the kings insisted that the Church in Ireland also break with Rome. Thus, religious differences were added to the existing ones of class and political loyalty. "Protestantism" was identified as "English" and alien by the subject Gaels. "Catholicism" was identified as "Gaelic" and alien by the ruling English. The Anglican Church was established as that of the island, with tithes due from all—a constant irritant to non-Anglicans, both dissenters and Catholics.

The resistance to the British was encouraged by Spain and the papacy, enemies of England at the time. This became another motive to Anglicize Ireland, to make sure that it would not serve as a springboard for an assault on England.

Areas resisting Anglicization were subjected to "plantation," with ownership titles given to the English for importing colonists to Ireland. Plantation in Munster was superficial, since few settlers actually did come, even though ultimate control of the land had passed to foreign owners. In Ulster, however, a different process took place and left the northeastern part of the island with an enduring problem.

Hugh O'Neill, Earl of Tyrone, led a revolt against Elizabeth I. At Kinsale in 1601, the Irish lost and the old Gaelic world finally collapsed. "The Flight of the Earls" in 1607 was followed by the plantation of Ulster, when great numbers of lowland Scots, usually Calvinists, were recruited to take over the land from the native Irish. For the first time, a new wave of invaders did not intermarry with the islanders, largely because of the recent legislation of the Council of Trent concerning Catholics entering into mixed marriages.

The governance of Ireland fell into the hands of the "New English," who controlled both parliament and the established Church of Ireland. The Catholics, both Gaels and Normans or "Old English," were subjected to civil disabilities, and deprivation of their lands. Derry was deeded to the London Merchants Guild, which renamed it Londonderry.

In 1641, when the English king and his parliament were at odds, the Gaelic Catholics of Ulster staged an uprising to regain their lands. Ireland became entangled in the English civil war between king and parliament, Cavalier and Roundhead. Charles I lost and was executed. Oliver Cromwell won and destroyed Drogheda. He dispossessed the Catholic and Cavalier Irish, rewarding his financial backers and soldiers with their lands. They became a Protestant upper class which owned the land, with the former landowners now simply working it.

After the restoration of Charles II in 1660, some Catholics regained their lands, but they were relatively few. In 1641 they had owned about three-fifths of the land; at the end of the Restoration period they owned no more than one-fifth.

One event of note during the rather peaceful reign of Charles II was the execution of Archbishop Oliver Plunkett of Armagh, a man of peaceful life and genuine loyalty, but caught in the web spun by the "popish plot" of 1678. He was declared a saint of the Catholic Church in 1975.

1685-1800: English Protestantism Victorious; Irish Nationalism

James II, Catholic brother of King Charles II, became the British king in 1685. James appointed Richard Talbot, Catholic duke of Tyrconnell, as lord lieutenant in 1687; he recruited a large number of Catholics into an Irish army. Tyrconnell held Ireland for James when the king was deposed from the English throne in 1688 and replaced by William of Orange. Loyal apprentice youths of Londonderry, who lived inside the city's walls, shut the gates of the city against Tyrconnell's men in 1689. (This event is celebrated by a parade of the group called "Apprentice Boys" each year in Derry on August 12.) James himself tried to negotiate the reopening of the city, but was unsuccessful. He set up a siege; relief ships sent by William of Orange broke the boom and ensured success to the resistance. This "siege of Derry" is an important symbolic event of Ulster Protestant tradition, and is the historical origin of the phrase still used today, "No surrender."

In July 1690, a major battle occurred at the Boyne River near Drogheda, fought by thirty-six thousand Williamite troops and twenty-five thousand French and Irish troops for King James. The twelfth of July is the day in Northern Ireland when Orange parades celebrate "The Battle of the Boyne" which established the yet existing British Protestant government in Ulster. Ironically, a *Te Deum* of thanksgiving was sung in St. Peter's, Rome, since the Papal States were then allied against Louis XIV of France, who backed James against the English. Religious differences rarely paralleled political and economic interests in Irish history.

The major battle of the war, at Aughrim in Galway, ended in defeat for the Irish. Limerick held out under Patrick Sarsfield until 1691, when a rather generous treaty was signed. Its spirit did not last; fear of an invasion from Ireland continued to plague England.

The "wild geese," thousands of Irish soldiers then fighting on the continent for the French and others, were a permanent threat to the English establishment. If they ever returned in force, they would surely be supported by the majority of the people. The English ruling minority therefore legislated privilege for themselves, as ruling minorities usually have done.

The Penal Laws (1695-1829) debarred Catholics from public life and office, from army, navy, and law, by prescribing qualifying oaths to the crown as head of the church which no Catholic could take. They made it illegal for Catholics to be educated (hence the establishment of "hedge schools"—open-air schools hidden behind hedges), to hold Mass in public, to own property, to own a horse worth more than five pounds, or to own any military weapons. The laws affected not only Catholics, but all religious minority groups of "Dissenters," especially Presbyterians. The Penal Laws ratified, as it were, the identification of oppressed classes in terms of religion.

The success of the American Revolution deeply affected Ireland. Spain and France supported the rebellion. Many of Washington's army were Irish emigrants, especially Protestants from Ulster. Henry Grattan urged Parliament to grant Ireland the status of an independent nation linked to London by a common crown and a common political tradition. He failed at the time, but soon after the loss of America it came about.

The British parliament renounced its claim to legislate for Ireland; the crown retained only veto and administrative power. For a short time the island was in form and theory an independent kingdom sharing a monarch with the neighboring island. An Irish Post Office was founded, as was the Bank of Ireland. The Customs House and the Four Courts were built. Dublin appeared to be a capital city, although political power was really withheld from Gaels and kept in English (Anglo-Irish) hands.

Attempts to reform the system so as to get political power to the Irish were failures. The moderate Volunteers in 1783 and the radicals led by Napper Tandy in 1784 had little effect and no success.

The uneasy coexistence of Irish and English took definite shape in 1784. Fearing that Catholics were stockpiling arms, northern Protestants created locally-based groups called "Peep-O-Day Boys," who broke into Catholic homes at dawn looking for arms. An Irish group known as "the Defenders" was formed for protection and was successful in the 1790s in forcing rents down. To counter the Defenders, a federated league of Protestants, called "the Orange Boys," was formed in September 1795. This was the origin of the Orange Order movement which has been an important force in Northern Ireland for almost two hundred years.

The French Revolution caught the interest of Theobald Wolfe Tone, a Protestant lawyer of Dublin, who spread the Republican principles of liberty, equality, and fraternity. Tone advocated cooperation of the underprivileged—Catholics and Dissenters— through the Society of United Irishmen in Belfast, and in Dublin with the help of Napper Tandy. At first they tried persuasion, and called representative conventions which in turn called for reforms. At war with France, Britain pressured the Dublin parliament into giving Catholics the vote—though they still were excluded from Parliament, judgeships and higher state offices. By 1798, a fierce conflict took place between the government and the United Irishmen helped by the French. Tone was captured and committed suicide before his impending execution.

The British prime minister, William Pitt, decided the best way to deal with uprisings in Ireland was to force a union of Great Britain and Ireland by dissolving the Dublin parliament and establishing a single parliament at Westminster. The Act of Union of 1800 meant that all laws pertaining to Ireland were to be made in London, in a House of Commons with 658 members, only one hundred of whom were elected from Ireland. It lasted until 1921.

1800-1905: Catholic Nationalism; The Famine's Effects; Parnell and the Land League

Robert Emmet's attempt at a rebellion in 1803 was unsuccessful, but his speech from the dock has influenced succeeding generations of Republicans. Daniel O'Connell, a Kerryman, became the great leader of the Catholic emancipation movement. He launched the Catholic Association in 1823. The clergy led local groups; a penny a month funded the movement among the peasants. Large protest meetings were held all over Ireland, calling for the granting of remaining rights to Catholics. In 1828 O'Connell, though ineligible, was elected to Parliament in Clare, the first Catholic so elected for centuries. In 1829 the Emancipation Act opened almost all public offices to Catholics. The Irish were coming to greater self-consciousness, and through nonviolent means—O'Connell's way.

Unfortunately for the future, at this time nationalism and Catholicism became so strongly linked politically that they became difficult to distinguish and usually impossible to separate. Much of the anger of the peasantry revolved around the tithe paid by all to the established church, the Anglican Church of Ireland. This was considered unjust by those not belonging to that church.

O'Connell's second great movement was toward repealing the Act of Union with Great Britain, and for this purpose he formed the Repeal Movement in 1830, imitating his Catholic Association of 1823. He rallied many Irish and some few English to the cause, but this time Parliament, which had been willing to grant emancipation, was adamantly opposed to "dismemberment of the empire." O'Connell died in 1847, disappointed but known in history as "The Liberator."

The Great Famine, 1845-50, changed Irish history. Figures given by historians differ widely. In 1841 over two-thirds of the population depended on agriculture for a living, and the potato was their staple. Blight in 1845 was fairly well compensated by government food and relief works, but an even worse blight in 1846 could not be countered by public relief. Hard winters set in, and mismanagement added to the horror. Many people panicked, and emigration became the only way out. Liverpool served as a gateway, but kept many poor Irish in its slums.

In "Black 1847" about one hundred thousand people sailed for Canada and two hundred thousand for the U.S.; about a fifth of them perished on the way. Three million people were on public funds, but not enough food was obtainable from England or anywhere else, even with donations.

The population declined from 8.5 million in 1841 to 6.5 million in 1851 and 5.5 million in 1871. Government response to the famine was so poorly managed that resentment developed. People felt that government policy showed "callous disregard for Irish suffering" (Beckett, *The Making of Modern Ireland, 1603-1923*). The government refused at the height of the famine to stop the exportation of Irish grain. This was especially painful for the Irish since people were starving while grain which could have been given away was being sold overseas for profit. A major result of the famine was a huge influx into the U.S. of Irish immigrants, whose sense of Irishness was based largely on hatred of Britain, often with convictions that the use of revolutionary violence was justified.

The Irish Republican Brotherhood (IRB), or the Fenians, was founded simultaneously in Dublin and New York in 1858. Dedicated to the one goal of independence from Britain, and convinced that this could be achieved only by physical force, the Brotherhood enrolled thousands of working-class men by 1865. Post-Civil War arms and officers arrived from the U.S., but not enough for the intended uprising of 1865, which had to be postponed until 1867, when it failed like that of Young Ireland in 1848. Fenianism waited fifty years; the IRB still existed in 1916, though its members were a tiny minority of the population.

Parallel to the *revolutionary* tradition of the IRB was the *constitutional* tradition of Gavan Duffy's Tenant League of the 1850s and Isaac Butt's Home Rule movement of the 1860s. The two traditions merged in Charles Stewart Parnell (1846-91), a Wicklow Protestant with an Irish-American mother, and Michael Davitt (1846-1906), a Catholic born of an evicted tenant-farmer from Mayo. In 1879, as another economic crisis threatened, they founded the Land League to prevent evictions, reduce rents, and transform tenant farmers into landowners.

In America, John Devoy influenced Clan na Gael, the American Fenians, to support the Land League, which combined all shades of nationalism from moderate home rule to republicanism in one great agrarian movement. The "land-war" of 1879-82 saw nonviolent resistance come to the fore: demonstrations, community relief for the evicted, legal defense of prisoners with support of their families, and the boycott—named after Captain Charles Boycott of County Mayo, who in 1880 found himself and his family reduced to isolation and helplessness by the non-cooperation of his tenant farmers. Troops and Orange volunteers from Managhan rescued him, but the name went into the language as meaning economic and often social ostracism.

Prime Minister William Gladstone consistently supported "justice for Ireland." In 1869 his "Church Act" disestablished and disendowed the Anglican Church in Ireland, placing religious denominations in legal equality. Ulster Presbyterians moved from hostility to British rule toward Unionist loyalism. In 1870 Gladstone's "Land Act," though largely unsuccessful, was a first step by the British government on the side of the tenants. A series of acts from 1881 to 1903 gradually abolished the old landlordism and enabled the peasant farmers to be owners of their land. This was agrarian revolution indeed.

The Ballot Act of 1872 set the stage for future developments since it established the secret ballot. Previously, votes were taken by a show of hands, and people were often intimidated into voting a certain way. After 1872, the number of people voting for home rule increased considerably.

Parnell now moved from his victorious campaign of land reform to home rule. The National League was his instrument. Gladstone supported home rule in the form of a devolved government elected by the Irish and legislating for Ireland within the British empire—much along the lines of Canada. He knew the opposition in Ulster, where the powerful feared loss of their position, but thought that an upper chamber of legislature, based on property and status, would insure their interests. Parnell's goal was for all Irish to share equally in home rule—all creeds and classes. Gladstone lost a vote in the Commons in 1886 on the issue of home rule, but at last made it clear that the issue was not merely one of "English versus Irish."

Parnell had an affair with Kitty O'Shea; when it was made public, Parnell divorced his wife in 1890. This scandal finished Parnell as leader of a united Irish Party, but Gladstone tried again in 1893 for a home rule bill.

Parnell's achievement has lasted. His demand for independent nationhood, and his willingness to gain it step by step within the system, set an example and a standard of political genius for others to follow.

Important non-political events followed soon after Parnell's downfall. William Butler Yeats led an aesthetic revival which went far to give Ireland a national literature, with heroic figures like Cuchulainn and Cathleen ni Houlihan. The Gaelic League was founded in 1893 by Douglas Hyde and Eoin MacNeill to preserve the Irish language and Irish customs in the face of English encroachments. Games (the Gaelic Athletic Association), dancing, drama, local and national festivals, Gaelic in the schools, pub-closing on St. Patrick's Day, and Irish parades for all suitable occasions were promoted. Before long it was a strong political force; a distinct culture should belong to a distinct nation-state. Young nationalists like Padraic Pearse, Plunkett, Ceannt and McDonagh were drawn to the revitalized IRB; Tom Clarke and Sean MacDermott played the theme, Get The British Out.

Parnell's Irish Party had regrouped in 1900 under John Redmond and continued to agitate for home rule by constitutional methods. They failed. Lord Randolph Churchill's 1886 slogans,

"Play the Orange card" and "Ulster will fight and Ulster will be right," had passed into glib mythology, later surfacing as "Home rule is Rome rule." Besides, the appeal in Ireland of the violence-prone revolutionaries was gaining adherents among the alienated, and the constitutionalists found the going difficult.

1905-66: Conflict of Unionism and Nationalism

Sinn Fein ("We Ourselves" or "Ourselves Alone") began in 1905 when Arthur Griffith in the *United Irishman* claimed that the 1800 Act of Union was illegal, and proposed Ireland return to Grattan's "dual monarchy," with its own parliament in Dublin. He offered a nonviolent alternative to Redmond's parliamentarianism, distinct from the Irish Republican Brotherhood's plan to use force as soon as opportunity offered.

In these years another small group was forming, made up of socialists and trade unionists in the cities, where the land revolution of the 1880s had had little effect. James Larkin and James Connolly organized the Irish Transport and General Workers Union in 1913, fought the employers in a bitter strike, and illegally established a Citizen Army to protect the strikers—an army that remained strong.

The complexity of the time is illustrated by the fact that in 1912 Pearse spoke for home rule, which was passed by the House of Commons in that year and was legally destined to become law in 1914.

A Dublin lawyer, Edward Carson, led the Unionist agitation in the North. Two hundred thousand signed the Ulster Covenant to use "all means" necessary to defeat home rule. The Ulster Volunteer Force, established illegally, and illegally armed from Germany, was ready to back a provisional government against the British if home rule became law. The British Conservative party under Bonar Law declared its support of Carson, and an impasse resulted. This idea of Ulster Unionists fighting the British in order to remain British is a paradox repeated in the 1960s and 1970s.

Another irony was the admiration of many Republicans for Carson as an Irishman unafraid of the British. An Irish Volunteer Force was started in Dublin, in imitation of the UVF. The outbreak of World War I in 1914 postponed the crisis, but *only* postponed it. Many of the IRB, through the Irish Volunteers, were waiting for their moment.

The Easter Rising of 1916 focused Republican self-consciousness. It was not so much the events of that terrible week as it was their aftermath which roused strong antagonism against the British among hitherto uncommitted Irish. Of the ninety rebels condemned to death, fifteen were executed between May 3 and May 12. Seven of those who had raised the tricolor over the General Post Office (GPO) and declared an Irish Republic died for their idea. The movement had its martyrs; Pearse's blood sacrifice was offered. Their declaration lives after them, and is recited by Irish-Americans at many gatherings. Its emotional appeal in this country is undeniable. Its romantic view of historical reality is questionable, and questioned by historians.

The next two years saw the sudden development of general sympathy with Sinn Fein. Threat of conscription ended with the end of the war, in November 1918, but had a major effect. The Irish Party's constitutionalism was more suited to peacetime than to these years, and the party won only six seats in the general election of December. Sinn Fein won seventy-three on an "Irish Republic" platform, and the Unionists twenty-six. On an island-wide basis, Sinn Fein polled less than a majority, 47.7 percent. The issue was not complete independence, but rather the greatest amount of independence obtainable without partition of the island. In other terms, it was for home rule as a dominion, with hope of further steps. Only a few Volunteers thought physical violence was a necessary step.

Sinn Fein honored its campaign promises and refused to take Westminster seats. Instead, they convened an Irish parliament, Dail Eireann, in Dublin with Eamon De Valera as head, Arthur Griffith as his deputy, and Michael Collins as military organizer. The Anglo-Irish war of 1919-21—"the Troubles"—followed, with guerrilla warfare, assassinations, raids, and reprisals. The "Black and Tans" achieved their infamous name as adventurers put into British uniforms to wreak atrocities on the Irish—or were they simply ex-servicemen pressed into action and left pretty much to themselves as they fought the guerrillas?

The "war" resembled that of the 1970s, and was equally unwinnable for both sides. In July 1921, a truce was signed, largely because of public opinion in Britain and the U.S.A. It led to a treaty in December which gave dominion status to the twenty-six counties. Excluded were the northeast six: Down, Antrim, Armagh, Fermanagh, Tyrone, Londonderry.

The Unionists in these six counties of what was called Northern Ireland (not "Ulster," which had nine counties) had already been given home rule of their own by the Government of Ireland Act in 1920. King George V had opened their parliament in June 1921, with Sir James Craig as prime minister.

David Lloyd George had imposed this dual settlement, and the Unionists accepted it as preferable to rule from Dublin. It provided for Irish representatives in Westminster from both Irish parliaments, and a common Council of Ireland to deal with cross-border matters. Sinn Fein had refused it flatly.

The December 1921 treaty set up the Irish Free State and gave Northern Ireland the option of pulling out—a foregone conclusion. The Boundary Commission was to adjust to the political realities. Nationalists thought it would cut into the six counties so deeply as to leave them unviable. Unionists successfully opposed any change, and the commission's report was never published. The six counties remained as they were, an integral part of the United Kingdom but with one-third of their population opposed to their political existence. Polarization was inevitable.

Nationalists in the six counties felt justified in refusing to cooperate with the Unionist government, and thereby were labeled disloyal, hostile to the state, and dangerous. Unionists felt justified in keeping local as well as province-wide government out of such hands. Religious affiliation became even more coterminous with political aspirations: "Protestant" Unionists and "Catholic" Nationalists. The dilemma has remained.

At any rate, the 1800 Act of Union had at last been superseded, at least in the twenty-six counties. In the South, Sinn Fein split. The pro-treaty party, led by Arthur Griffith, carried the Dail by sixty-four votes to fifty-seven in January 1922. The anti-treaty party, led by De Valera, lost the June general election. A disastrous civil war followed, lasting until May 1923, leaving its heritage of bitterness. The civil war had the effect of shifting attention in the Republic away from Northern Ireland and toward domestic, especially economic, issues. The original Act of Parliament formed a Council of Ireland which would have brought the two parts of Ireland together in discussions to resolve their differences, leading to eventual unification. However, points mentioned below postponed this process until the Sunningdale Agreement in 1974.

William T. Cosgrave succeeded Griffith as head of state. De Valera and his party, Fianna Fail ("Warriors of Ireland") stayed out of electoral politics until 1927; his acceptance of the Free State as the legitimate government earned him the title of "traitor" from the hard-line anti-treaty group. Many of the latter emigrated. They still refer to the present Dublin government as "The Free State"; it is not a compliment.

In 1932 De Valera formed his first government, and remained in office until 1948. He produced a new constitution in 1937, declaring Ireland to be a sovereign, independent, and democratic state with de jure right to govern the entire island (Articles 2 and 7). This divergence from the 1921 treaty remains as a major irritant to Northern Unionists and for many is sufficient reason for continuing deep distrust of Southern governments.

Ireland remained neutral during World War II, despite pressure from President Roosevelt. The first postwar election in 1948 brought in a coalition government of Fine Gael ("Gaelic Family"), labor, and others, which put the Republic or Ireland Act through the Dail in 1949 as the final step in withdrawing the twenty-six counties from the Commonwealth and from all fealty to the British crown.

In the North, sectarian strife had recurred in 1922 and in the early thirties. The Unionist Party held power throughout the province; the Labour Party never made headway. The Unionists always held two-thirds to three-fourths of the seats at Stormont. Of the thirteen members of the Westminster parliament, eleven were almost always Unionists and supported the British Conservative Party. Lord Craigavon was prime minister between 1921 and 1940. To him is attributed the "Protestant parliament for a Protestant people" sentiment and the "Hire your own" advice. J.M. Andrews held the office from 1940 to 1943, when Lord Brookborough followed him and served until 1963. Captain Terence O'Neill was prime minister from 1963 to 1969.

These were difficult years. The two main industries, shipbuilding and linen, fell on hard times. Unemployment reached twenty-eight percent in 1931, and was still twenty percent in 1941—despite much emigration. Eire's wartime neutrality of course sat badly with the North, although many Irish volunteered for the British army, and on one notable occasion in 1941 the Dublin fire department raced to Belfast to help after a German fire-bombing. Londonderry became the port where American naval vessels berthed, and many U.S. troops passed through Northern Ireland.

Some cooperation between North and South occurred in the fifties: railways, fisheries, power—common areas with minor political ramifications. But the old issues remained. Westminster passed the Ireland Act of 1949, promising that Northern Ireland would not cease to be part of the United Kingdom without consent of its parliament. A violent campaign of the IRA, especially along the border, occupied much of 1956-62.

Encouraging steps were the 1965 meeting at Stormont between Captain O'Neill and Mr. Sean Lemass, head of the Dublin government, and the Anglo-Irish trade agreement that same year. In 1964 Stormont recognized the island-wide Irish Congress of Trade Unions. Ireland entered the United Nations in 1955, and sent troops to serve in U.N. forces in Lebanon and Cyprus.

1967: The Situation Just before the New Troubles

A summary of the situation in the North in 1967 will provide some elements against which to evaluate the chronology which follows. A reminder: no short treatment can possibly be comprehensive.

In Northern Ireland, the Unionist government had controlled virtually all aspects of civil life for the entire forty-six years of the province's existence. Their two-thirds majority in the six counties had persisted despite the higher minority birthrate, largely because of emigration which the minority felt was forced on them by discrimination in hiring. Captain O'Neill was trying to follow a moderate course, but an adamant Unionist group was resolutely opposed to any concessions that in their view would threaten the majority's control and their way of life. In the sixties, Ian Paisley appeared as the demagogic and very effective leader of the extreme right in his Free Presbyterian Church and at Stormont. His influence grew and grew.

The Nationalist Party under Eddie McAteer of Derry had little effect on policies. Even where they were a majority, they rarely gained local political power because of gerrymandering by the majority Unionists. The minority Catholics had little hope that they would ever be more than second-class residents in a province where their families had lived for centuries. The IRA was dormant, though a small Republican group continued to dream of change.

The majority Protestants felt that their right to govern was undeniable, as their long-time residence in the six counties testified— longer, for instance, than European Americans had lived in the U.S.A. Many Unionists genuinely believed (and still believe) that they acted fairly in regard to the minority, despite the minority's refusal to cooperate with the Northern institutions. The police and their auxiliaries, the B-Specials, kept order in the state. Three thousand soldiers were garrisoned around the province—the only army needed. "Law and order" were provided for all who would accept the state.

The poor existed in both communities. Housing on the Loyalist Shankill Road was like that on the Republican Falls Road: tiny rowhouses with outside privies in back, cold-water taps, few amenities in the streets. Unemployment was worse on the Falls but bad on the Shankill. A main difference was that the Shankill people in general felt that Stormont was "their" government and would protect their interests, whereas the Falls people in general distrusted Stormont and saw few signs of betterment for themselves.

Their common Christianity had not yet come home to them as a reconciling factor. Indeed, it unfortunately split along political and historical lines so as to reinforce the cultural and social divisions expressed in segregated neighborhoods and neighborhood schools. Vatican II had opened up the Roman Catholic Church to the other Christian churches in a way unforeseen in the fifties; its effect was slow in reaching the hard-line areas of the North. Working class Protestants lived, worked, played, studied, shopped, drank (if they did), worshipped, and thought in their own areas and in their "British" way, which they knew was good. Working class Catholics did the same in their own way in "Irish" areas. They rarely encountered each other in the city streets; their pastors practically never met together. Such separation necessarily begot wary ignorance, which in turn gave birth to distrust, anger and eventual bitterness toward "them."

This chapter closes with a quotation from *Violence in Ireland: A Report to the Churches,* where the ecumenical group comments:

The historical background, although it can be summarized in this matter-of-fact way, had induced on both sides a depth of feeling which is difficult for the outside observer fully to appreciate and which is undoubtedly strengthened by the religious dimension. On the one hand there is the profound inner conviction that the British presence has for centuries brought nothing but suffering, humiliation and neglect to the Irish, a conviction that does not always lose its potency when somewhat qualified by objective historical study. On the other hand there had been an attitude based on the strange amalgam of superiority and insecurity that characterizes a minority when it is maintained as an elite by an external power. The use against the British presence, whether in the whole island or since 1920 in Northern Ireland, of methods held by their users to be a justifiable use of force on behalf of their nation, has seemed to the unionist community not only to constitute illegitimate violence but also to be a direct menace to which it must respond with counter-violence if British protection wavered or failed. We have seen in recent years how very strong remains the determination to maintain an identity distinct from that of the Irish majority and to demand political institutions that will guarantee the distinction.

Folk art in Londonderry depicts King William III. The King remains a symbol for many people of Protestant domination in Northern Ireland.

Chapter 5
The New Troubles

The last fourteen years in Northern Ireland have constitued an exceptional history. To many observers, it is a story piling horror upon horror. If there is any "sense" to what has been happening there, the logic is invisible. Why does all this violence continue?

Events in Northern Ireland do have causes, and many of the major forces are discussed in chapter 3. Significant events and turning points caused major developments later on. With hindsight, it seems fairly easy to see patterns and trends. At the time, to be sure, all was chaos and turmoil. In 1967 and 1968, there were clearly the early beginnings of a new movement, shaking off the dust of two generations—an integrated civil rights movement with a nonviolent strategy.

The second significant period was 1969-72: it was during this time that the Social Democratic and Labour Party (SDLP) and the Alliance party were born, British troops were called in, the IRA split into two main groups, and internment was introduced. The most important year, if it is possible to single out one, was 1972. This year saw Bloody Sunday, Bloody Friday, and the imposition of direct rule. The violent events were watersheds in terms of lethal intention to maintain control and power. The implications of direct rule are clear, since Northern Ireland is still in 1982 without its own provincial government. By the end of 1972, the lines were drawn.

The years 1973-75 saw an attempt by the British authorities to encourage a workable government in which Catholics and Protestants would share power. But the 1974 work stoppage indicated to many that this strategy would not succeed.

The Sunningdale Agreement continued the British government's 1949 position, which is still in effect: if the majority of Northern Irish people want to leave the United Kingdom, the British government will not stand in the way.

Nineteen seventy-six to 1978 makes up a fourth period, ushered in by the Peace People and the short-lived but widespread hope that perhaps now peace would finally break out.

The next definable period was 1979-81, marked especially by prisoners' actions and the strong campaigns of the Provisional IRA to develop support and to keep their political and military initiative. That period ended when the hunger strikes failed in 1981.

Examining the statistics of fatalities on page 204 also offers a valuable picture of the last fifteen years. The highest number of fatalities of any one year in terms of politically motivated killings took place in 1972. In 1977, the total number of people killed was two-thirds less than in 1976. The campaign of killing prison officials did not begin until 1976, which roughly coincided with increased political activity on the part of prisoners. Yet it is impossible to imagine what it has been like for Northern Irish people to live through this period, when not one month has been free of murders since at least January 1972.

Many observers have noted that Northern Ireland is governed by the politics of the last bullet. The latest violent event sets up a new polarization and enmity which thoroughly change the perceptions of the recent past. Previous events may be wiped out or rearranged in unexpected ways. Sometimes the more heinous or violent the latest atrocity has been, the more thorough is the rearranging.

Finally, to answer the question "Why does all this killing continue?", we need to remind ourselves that the waves of violence have created seemingly permanent layers of fear, which remain and create new poison and alienation and bitterness. It is as though Northern Irish people are prisoners in the violence and fear they themselves have created.

The last fifteen years in Northern Ireland have witnessed amazing events; thus, no recounting can possibly be complete. But it is important, especially for people not living in the province, to understand the sequence and the context of the major events that have occurred, so as to better understand present and future developments. Detailed analysis of many issues, as well as background information on organizations, are given in other chapters.

1967 Beginnings

In January, people from majority and minority communities formed the Northern Ireland Civil Rights Association (NICRA). Through nonviolent action, NICRA sought to achieve reforms in laws which govern jobs, housing, and voting rights. In December, the prime minister of the Republic, Jack Lynch, visited Prime Minister O'Neill at Stormont and was heckled by Ian Paisley and his supporters.

1968 Civil Rights

In August, the first civil rights march took place from Coalisland to Dungannon, about four miles. Between twenty-five hundred and four thousand people took part. The main issue was to protest local housing policies which discriminated against Catholics. Fifteen hundred Loyalists held a meeting there, too; police kept the two crowds apart. In October, despite a government ban, NICRA sponsored a civil rights march in Derry; about two hundred took part, and TV reported it. Police blocked the march, then attempted to break it up by beating people with batons. Rioting and stonings continued throughout the night, and at least eighty-eight people were injured.

In November, the Northern Ireland cabinet proposed a five-point reform program, including a points system of housing allocation, an ombudsman, a voting franchise report, a review of the Special Powers Act, and the setting up of the Londonderry Development Commission. On the thirtieth, an approved civil rights march in Armagh was forcibly opposed by one thousand people led by Paisley and Major Bunting, who was later jailed for illegal assembly. In December, Prime Minister O'Neill gave a famous "Ulster stands at the crossroads" speech. In spite of 150,000 messages of support for O'Neill's reforms, William Craig opposed them and was dismissed as Minister of Home Affairs.

1969 Enter British Troops

This year saw numerous demonstrations. British troops were sent in to protect the marchers. The government took action by establishing a Civil Rights Commission to report on various important events. In January, the People's Democracy organized a civil rights march from Belfast to Derry, about 120 miles. On January 4 the march—then consisting of about two hundred people—was attacked at Burntollet Bridge outside Derry. Eighty police were on hand. A number of people were beaten up. A similar march in Newry ended in violence on both sides; NICRA blamed "agitators." The government established the Cameron Commission to inquire into the causes of the violence in the North from 1968 on.

In April, Bernadette Devlin was elected to the Westminster parliament from Mid-Ulster. Prime Minister O'Neill resigned under duress after his government made concessions on the "one man, one vote" issue for local elections. Major James Chichester-Clark succeeded him by winning an election from Brian Faulkner.

Full-scale riots occurred in Derry and Belfast in August. Jack Lynch asked the British government to request a U.N. peace-keeping force in Northern Ireland. Lynch's statement became famous: "We shall not stand idly by." In riots in Belfast, a row of houses on Bombay Street burned down. People erected barricades between the two communities in Belfast and Derry to prevent mobs from crossing. Local citizens' groups developed alternative (although temporary) neighborhood governments which were independent of city governments. The first death from sectarian fighting occurred. Extra British troops were flown in for the first time and welcomed by the minority as protectors. The Scarman Tribunal was appointed to investigate the August riots. The government established a mixed Community Relations Board (later, Commission)—none had existed before. Many families who lived in integrated neighborhoods moved into their "own" areas. The "Peace Line" was erected in Belfast—a wall of sheet metal, barbed wire or brick which blocked certain roads, dividing neighborhoods and keeping the two communities apart.

Over strong Unionist objection, the Hunt Report urged reform of the police and the end of the Ulster Special Constabulary (B-Specials). The Ulster Defence Regiment (UDR) was set up, six hundred strong, often accused of being the B-Specials under another name although a number of Catholics joined. The voting age was lowered to eighteen in December. Finally, Bernadette Devlin was sentenced to six months in Armagh jail. She was "Man [*sic*] of the Year" in the *Sunday Independent*.

1970 IRA Split

In 1970, important events occurred on the streets, and new political lines were drawn in Northern Ireland with the creation of new political parties, SDLP and Alliance. In January, the Irish Republican Army (IRA) split into two wings: Provisionals and Officials. The Ulster Defence Association (UDA) appeared as a counterpart vigilante group in the Protestant community. Eastertime parades ended in riots against troops in West Belfast; tear gas was used.

In the electoral politics arena, Paisley was elected to Stormont from County Antrim. The non-sectarian Alliance Party was formed, with Oliver Napier as leader. Neil Blaney and Charles J. Haughey were dismissed from the Republic's cabinet after allegations that they had assisted gun-running to the North. (Charges were later dismissed.) Paisley was elected to Westminster, as were Independent-Unity candidate Frank McManus, Bernadette Devlin and Gerry Fitt. Unionists retained eight seats.

For two days in July, the army imposed a curfew on the Lower Falls area of Belfast and conducted a house-to-house search for arms. Rubber bullets, used by the British army, were rumored to be made in the U.S. The Social Democratic and Labour Party (SDLP) was formed, with Gerry Fitt as leader. This left-of-center minority party works for civil rights and eventual reunification of Ireland by consent of people in the North. Sinn Fein opposed it, and the Alliance Party attacked SDLP as sectarian.

By November, the UDR had 201 officers and 3,668 others; sixteen percent were Catholic. One-third of the members were authorized to hold weapons at home. On another note, the "Movement for Peace in Ireland" was launched in Belfast and Dublin, to help form opinion and promote peaceful discussion. In

December, Jack Lynch said the government of the Republic would introduce internment without trial if necessary; Chichester-Clark said it would be used only as a last resort in the North.

1971 Internment

The most important development in Northern Ireland this year was internment.

In August, after many denials that it was imminent, and much preparation for it on both sides, the government introduced internment, the procedure of arrest and indefinite detention without specific charges or public trial. On August 9, 363 people were arrested, only two from the majority. Two hundred homes were burned in the Ardoyne section of Belfast. Some seven thousand people fled Belfast temporarily to five camps hastily set up in the Republic. Allegations were made that some people were treated brutally by British troops, nine cases were verified later by the Strasbourg Court (see 1977-78). Amnesty International and the Red Cross also investigated. The Compton Inquiry was established to investigate these charges. The SDLP, NICRA, and others called for a boycott of the collection of local taxes ("rent and rates") to protest internment. This campaign, which lasted as a major focus for nine months (and officially for some years) cost local government about sixty-five thousand pounds a week. British troops numbered twelve thousand; the UDR numbered about ten thousand.

The first soldier to be killed in Northern Ireland since 1969 met his death in a Protestant area in February. Explosions increased. A prayer service for peace in Ulster Hall was attended by over a thousand people. Maurice Hayes of the Community Relations Commission recommended introducing proportional representation to local elections and reducing the number of gun licenses (102,112 weapons were registered in Northern Ireland on 73,193 firearms certificates and permits.). Provos and Officials shot at each other on the Falls Road, Belfast for two days.

In March, Chichester-Clark resigned "to bring home the realities" of the situation. Brian Faulkner was elected over William Craig, who spoke of re-arming the RUC, restoring the B-Specials, and defying the British if direct rule were attempted.

In May, the "Contraceptive Train" protest took place: Dublin women bought contraceptives in Belfast and declared them to Irish customs to protest against the Republic's law against their sale.

It was reported in June that multinational corporations had provided one-third of the new jobs since the war. DuPont announced a seven million pound ($17,080,000) expansion of its Derry plant, with 180 new jobs provided.

In July, Faulkner expressed satisfaction with the first inter-party meeting at Stormont, but later SDLP boycotted Stormont. Paisley offered to be "loyal opposition." Official unemployment figures showed the highest unemployment in nineteen years: forty-three thousand—10.1 percent for men, 5.4 percent for women. Rioting, explosions, and arrests increased. There were ninety-two explosions in July alone. British Home Secretary Reginald Maudling on one occasion said a state of "open war" existed between the IRA and the army; this phrase has been used ever since by the IRA to "justify" its claim of being "at war with the Brits."

1972 The Year of the Killers

The year 1972 was pivotal in Northern Ireland. In many respects, it was like 1968 for the United States: major violent events took place, and the country was never the same again. Paramilitary groups took major initiatives in 1972, and their activities have been a central fact of life in Ulster since then. The government structure disintegrated, and many of the struggles of succeeding years have been about finding a workable replacement.

The year was marked by five major events:

1. *Bloody Sunday* occurred on January 30 when fourteen men and boys were killed by paratroopers at a banned civil rights rally in Derry. (Thirteen people died that day; one person died later from his wounds.) The troops claimed to be returning fire. (See the Widgery Report in chapter 2.) Two days later, the British embassy in Dublin was burned down, with a huge crowd looking on. Many developments stem from Bloody Sunday.

2. *The British Government* imposed direct rule in March. The provisional government at Stormont was closed down. Initially,

this was seen as a victory for the minority, since the majority had governed since 1922 in what many regarded as a prejudicial manner. The minority hoped that the British government would usher in needed reforms, doing away with prejudicial laws and practices.

3. *Derry Women's Peace Initiative* in May: A Catholic soldier, George Best, came home to the Creggan in Derry on leave from British army service in West Germany. He was killed by the Official IRA as a traitor to his own people. Two hundred women and children demanded that the Official IRA get out of the Creggan and the Bogside, both militant Catholic areas of Derry. Later, they said the same thing to the Provos. Thousands joined prayer rallies for peace. A few days later, the Officials announced a ceasefire, since "the overwhelming desire of the great majority of all people of the North is an end to military action by all sides." In June and July, women delivered thousands of signatures on petitions calling for peace.

4. *Bloody Friday,* July 21. Twenty-two Provo bombs exploded in Belfast within seventy-five minutes, terrorizing the city. Eleven people were killed and 130 people were injured. The event was condemned by all other groups.

5. *Sectarian assassinations multiplied*. An investigation by the Catholic Ex-Serviceman's Association reported seventy-two assassinations; fifty of the victims were Catholics, and many of the others were Protestants with Catholic friends.(

From 1972 onwards, Northern Ireland events become more complex and difficult to follow. We have arranged them under the following headings: demonstrations, IRA actions, Unionist actions, government actions (in Northern Ireland, Britain, or the Republic), elections, prisoners and courts, bombings, U.S. actions, peace initiatives, and other events.

Demonstrations: All parades were banned for the year, but the Grand Orange Lodge and a few Unionist leaders said they would not be bound by the ruling.

IRA actions: The Official IRA bombed the officers' dining hall at Aldershot, England, killing seven. In March, the Provos announced three conditions for ending their campaign: army withdrawal, amnesty for political prisoners, and the abolition of Stormont. Libyan President Khadafy's remarks on the IRA led to the search of a Libyan ship in the Belfast harbor; no arms were found. *Eire Nua* presented the Provos' proposal for a new Ireland, including a nine-county Ulster with its own parliament. When street fighting became intense, bus companies stopped service on some routes in both communities. Freelance "Black Taxis" began to operate on dangerous roads in Belfast, under "protection" of paramilitaries on both sides, who probably receive a share of the profits from the service. Sean MacStiofain, Provo leader, was sentenced to six months for being a member of the IRA and went on a hunger strike. Church leaders succeeded in persuading him to end the hunger strike, and he disappeared from public life for years.

Unionist actions: The Ulster Vanguard movement was formed by William Craig to unite Loyalists. A month later, seventy-five thousand people attended a Vanguard rally in Belfast. Craig called for a two-day work stoppage after direct rule was imposed; 190,000 responded. The UDA set up temporary no-go areas to protest no-go areas in minority estates. ("No-go areas" were parts of a city that were policed by members of a paramilitary organization. Travel through these areas was restricted by road blocks and check points.) A few months later, the UDA set up permanent no-go areas in Belfast; seven thousand masked men faced the army with clubs, but finally agreed on joint patrols. Reports said that twenty thousand armed UDA volunteers were ready.

Government actions: British Prime Minister Heath and Home Secretary Maudling said the majority in Northern Ireland could not be bombed into a united Ireland, but the minority had to share properly in the country's life. Faulkner demanded an end to violence, the restoration of a strong Stormont, and a refusal to negotiate with enemies of the state. In July, a meeting between Provo leaders and Secretary of State for Northern Ireland William Whitelaw resulted in these Provo demands: (1) recognition that all people of Ireland must decide the island's future; (2) declaration of intent from the army to leave by the end of 1975; (3) amnesty for political prisoners. In England, Labour Party leader Harold Wilson met with five Provo leaders. All no-go areas were dismantled by the end of July, allowing police and army to enter these areas for the first time since 1969. The RUC advertised a confidential security phone number for people who wished to give information on crimes. The Darlington Conference on the future of Northern Ireland involved only the Unionists, the NILP and Alliance; other parties boycotted it. A "Green Paper" of the U.K. government outlined the plans of the various parties in Northern Ireland.

Bombings: A no-warning bomb in the crowded Abercorn Restaurant in Belfast killed two and injured 130. Both IRA wings denied responsibility. In mid-April, thirty explosions occurred throughout Northern Ireland. In May, the IRA fire-bombed the huge Belfast Co-operative store with damage of ten million pounds (twenty-five million dollars) and loss of 750 jobs. The Derry Guildhall was twice bombed and severely damaged.

U.S. actions: A month after Bloody Sunday, the Foreign Affairs Subcommittee of the House of Representatives held hearings on Northern Ireland. The U.S. refused a visa to Maire Drumm, as it had to Joe Cahill earlier; both were important Provo leaders.

Additional peace initiatives: Leaders of the four main churches issued a joint statement calling for an end to the violence. Rev. Joseph Parker, whose son Stephen was killed on "Bloody Friday," began 'Witness for Peace' with a fast outside Belfast City Hall and a banner with crosses for those killed.

Other events: Bishop Cahal Daly said it was morally wrong for Catholics to belong to the IRA since it was illegal and acted against democratic institutions of the state. U.N. Secretary-General Kurt Waldheim offered to help in the Northern Ireland crisis, but the U.K. government turned him down. Maurice Hayes, chairman of the Community Relations Commission, resigned in protest against government inaction. Amnesty International found that army ill-treatment of internees in August-November 1971 "amounted to brutality." Two days before direct rule, a poll in the *Belfast Telegraph* showed a Westminster takeover was rejected by seventy-two percent of Protestants, supported by seventy-five percent of Catholics. Because of the danger of car bombs, such vehicles were banned from city centers; the army said it would blow up unattended cars. A pregnant Ballymurphy woman was tied to a lamppost, beaten, tarred and feathered, then told by Provos to leave home within forty-eight hours. She had been judged by an independent citizens' court in a no-go area. These courts in Belfast and Derry lasted for a few years as alternatives to recognized courts. Whitelaw allowed "special status" in Long Kesh to Crumlin road prisoners on hunger strike, both Republicans and Loyalists.

Robberies, usually thought to be for support of paramilitaries, took place all over the province. The Northern Ireland Housing Executive announced it would rebuild houses burned down in 1971 after introduction of internment. A BBC poll said fifty-five percent of the British people wanted troops withdrawn from Ulster. The Republic voted overwhelmingly to delete the "special position of the Catholic Church" phrase from article 44 of the 1937 constitution. Seven Catholic churches were damaged during the year in Northern Ireland.

1973 The British Try

The most important events in 1973 were government and Unionist initiatives and two important elections. In March, a British "White Paper" proposed an eighty-person Assembly elected by proportional representation, security by Westminster, and a Council of Ireland for North-South discussion of common matters. Craig and Paisley denounced it, as did the IRA; others accepted it. Whitelaw moved toward forming a power-sharing executive, composed of six Unionists, four SDLP members and one Alliance member, with Faulkner as chief executive and Gerry Fitt as deputy chief. In December, the Sunningdale Conference with U.K., Republic, and Northern Ireland representatives issued an important agreement: as promised in 1949, Northern Ireland was to remain part of the U.K. as long as the majority so wished.

Other developments:

Unionist actions: The United Loyalist Council called a successful one-day strike in February. The Ulster Freedom Fighters, a Loyalist group still more extreme than the UDA, was formed. Tommy Herron, former UDA chief, was kidnapped and killed. In December, the United Ulster Unionist Council (UUUC) was set up to oppose Faulkner's Unionists; the Ulster Army Council was also formed, including many Loyalist paramilitary groups.

Government actions: Great Britain and the Republic became members of the Common Market (EEC). In the Republic, a coalition of Fine Gael and Labour won the election, with Liam Cosgrave as prime minister. Erskine Childers was elected president of the Republic. The Northern Ireland (Emergency Provisions) Act replaced the Special Powers Act of 1922.

Elections: Out of 519 winners, local elections in Northern Ireland gave Unionists 210 seats, Democratic Unionist Party (DUP) 13, other Loyalists 68, SDLP 82, Alliance 53. Proportional representation in the Northern Ireland Assembly gave the Unionists an overwhelming majority.

Prisoners and courts: Prisoners in the Republic claimed political status, but were refused despite a hunger strike. The case against British troops, arising from their behavior toward arrested people at the start of internment, opened at the European Court of Human Rights.

Bombings: In March, two bombs in London killed one and injured 180; the Price sisters and others were jailed for it later. The pillar of the Walker Memorial in Derry was destroyed by a bomb.

Peace initiatives: Leaders of the four main churches notified the Vatican and the World Council of Churches that what was happening in Northern Ireland was not a war of religion. Peace Point was formed to provide media with information on the "better side of life" in Northern Ireland. The first Ballymascanlon meeting of Protestant and Catholic leaders took place.

Other events: The Littlejohn brothers were sentenced for a Dublin bank robbery after claiming they worked for the British Ministry of Defence, which strongly denied this. From January 1972 to September 1973, 124 Catholics and sixty-nine Protestants were assassinated.

1974 Power-Sharing—A Failed Experiment

This year is remembered for the powerful Unionist reaction to power-sharing.

It came in the form of a massive "work stoppage" organized by the Ulster Workers Council, May 14-28. This action told the British government and non-Unionists in the North that the Council of Ireland was not acceptable and that the Unionists had the energy to block it. They did; the Northern Ireland power-sharing executive died as a result.

1974 is also remembered for a major peace campaign initiated by church leaders in December. The action was successful in that an IRA ceasefire held for a few months and some hope was generated.

Events leading up to the work stoppage: When the new Northern Ireland executive took office in January, the UUUC rejected the Sunningdale Agreement, and Brian Faulkner resigned as head of the Unionist party. Paisley and other Unionists disrupted the first meeting of the executive. Hundreds of signature centers were set up for anti-Sunningdale petitions. Some months later, Paisley presented 313,000 signatures calling for an end to the Northern Ireland executive.

Work stoppage: The Assembly voted in the Sunningdale Agreement and the work stoppage began on May 15 as ports were closed and power was cut off. Businesses were shut down; imports and exports stopped. Transport was disrupted, bombs went off, and mail and phone services were affected. Barriers went up on some streets. Troops were called in to keep gas stations open. Faulkner resigned on May 28, the executive collapsed, and direct rule was restored. This massive demonstration of Unionist power is remembered to the present time as a British failure to control violations of law by the majority.

Church peace initiative: A Joint Campaign for Peace was begun in mid-December by the four main churches. At the same time, some church leaders met independently with Provisional IRA leaders at Feakle in the Republic. They succeeded in establishing a ceasefire that lasted some months.

A more detailed account of the work stoppage appears in chapter 3; for more details of church initiatives, see chapter 6.

Other events important in 1974:

IRA actions: The Irish Republic Socialist Party (IRSP), with Seamus Costello as leader, formed as a breakaway group from the Official Sinn Fein.

Government actions: Harold Wilson became Labour prime minister of Britain and Merlyn Rees became minister for Northern Ireland. Rumors spread that Special Air Service (SAS)-trained plain clothes soldiers were working in Belfast and Derry. Since 1969, the U.K. had paid 84.8 million pounds ($198.43 million) in property damages and 10.74 million pounds ($25.53 million) for criminal injuries to people. In Birmingham, bombs killed twenty, injured 182, and led to the Prevention of Terrorism Act. This made the IRA illegal. In England (later also in Northern Ireland), it gave the government power for six months to arrest and expel suspected terrorists. The IRA denied responsibility for the bombing. In Dublin, a Criminal Trial Act provided for trial in the Republic for some offenses committed in Northern Ireland.

Prisons and courts: The Price sisters ended their 206-day hunger strike (after they had refused to eat for thirty-nine days, they were force-fed for 167 days); they were transferred to Armagh jail. In October, prison riots in Northern Ireland wrecked many buildings.

Other events: A German industrialist was kidnapped and killed; his body was found some years later. (It has been unusual that industrial figures have been assassinated in Northern Ireland.) Fr. Edward Daly was consecrated bishop of Derry. Violence since 1969 had claimed one thousand lives. Garrett Fitzgerald of the Republic said in the U.S. that Northern Aid gave the IRA much support, and the rest came from intimidation and bank robberies. Bishop Daly said internment had brought younger and more irresponsible leaders to the militants. An assassination campaign, mainly against Catholics, escalated. Rev. Joseph Parker, founder of Witness for Peace, emigrated to Canada. The UDA and Sinn Fein leaders visited Libya simultaneously (but not "together", they claimed) to talk about financial matters, like off-shore oil. Over one hundred thousand signatures on a petition to end internment were collected by a magazine in the Republic.

1975 The Constitutional Convention

After the turmoil of the previous year, 1975 was quiet by comparison. There were few dramatic developments, yet initiatives were important for setting the stage for future events. The central event this year was the Constitutional Convention, a government initiative to assist political parties in Northern Ireland to work together and form a workable government. Since Loyalists held over half the convention seats, there was little question as to its outcome. But the experience did enable political figures to discuss issues.

In addition, the IRA ceasefire lasted for a few more months, and thousands of people attended peace services in Belfast and Dublin.

Other important events and developments:

Paramilitarist actions: Feuds broke out between the O-IRA and IRSP and between the UDA and UVF in March. Another IRA feud developed in October, lasting two weeks. A conference in Holland of paramilitaries from both sides discussed cooperatives for released prisoners.

Unionist actions: Loyalists began to police their own areas after continued friction with the RUC. The UVF was declared illegal again after they had murdered eleven people in October.

Government actions: Rees announced the end of "special category" status for new prisoners, beginning March 1976. (This set up conditions for protracted campaigns regarding the status of prisoners. This issue is still unresolved, eight years later.) Internment was officially ended.

Bombings: On one day in September, twenty bombs exploded all over the province, injuring many. Provos claimed bombings which occurred in London. Bombings on the border were claimed by the Red Hand Commandos, a Loyalist group.

U.S. actions: Forty-five Northern Ireland leaders came together at Amherst, Massachusetts, for a forum organized by Boston Irish-Americans; participants represented community, paramilitary, and peace groups, politics, church, and media.

Other events and developments: Doctors reported two deaths and forty injuries from the firing of 3,300 rubber bullets since they were first used in August, 1970. Unemployment in Northern Ireland was 54,977, 10.6 percent overall. A Gallup poll in England showed sixty-five percent wanted troops out, compared with thirty-four percent in 1972.

1976 The Peace People

This year is remembered for the Peace People. They appeared dramatically and created, for a little while, energy and hope. At rallies and marches in Belfast, Catholics and Protestants walked in each other's areas for the first time in their lives. They all demanded peace and an end to the killing and murder. Controversy and criticism about the Peace People developed just as dramatically; a fuller account is given in chapter 6. The point remains that many Northern Irish people were heady with the new-found energy and hope that peace just might be possible.

Other events important to note:

IRA actions: Frank Stagg died after sixty days of hunger strike. In April, thousands attended a banned Sinn Fein rally in Dublin.

Unionist actions: Maire Drumm, former vice-president of Provo Sinn Fein, was murdered in the hospital.

Government actions: The Constitutional Convention ended with little accomplished except a hardening of positions. Liam Cosgrave, the Republic's prime minister, asked the U.S. Congress to help halt American funds for the Provos. James Callaghan was elected Labour prime minister of Britain; Roy Mason became secretary of state for Northern Ireland.

Prisoners and courts: March saw the end of the special category status for newly convicted prisoners. Two prison officials were killed by PIRA, the first of a number of murders of such officials. The European Commission of Human Rights found the U.K. government guilty of using "torture" in August 1971.

Bombings: Christopher Ewart-Biggs, U.K. Ambassador to Ireland, was killed by a bomb. Derry Provos wrecked the center of Portrush, with six bombs causing a million pounds of damage. In December, Provo bombs destroyed seventeen shops in Derry.

Peace initiatives: A special commission of the Irish Council of Churches and the Catholic Church issued the book, *Violence in Ireland*.

Other events: Two events in south Armagh were especially violent. Five Catholics were killed by masked gunmen. The next day, ten Protestants were machine-gunned to death after being stopped and forced out of their bus. The one Catholic on the bus was spared. The U.K. closed three maintenance bases in Northern Ireland, costing two thousand jobs.

1977 A Quiet Year

Nineteen seventy-seven is noted for its relative lack of violent incidents. The number killed was 112. This was fewer deaths than in any year since 1971, with 173. The year saw only one-third the number of violent deaths than 1976, with 296.

The Peace People continued to enjoy their wave of popularity and media attention, as well as controversy. Their winning the 1976 Nobel Peace Prize returned them to world attention.

Finally, Paisley tried to organize a workers' strike, sponsored by the Ulster Union Action Council (UUAC). Workers refused to strike, and stayed at their jobs despite intimidation.

Other important events:

Government actions: The British government began its strategy of "Ulsterization" of security, by phasing in the RUC and UDR to do jobs formerly done by the army. The army announced that it would computerize information about Northern Ireland people. In the Republic, Jack Lynch's Fianna Fail party won the June election. Queen Elizabeth II visited Northern Ireland in August.

Prisoners and courts: Twenty-six UVF men were sentenced to a total of seven hundred years for murder and bombings. Demonstrations and hunger strikes were part of a protest against conditions at Portlaoise Prison in the Republic.

U.S. actions: Senator Kennedy, Senator Moynihan, Congressman O'Neill and Governor Carey issued the first of their annual appeals for peace on St. Patrick's Day. President Carter issued a statement on Northern Ireland, supporting a peaceful solution involving both communities.

Peace initiatives: Corrymeela hosted an important peace conference, drawing numerous delegates from nine peace groups.

Other events: Brian Faulkner died. Tomas O Fiaich was appointed Roman Catholic primate of all Ireland, Cardinal Conway having died the previous year.

1978 Transitions

This year saw the disappearance of certain forces and the emergence of new ones. Army check-posts and barriers came down in many cities, since fewer violent acts were occurring. There were only eighty-one deaths this year connected with political motives. But people's attention turned more and more to prisoners, their rights and conditions, and the many complicated issues related to the courts and laws.

Other important events:

IRA actions: In November, the P-IRA launched a winter offensive, planting bombs in many cities.

Unionist actions: The UDA announced it would campaign for a British withdrawal and an independent Northern Ireland state.

Government actions: Jack Lynch announced his recommitment to a united Ireland.

Prisoners and courts: Since November 1974, 3,375 people had been detained under the Prevention of Terrorism Act. Twenty-five hundred people marched to support political status for prisoners at the Maze prison.

Bombings: In February, the La Mon Restaurant bombing in Co. Down killed twelve and injured twenty-three. Revulsion on all sides; the P-IRA, claiming responsibility, apologized.

Peace initiatives: The Peace People launched an initiative to replace the Emergency Powers Act with standard judicial procedures.

Other events: A state-sponsored agency reported that Catholic unemployment was two-and-one-half times Protestant unemployment. Archbishop O Fiaich said the British should indicate an intention of ultimate withdrawal, a position advocated by many. David Cook, a member of the Alliance Party, was elected Belfast mayor. A public opinion poll in Britain found fifty-three percent of respondents in favor of troop withdrawal. Amnesty International reported on RUC treatment of suspects, finding evidence of RUC malpractice. Unemployment stood at 13.4 percent (whole of U.K. was 6.6 percent).

1979 Trial by Non-Jury

One important issue which developed this year concerned the methods that police used to interrogate prisoners. An Amnesty International team investigated seventy-eight complaints of ill-treatment at the Castlereagh interrogation center in Belfast. The Bennett Report recommended that closed-circuit television be installed in interview rooms and that suspects have access to a lawyer after forty-eight hours. These and other recommendations were accepted by the government.

Other important issues:

Demonstrations: About eight thousand Sinn Fein sympathizers marched through Belfast to demand the withdrawal of British troops.

IRA actions: The Provisional IRA claimed responsibility for killing 79-year-old Lord Mountbatten and relatives in Donegal. A bombing incident in Co. Down the same day killed eighteen British soldiers. In November, the Provisional IRA set off numerous bombs on one day in Belfast.

Government actions: Margaret Thatcher became Conservative prime minister of Britain. She chose Humphrey Atkins as secretary of state for Northern Ireland.

Prisoners and courts: The Shankill Butchers, a Loyalist gang of eight men responsible for many murders, were sentenced on charges of murder, kidnapping, and possession of firearms.

Bombings: Airey Neave, Conservative M.P., was killed by the Irish National Liberation Army as he was leaving Westminster.

U.S. actions: Congressman Tip O'Neill and other members of Congress met with Northern Ireland leaders. The U.S. State Department banned the sale of heavy revolvers to the RUC.

Other events: Uranium traces were found in Donegal and mining companies began explorations. Archbishop O Fiaich was made cardinal for all of Ireland. The Pope's visit to the Republic drew massive crowds, but he did not travel to the North.

1980 Hunger Strikes, Part I

The overwhelming events this year were the hunger strikes in the fall. They riveted world attention on Northern Ireland again. Behind these events, however, was the longer and more complex H-Block campaign which had been gathering strength over previous years (see chapter 3 for a detailed discussion).

In March 1980, marches and rallies to support the H-Block prisoners became common. Chaplains in the Armagh Jail held sympathy strikes, and American support rallies took place. A committee of the Irish Council of Churches recommended an official study of prisons. Then in October, seven Republican prisoners began hunger strikes. They lasted with increasing tension and polarization until December 18, a total of fifty-three days. The fact that both the Provisional IRA and the government claimed victory left the issue dramatically unresolved, as events in 1981 were to show.

Government actions: In July, the British government issued a discussion paper on the future government of Northern Ireland. The paper proposed that a given percentage of votes would mean the same percentage of seats on the executive, or that a majority-rule executive would be balanced by an Assembly council. In December, high-level talks took place among Secretary of State Atkins, Thatcher, and Haughey to examine ways in which Northern Ireland and the Republic might cooperate. The army announced that phone-tapping was widespread. Troop levels were reduced in Derry and West Belfast.

Peace initiatives: Two Catholic and Protestant leaders, Gerry Clifford and William Arlow, were chosen by their churches to promote reconciliation and inter-church cooperation in Northern Ireland.

Other events: The total death toll since 1969 reached two thousand this year.

1981 Hunger Strikes, Part II

Many people consider this to have been the most important of recent years, second only to 1972, at least in terms of worldwide attention and circles of influence. The prisoners' hunger strikes were so dramatic that they were followed on a daily basis even in distant countries. But other events occurred in Northern Ireland, too, which had far-reaching effects there: the Anglo-Irish talks, Ian Paisley's campaigning, and severe unemployment.

The hunger strike campaign: Begun in 1980, this campaign resumed in earnest this year. Bobby Sands, an IRA prisoner, began his hunger strike on March 1, ostensibly because the British government did not keep its agreements for prison reforms made in December 1980, at the end of the first hunger strike series. Eventually, ten men starved themselves to death between May 5 and August 20. The campaign finally ended on October 3, when family members of striking prisoners and Catholic clergy encouraged an end to the strike. Massive demonstrations had taken place in Catholic neighborhoods. A great deal of support had developed for the Republican cause and for the general concept of "Irish liberation" (as seen from abroad). Emotional and frequent demonstrations took place in the U.S., the Republic, and elsewhere outside Northern Ireland.

The hunger strike attracted intense worldwide attention to Northern Ireland. The society there was fiercely polarized; many observers felt that "community relations" work of many years suffered a major setback. Three days after the strike ended, the British government announced changes in prison conditions. Prisoners were allowed to wear their own clothes, rules were relaxed for movement inside the prison, as were parole rules, and more visits were allowed.

The Anglo-Irish talks: Discussions between representatives of Ireland and Great Britain often took place at the prime minister level. Despite reassurances to the contrary, Paisley and others became convinced that plans were developing to "sell out" Northern Ireland to the Republic. The November talks discussed issues such as an inter-governmental council, cooperation, security improvements, and an inter-parliamentary body.

Paisley's activities: Partly in response to the enormous support for the hunger strikes and to the Anglo-Irish talks, Ian Paisley developed a campaign called the "Carson trail," named after Edward Carson, Unionist leader of 1912-22. Paisley used this campaign to gather support and attack opponents. It culminated in a "Day of Action"—November 23—when a Belfast rally and a Newtownards march took place.

Unemployment: The unemployment level (Northern Ireland is always the highest of all areas of Great Britain) continued its relentless increase. By August, male unemployment reached 21.1 percent, female 13.3 percent. The total was 109,153, or 18.9 percent.

Other important events:

IRA actions: Bernadette and Michael McAliskey were shot and seriously wounded: the motive was thought to be related to Mrs. McAliskey's prominence as an H-Block campaigner.

Unionist actions: The Unionist Party of Northern Ireland announced it no longer was willing to consider sharing power with the SDLP....The UDA announced that the New Ulster Political Research Group had become the Ulster Loyalist Democratic Party....The Reverend Robert Bradford, Official Unionist M.P. for South Belfast, was shot dead by P-IRA gunmen as he was meeting constituents.

Government actions: James Prior was appointed secretary of state for Northern Ireland.

Elections: In the Republic, Garrett Fitzgerald was elected prime minister in a Labour coalition government....In Northern Ireland, local elections were held in May. In the North, by a small margin, the Democratic Unionist Party (DUP) won more votes than the Official Unionist Party (OUP). Alliance and SDLP lost seats. In general, the outcome was seen as a victory for polarized positions and a loss for moderate positions.

United States actions: Kennedy, Moynihan, O'Neill, and Carey formed a new organization, "Friends of Ireland," seeking peace in Northern Ireland.

Other events and developments: The DeLorean Motor Corporation announced it needed a ten million pound ($20.2 million) government loan as cars began to be produced in Belfast....It was revealed that Northern Ireland received more aid from the European Parliament than any other European region.

1982 The Assembly Election

The central political event of 1982 seemed to be the election for the seventy-eight-member Northern Ireland Assembly in October. For ten years, Northern Ireland had not had a functioning provincial government; direct rule from London had been established in 1972, the Stormont parliament was closed, and laws were made by the British parliament. The Provisional Sinn Fein party ran candidates, and five of them won (ten percent of the vote). This was a major victory for Provisional Sinn Fein. It should also be noted that the election brought out a larger than usual Catholic vote, although overall forty percent of the electorate abstained from voting. Provisional Sinn Fein announced that it would continue its policy of refusing to serve once its candidates won in an election. The Alliance Party won ten seats. The Official Unionist Party won a few more seats than Paisley's Democratic Unionist Party; the latter won three percent fewer votes than in the previous elections.

IRA actions: The Provisional IRA was responsible for exploding a car bomb in London in June as royal guards were parading on horseback. Eleven people died as a result of the explosion. Universal condemnation followed. In December, the INLA claimed responsibility for exploding a bomb in Ballykelly (in Co. Londonderry), killing sixteen people.

Elections: In the spring, Charles Haughey won an election in the Republic. But he lost in the fall to Garrett Fitzgerald, who formed a coalition government with the Labour Party.

Other issues: Late in the year, John De Lorean, the American car manufacturer formerly with General Motors, was arrested and charged with involvement in a cocaine deal. His car company, which opened a factory in Dunmurry (outside Belfast) in 1978, was criticized for absorbing large amounts of money but employing fewer workers than economics had hoped. The factory was scheduled to close in May, but fifteen hundred workers temporarily took over the plant in a vain attempt to keep it open. De Lorean also tried to keep the plant open, asking for more loans from the British government. He was unsuccessful.

Unemployment figures continued to have a major impact. Total unemployment in May 1982 was 19.7 percent (112,978); male unemployment was 24.2 percent, female unemployment 13.7 percent.

After fourteen years of intense and painful turmoil, the conflicts and contradictions of Northern Ireland remain. The landscape has changed, but the main issues continue unresolved. People who live there will never be the same as before 1969. Although many people have found ways of communicating across the divides, murders continue. Fear accumulated over this period drains away only very slowly, and it seems to be ever-present at differing levels. Yet the past fourteen years have witnessed not only brutality and bitterness; they have also seen courage and humanity act in the midst of terror and violence.

Lynne Shivers

"Children's memories of Operation Motorman in 1972 in the Bogside, Londonderry. Operation Motorman was a British military operation to break up barricades, thus allowing British soldiers and Ulster police to patrol Catholic areas once again. For a time, some Catholic areas in Londonderry and Belfast were closed to military and police authorities."

Chapter 6

The Search for Alternatives

Of the countless groups in Northern Ireland which search for alternatives to violence, a few stand out as exceptional. The groups profiled in this chapter offer visions of what Northern Ireland society might be; they offer practical models for application elsewhere. The groups represent constituencies or influential viewpoints; some of them have created openings through which new options have developed. All of them have provided fresh hope for solutions to the problems of poverty, unemployment, lack of social services, and the violence which has produced murder, fear, and alienation.

Some of these groups have a clear commitment to nonviolence; other groups might not use the word, but their action speaks loudly. Why do we place importance on groups which carry out their work through nonviolent strategies? We often hear of those who use violence in both communities for opposite ideologies; we seldom hear of the nonviolent, who do not make "news" that our media seem to want to report.

By nonviolence we do not mean a vague do-good-ism or an absorption in one's own purity or passivity. We refer to a method of social change which commits participants to (a) non-injury, (b) truth, and (c) the willingness to take on suffering if that is necessary to interrupt the spiral of violence in society. We refer to actions which are alternatives to violence. In nonviolence theory, means are as important as goals, since means are the *end in process*. The commitment of nonviolent groups is just as strong as that of groups which have chosen military strategies; they are committed to creating a just and decent society for all.

It is as though there is a second level of struggle in Northern Ireland, whose work does not often make newspaper headlines, but which confronts direct forms of violence as well as structural forms. Thousands of people working through nonviolent organizations constitute not a paramilitary army, but an invisible force dedicated to action and determined to use only nonviolent methods—something neither army nor police may risk.

These activities assume their proper importance when we are aware of the enormous upheaval which has taken place in Northern Ireland since 1968. Political events have led to successive changes and upsets in government structures. Representative provincial government has been suspended; the responsibilities of elected local councils have been drastically reduced. All this has had repercussions in ongoing administration, creating both gains and disruption. Some of the groups here described help to provide either substitute or supplementary voluntary social services, often funded substantially from official sources. Sometimes this has arisen through the official services being effectively excluded from a particular area or section; it also implements the official policy of cooperation between voluntary agencies and the services carried out by government agencies.

Other groups represent important citizens' initiatives. We can describe only a few of the literally hundreds of community associations, peace groups, cooperatives, and action groups which are creating important alternatives in Northern Ireland.

What do these organizations do? Here is a brief survey of some activities, not at all inclusive. Community associations provide places for children of both communities to play together and for adult conferences to be held. Groups provide refuge against street violence and give support against intimidation. A few groups help people emigrate who have received death threats or who want to leave paramilitary organizations. Peace groups have organized petitions, rallies, vigils, and marches for peace. Cooperatives provide skill-training and employment. Hundreds of drafts and proposals and analyses have been written. Some groups lobby for changes in laws they consider unjust. A few groups offer courses in peace studies. Some groups encourage and implement North/South links and connections across the border. Many groups undermine the sectarian division by arranging for Catholics and Protestants to mix, thus breaking down the fear and ignorance which each community has of the other.

We discuss these groups as examples, to give some idea of the scope of such activities and to offer ample evidence that Northern

Ireland is much more than "a place where a war has been going on." Peace, too, is being "waged," and justice accompanies it in the areas of community development, peace education, voluntary relief activity, and human services.

THE CHURCHES

Churches in Northern Ireland have sometimes been criticized for lack of initiative toward ending the conflict. Some of this criticism may be justified; the churches themselves have so confessed. But the churches should not be criticized on the mistaken assumption that the conflict is essentially a religious one. We do not accept that perspective (see introduction), but understand how some people might. The churches, their leaders and members, could have done more before 1969 to prevent the causes of violence from reaching the point where open conflict became inevitable, and since 1969 to stop the fighting. But, in our view, they deserve the strongest congratulation for initiatives they have taken.

From 1968 on, laity and clergy have taken leading roles on the streets and in meetings to calm emotions and defuse riots. Displaced and dispossessed persons have been sheltered, fed, and cared for again and again. The vast majority of the clergy have preached understanding and patience; funeral sermons by clergy have usually urged forgiveness of killers rather than revenge.

Many peace groups, North and South, were originally church–related, and still draw support from church ties. All the churches have services for the poor and the suffering, such as "Protestant Relief" and "Catholic Charities." The churches' Central Committee for Community Work, with Jean Currie as liaison officer (spring 1982) was set up to foster interdenominational cooperation on social concerns.

Church leaders regret that they did not meet effectively across the social divisions until 1968 or 1969. But since then they have met almost monthly, spoken out together, and established cooperative agencies which have significantly affected the situation.

The churches set up a Joint Group on Social Questions in 1970, whose working parties have issued excellent studies, including

Violence in Ireland. They set up the Ballymascanlon Conference in 1973 for top-level discussion of ecclesiastical themes both doctrinal and pastoral; the conference has also set up working parties to deal with sensitive issues.

Among the other initiatives taken by the churches, two in particular should be noted: the Peace Campaign, and the Feakle meeting with the Provisional IRA.

Churches' Joint Peace Campaign

Between December 1974 and Easter 1975, four major churches—Roman Catholic, Presbyterian, Methodist, and Church of Ireland—initiated a joint campaign for peace. Other churches joined. The campaign included full-page advertisements in newspapers; speeches, sermons, and ecumenical services; rallies and marches; posters, petitions, and prayers. A number of meetings took place between church leaders and the highest government officials of the United Kingdom, Northern Ireland, and the Republic. This joint campaign in 1975 helped to raise hopes and create a climate of opinion for peace in Northern Ireland. Politicians of all parties have met with church people to hear suggestions for nonviolent action in the search for civil consensus.

Feakle Initiative

In late 1974, eight Protestant church people from Ireland and Britain, not representing their denominations or a council of churches, but acting only as individuals, contacted the Provisional IRA and arranged a meeting at Feakle in County Clare, in the Republic. Five Provisional council members and two Sinn Fein representatives were present. The church leaders frankly expressed their convictions about Protestant attitudes toward Provo violence and their hopes for the future. The Provisionals appreciated this, as well as the courage displayed by these leaders in talking to them.In fact, the council had to depart Feakle hurriedly, to escape arrest by Southern security forces.

The outcome of the meeting was a Provisional IRA agreement to a ceasefire over Christmas, with an indefinite extension if the

British government showed itself sympathetic to negotiations. The church leaders contacted Merlyn Rees, Secretary of State for Northern Ireland, and the Northern Ireland Office entered into further discussion with Sinn Fein, the legal political arm of the IRA. At this point the churchmen withdrew from the process, except to act as consultants when the negotiating parties called on them.

We should pay tribute to all concerned in the Feakle meeting. The churchmen involved were risking their professional careers, and knew it. The Provisionals risked their credibility with their own supporters, and therefore their lives. After initial criticism and the subsequent success of the extended ceasefire, the church leaders were honored for their courage and prudence. (The ceasefire broke down in the spring of 1975.)

Irish Council of Churches

The Irish Council of Churches has eight members: Church of Ireland (Anglican), Methodists, Presbyterians, Non-subscribing Presbyterians, Quakers, Lutherans, Moravians, and the Salvation Army. In 1980, David Beakley succeeded Rev. William Arlow, secretary since 1975. David Stevens is the projects officer, and Rev. John Knox was the peace education secretary until late 1982. The member churches meet bi-annually to plan and decide on joint programs; the executive committee meets six times yearly, or more often if needed. Roman Catholics attend meetings as official observers, and are members of many of the joint working parties, as well as the Interchurch Emergency Fund for Ireland. The latter consists of six delegates from the Irish Council of Churches and six selected by the Roman Catholic hierarchy. It meets bi-monthly to deal with ecumenical and relief aid funds from Europe and America.

The Irish Council of Churches acts as liaison with the British Council of Churches, the Conference of European Churches, the Canadian Conference of Churches and the National Council of Churches of Christ in the U.S.A., whose Ireland office was staffed by David Bowman, S.J., from 1972 to 1979.

The work of the Irish Council of Churches is divided into ecumenical relations among churches and issues related to the war and violence. Northern Ireland is a society where church identification is important. For many it is a source of pride and cultural heritage; but it is also for others a source of alienation and division. As a result, ecumenical work is an uphill task; for example, talks on mixed marriages almost broke down in 1979.

Rev. John Knox developed peace education through issuing joint school programs with the Dublin-based (Catholic) Irish Commission for Justice and Peace.

Some of the churches' initiatives related to the war and violence are detailed earlier in this chapter.

The Irish Council of Churches has serviced the Joint Group on Social Questions and the Ballymascanlon Conferences, which have formed a number of working parties on such issues as internment prison conditions, drug abuse, alcohol, housing, underdevelopment in rural Ireland, and the environment. The joint *Report on Violence in Ireland* has been the most important study of all; it has been a most helpful document in the preparation of this book (see bibliography). In the last year, the Irish Council of Churches began a new program of ecumenical youth work. This program encourages children of different churches to play together and share projects. In a society where suspicions of different church identifications exist, this activity has potential importance. In 1980, the Irish Council of Churches published a study booklet entitled *What the Bible Says About Violence*, distributed widely in schools. Other projects, too sensitive to be detailed here, are carried out officially and unofficially by the Irish Council of Churches, by its member churches, or by individual clergy. But to list even the above projects shows that the churches of Northern Ireland have, on the whole, taken constructive and important nonviolent initiatives for peace over the last ten years.

Society of Friends

The Society of Friends (Quakers) in Northern Ireland is a small church, but because of its pacifist testimony, its members have been more active in addressing issues of violence and social disruptions than some would expect from its numbers. Individual Friends addressed themselves to social disruption as the present "Troubles" began. Denis Barritt, up to August 1980 secretary of the Belfast

Volunteer Welfare Society, and Arthur Booth, of the Northern Friends Peace Board, co-authored a small book entitled *Orange and Green: A Quaker Study of Community Relations in Northern Ireland* (1969 and 1972 editions). When internment began in August 1971, Friends opened one of their meeting houses in Belfast as a shelter for children when their areas were scenes of heavy fighting.

The Ulster Quaker Service Committee began in 1969 as an expression of the Quaker peace testimony. Its first project was to initiate a waiting room for visitors at the Long Kesh prison. Volunteers served tea and provided a place to wait while visitors' papers were processed. This "canteen" has continued unbroken since before internment, and women volunteers from the Quakers and a number of churches have rotated responsibilities. An advice center and a playgroup for children, both under Quaker care, have been added to the services available to visitors at the Maze.

The Service Committee also bought a mini-bus to use for a "Meals on Wheels" program to transport children on day trips, and to transport older people, especially when street fighting disrupted public transportation. As with a number of other groups, Friends helped to raise money for brief children's vacations in Scotland and elsewhere outside Northern Ireland. When very heavy fighting erupted in the summer of 1969, thousands of people from Belfast fled their homes. Experienced in relief work at other times, Quakers helped organize an orderly evacuation, providing needed blankets and food.

Recent Friends' projects include training young men to rehabilitate houses, staffing a day-care center with volunteers, making available a mini-bus for use by other service organizations, and running a "holiday scheme"—that is, enabling families to have vacations inside Northern Ireland.

The most ambitious of recent service committee programs has been establishing the Quaker Cottage outside Belfast on Black Mountain. Begun in 1980, the cottage was repaired and made ready for numerous programs for children living in deprived areas. Activities have included pottery, arts and crafts, games, and hiking; a playground was built, and facilities increase as funds and labor permit. Some of these projects are not unique to Friends. They are expressions of Friends' peace testimony, seeking to create human relief in times of turmoil.

Irish Mennonite Movement

The Irish Mennonite Movement arose out of the conviction of a need for an evangelical peace church in Ireland. In the early 1970s, Mike Garde contacted British and American Mennonites. John Howard Yoder (author of *The Politics of Jesus*) visited Ireland in 1975, and Mennonites were resource leaders for a time at Glencree (See below).

Many peace organizations in Ireland, North and South, use volunteers. This is a strategy with certain weaknesses. An alternative is a community based on the Gospel, peace, and the poor. Such a community has been established in Dublin. Its members intend that it be self-supporting, work from the communal basis, and explore the roots of the conflict in Ireland. At present, members work through other groups and initiatives, e.g., *Dawn Magazine*, Student Christian Movement, and Glencree. Members hope to address local neighborhood issues and to increase participation by Irish people (the community now included Irish, German, and American adults, plus three children). They hope to link with other communities which espouse similar life styles and issues.

Community members see the need to analyze the religious roots of political and civil violence, the influence of hierarchical religious systems in the churches, the educational divisions in Northern Ireland, and various aspects of mixed marriages.

PEACE ORGANIZATIONS

The Community of the Peace People

The Community of the Peace People stemmed from a tragedy in August 1976, when Danny Lennon, an IRA member, was shot by the British army; Lennon's car crashed into Ann Maguire and her children, three of whom died. That evening, Betty Williams went on province-wide television to plead for an end to all the killing. Ann's sister, Mairead Corrigan, heard the broadcast and, with Betty, founded the Community of the Peace People. Ciaran McKeown, a journalist, joined them a few days later.

In the first five months, the "Peace Women" (as the media labeled them) sponsored at least fifty marches or rallies in Northern Ireland, the Republic, or Great Britain. Soon they were known as the Community of the Peace People. The Peace Declaration and the statement of intention, called the "Price of Peace," gave initial focus. The rally phase was followed by the hard work of forming an organization. Membership has been Catholic and Protestant, middle-class and working-class, with probably more women than men.

The Community of the Peace People has been distinct from other nonviolent action groups in Northern Ireland on four counts: (1) It has maintained a high commitment to nonviolent action. Other peace groups carry out a nonviolent strategy, but the Community of the Peace People has used the term deliberately and consciously. (2) It has insisted that its structure be decentralized so that local groups would be encouraged to develop leadership skills. Critics question how successful this has been. (3) It has strongly encouraged a redefinition of "politics" and this has led to criticism and misunderstanding. The Peace People's view has been that electoral party politics in Northern Ireland can only perpetuate sectarian divisions. The Peace People have encouraged, instead, the development of "community politics," that is, local initiatives to improve the quality of life along lines defined by the community itself. Critics have predicted that Peace People leaders would therefore run for elections, but this has been denied. (4) Finally, a central goal has been to create a nonviolent society in Northern Ireland, not just to end the present violence. This goal arises from the understanding that injustice and bigotry make recourse to the gun the normal form of conflict resolution.

For some time, Peter McLachlan (formerly a Unionist member of the Stormont parliament) was executive secretary of the Peace People Trust, which issued loans and grants in order to encourage employment on the local level. Local Peace People groups proposed projects that could be undertaken locally, whether developing local employment and "cottage industry," or building a community center, or replacing sports equipment in a youth club. Some simply brought people together to visit. Some helped people move to other housing. Some helped individuals who were being intimidated to leave Northern Ireland and resettle elsewhere. Some visited prisoners. Young people contacted other teenagers and encouraged them to consider nonviolent strategies. The Flying Squads are composed of teenagers and adults who visit various sections of Northern Ireland selling the bi-weekly newspaper *Peace by Peace* and building communication across neighborhood divisions. Some people helped shopkeepers stay open during the May 1977 strike.

In 1977, Betty Williams and Mairead Corrigan were awarded the Nobel Peace Prize. The award specifically cited them for their courage in taking action when they issued the call for peace. A number of positive and negative consequences developed. Worldwide publicity led people who otherwise ignored Northern Ireland to pay attention to the conflict and the issues behind it. Hope once again grew that perhaps peace was possible. On the negative side, with media attention, the organization grew too fast. It was criticized for receiving credit for what other organizations had been doing for years. The two women kept their monetary award; years later, Peace People leaders admitted that this cost the organization credibility.

In February 1980, Betty Williams resigned from the organization for personal reasons, and Peter McLachlan was asked to resign. These events followed Ann Maguire's suicide three weeks earlier, a blow to many Peace People members.

The double shock that the Peace People suffered in 1980 led many to question if the organization had enough credibility and resources to continue its programs. Members now maintain that internal contradictions have been removed and that even deeper agreement exists about future programs. Any organization that receives heavy media coverage will be judged harshly when it weakens. In 1980, the Peace People published two booklets about the Emergency Powers Act. One was a guide for young people who might be arrested; the other was designed to help adults consider how the emergency laws might be rescinded and normal laws established. Another focus area in 1980-81 was to developing discussion on political consensus and "new politics." This meant encouraging debate among leaders of disparate organizations. organizations.

In the summer of 1981, a conference was held on the topic, "Administration of Justice," chaired by Lord Gardiner. Working groups were set up following the conference to deal with various issues—for example, individual complaints and emergency laws.

But many of the Peace People's programs and activities have been cut back or eliminated. There is no question that much of the driving force has diminished in the organization. Most initiatives now come from local groups rather than from the leadership. But many members remain committed to the original strategy and vision.

Corrymeela

The Corrymeela Community is a visible effort in Northern Ireland to provide services at a time of great social upheaval. Founded by Rev. Ray Davey in 1965, long before the latest troubles began, the community is an impressive example of ordinary people creating an alternative to the animosity which, for many, is synonymous with Northern Ireland. Corrymeela, "Hill of Harmony" in Gaelic, is a symbol of hope, a refuge where thinking and planning can be pursued without fear of who might overhear or take offense.

All the present Corrymeela programs at the two centers in Ballycastle and Belfast were developed to meet particular needs as they arose. Programs will change as social needs change.

People can go to Corrymeela to get away from urban violence and stresses, and to recover from tragedy like loss of family or home. Bereaved people have special needs of comforting, and Corrymeela tries to provide for them. They say, "It is not enough to bring people out of violent situations and send them back in: we have to bring people to look hard and honestly at the causes of violence and what we can do about them."

Corrymeela staff stress that they do not offer pat answers; they see their job rather as one of raising questions. The center is available for groups on all sides of the conflict. Since 1965, Corrymeela has been an open door to thousands of individuals who have been the victims of violence, fear, and intimidation, as well as those who suffer from the personal and social pressures of densely populated urban areas. This is not just first-aid work, though that would be valuable enough; staff help people to face the realities they live in and help them after they return to their homes.

Conferences are held there by a variety of groups; Corrymeela is known as a place where all sides can get a hearing. Recent conferences have dealt with the political future of Northern Ireland, waging peace, violence and the media, women in society, family life in a violent society, the police and community, understanding grief, political independence in the North, prisoners' rights, community work, and unemployment.

The Corrymeela Youth Program provides a place for youngsters to be part of a mixed (Catholic and Protestant) group, still a rare phenomenon in Northern Ireland. While the youth program is largely recreational, it also encourages teenagers to reflect on what is happening in their lives and their communities.

A school program enables schools to bring students to Corrymeela for a day or a week. They are encouraged to pair with schools across the sectarian divide.

A summer work-camp program provides outdoor construction experience and recreation. Participants learn to build rather than destroy.

Daily prayer programs are attended by Protestants and Catholics together, and are often led by lay people rather than by clergy. Corrymeela believes that religious faith is the central healing force in the world, especially in Northern Ireland where too often Christian faith and practice have been distorted and perverted.

Rev. John Morrow has followed Ray Davey as leader; Derick Wilson is program director, assisted by Rev. Douglas Baker of the United Presbyterian Church U.S.A.

Staff at the Ballycastle center consists of sixteen people; half are permanent, half are volunteers who work there for a year. Some Americans have been accepted there. It is important to note, however, that aside from the staff, the center is not residential. Visitors cannot stay overnight except when they are attending a conference.

The center itself consists of a main house, which has bedroom space for fifty, offices, conference rooms, a dining room and kitchen; a Youth Village of sixteen two-bed chalets; the rebuilt work-camp cottages accomodate thirty (the work was done by apprentices, learning their trades); and Coventry House, where the staff live. The Croi (Heart) is a small communal worship center where groups can also meet. Corrymeela can accommodate up to 120 visitors at one time, but does not want to grow beyond that size.

Corrymeela also has a Belfast office with a staff of four, which works closely with people in the city. A steering committee of about one hundred members has the major responsibility for directing Corrymeela's work. Local groups are forming in Northern Ireland as well: four or five in Belfast, six dotted around in smaller cities. People occasionally wonder if Corrymeela will be irrelevant when the shooting stops in Northern Ireland. As Ray Davey says, "Corrymeela started before the shooting began. When the violence ceases, then the real work begins." Its programs and directors are flexible enough to change as social needs change. Corrymeela would be an important place anywhere, but it has special value being where it is, providing hope, tangible sustenance and vision in the context of a community, with links around the world.

In the spring of 1981, Corrymeela and Glencree jointly sponsored a conference at Queens University in Belfast on "Models of Political Cooperation." This was an attempt to explore a number of issues concerning cooperation between Britain and Ireland. The issues included economic forces, constitutional arrangements, and statehood; some were well-known, others less so. This conference is an example of the attempt by Corrymeela and Glencree to address wider issues concerning North and South.

Glencree

Glencree is the only peace center with conference and dormitory space in the Republic of Ireland. Founded in 1974, it is located twelve miles south of Dublin in the Wicklow Hills.

Four major programs take up Glencree's energy: reconciliation, hospitality, communication, and peace education. Glencree has hosted people from Northern Ireland who need a break from sectarian conflicts. Special groups who have taken advantage of Glencree hospitality include families, battered wives and their children, older people, and mixed groups of teenagers.

Glencree's seminars attract participants from long distances, dealing with such issues as law, youth training, violence and nonviolence, and pluralism in the Republic. Work camps take place throughout the year, attracting teenagers from Britain, Germany, Holland, Belgium, France, Canada, and the United States. This work also helps develop Glencree, transforming it from its former life as an army barracks to its present life as a reconciliation center. Finally, Glencree is currently engaged in a program of developing close links with schools and universities—creating a library and audio-visual resources in peace studies, and planning research in the areas of justice and peace. A series of seminars for high school students introduces participants to the rich field of peace and nonviolence. At present, extensive work is done with schools.

Glencree may seem similar to Corrymeela, and in some respects it is. But it is surprising how different the two places feel. Corrymeela has developed out of meeting emergencies and family crises and concerns. While Glencree originally emerged in response to the Northern situation, it has grown through meeting social issues. Although the two centers are in frequent communication with each other, there are no administrative links, and each sees its own program as meeting particular needs in its own society. Occasionally people from the Republic attend events at Corrymeela; a little more frequently people from Northern Ireland visit Glencree. But basically they are intended to serve the places in which they are located. Glencree's contributions far outweigh its visible programs, since its presence has influenced people's thinking, and will no doubt stimulate other programs to develop elsewhere.

Southern Movement for Peace

The Southern Movement for Peace started at the same time as the Community of the Peace People (1976), but is autonomous and is concerned primarily with the situation in the Republic. Brendan O'Regan in Killaloe and Ursul O'Neill in Athlone have led this movement, with much decentralization of responsibility. Its main goals are to strive for an end to injustice and violence in Ireland, thereby supporting a just and lasting peace in Northern Ireland. They promote friendship across the borders. They encourage understanding through discussions between Northerners and Southerners, work with other organizations toward the same goals, hold interdenominational services, arrange adult education courses, and in general facilitate various contacts between Northern Ireland and the Republic. Inter-group visitations are especially encouraged. The Southern Movement gets cooperation from churches, commercial organizations, sports clubs, labor unions, voluntary groups, professional and cultural associations, and is spread throughout the Republic.

Peace Point

If having your office bombed is a mark of how important your work is, then Peace Point wins a prize. (So do the Presbyterian and Methodist Church centers and some other peace groups as well.) Its office was destroyed in December 1976, when the store below was bombed. Records were completely ruined. Within a few weeks, however, Peace Point was working again. It was small, but the only reconciliation group which combined peace education and community development work, and the only peace organization in Ireland with committees north and south of the border. Outsiders must understand that peace and community development are inextricably linked. Since 1973, Peace Point had tried to establish communication between peace groups and local community development groups, of which there are about five hundred in Northern Ireland.

The three staffers in Belfast, with the help of a small committee and an academic advisory group, assisted people working in their local areas to reflect on their own situations, identify problems, establish priorities, and develop long-range planning. Peace Point also took training programs into local areas. Topics of workshops in 1976 included the nature of power, social justice, and conflict resolution. In the autumn of 1977, Peace Point initiated and organized courses in human relations and group-leadership training in Belfast, which in 1978 were extended to other areas in Northern Ireland. The courses were well attended in 1978-80. Dr. Henry Grant directed these courses which were co-sponsored by the Community of the Peace People and Corrymeela; Sheelagh Flanagan was office organizer; Sean Cooney was community peace worker until 1979.

Peace Point also did valuable work in organizing hospitality for Americans and a number of Europeans, for example, the 1967-77 tours of Church Women United and the Journey of Reconciliation.

In January 1977, Peace Point co-sponsored an important conference at Corrymeela called "Waging Peace," which facilitated communication among a number of peace groups and community organizations. Peace Point obtained a research fellowship at Queens University for Dr. Joseph J. Fahey, the director of an American peace studies institute at Manhattan College, New York.

Peace Point's main work in Northern Ireland was to help local organizers reflect on their work; to connect peace and reconciliation activities with community organizing and development; to develop the concept of peace studies; and to help visitors understand the enormously important work going on there. Peace Point's symbol was a dove with the body forming a hand; the five fingers represent communication, dialogue, education, reconciliation, and peace. The organization lived up to its name—a focal point for the creation of peace.

Peace Point programs ceased in 1981 due to lack of funds.

Women Together

Women Together is the only organization in Northern Ireland whose membership consists only of women working for justice, peace, and reconciliation. Along with Peace Point, its office was destroyed in December 1976, but within weeks the organization was working again. Women Together was formed through the initiative of Ruth Agnew and Monica Patterson, who organized a few local groups which came together for their first public rally in September 1970: four hundred women gathered from different parts of Belfast, especially areas which had seen fierce fighting. Women Together has mainly been based in Belfast, where much of the fighting has occurred. Saidie Patterson headed the group from 1973 to 1976; she won the World Methodist Council's first Peace Award in 1977. The present chairman [sic] is Irene Carson.

The main goals of Women Together are: "(1) to bring together women who believe that violence, with all its heartbreak, must be banished from Northern Ireland; (2) to give them the corporate strength to resist undesirable pressures and to use their influence for peace in their homes, their street and their neighborhood; (3) to foster a sense of pride in their locality and enable them as a group to bring effective pressure on the local authorities to fulfill their obligations; (4) to offer them a wide range of activities in which they can engage as a relief from their home commitments and a means of working together.''

From the beginning, Women Together created an impressive reputation based on several activities: separating rival gangs in riots by physically intervening; stopping children and young people from setting fire to property; dispersing a gang of knife-wielding youths who were attacking a boy from the ''other side''; defending neighbors from having their windows broken; going out at night to talk with neighbors in unsettled areas. Women Together members also engage in cleaning up churches and homes after bomb explosions, sweeping streets after riots, cleaning up community centers to make them usable by local community groups, and organizing bus trips for people who need to leave their areas for brief vacations. Women Together prints a quarterly newspaper. To the outsider, these activities may not seem spectacular, nor geared to ending the conflict. The fact that they take place at all is what really matters.

One event which Women Together organized in the autumn of 1977 was a fashion show located in Belfast. Participants marveled that it could take place and that it was so well attended. We must remember that occasions which are ''normal'' elsewhere are often exceptional in Northern Ireland. Such ''ordinary'' things are great encouragements.

At the present time, Women Together has six or seven local groups; they are as mixed as possible. One group provides hospitality (with other organizations) at the Maze prison visitors' center. The groups send representatives to a monthly council meeting which makes decisions for the whole organization. Hospitality, neighborly care, and informal times over a cup of tea provide opportunities for personal caring in a situation which makes ordinary human contact difficult. Women Together has been responsible for helping to establish a climate of reconciliation and communication, so necessary for the building of peace in Northern Ireland.

Protestant and Catholic Encounter (PACE)

Protestant and Catholic Encounter (PACE) was formed in 1969. Its major goals are "(1) to promote harmony and good will between the religious and political communities in Northern Ireland; (2) to demonstrate that, although people may be separated by difference of conviction, there are many activities in which they can unite freely in order to work together for the common good of all; (3) to work with all those who desire the establishment of a social order based upon justice and charity, and enlivened by mutual respect and understanding, thus leading to the elimination of the factors which produce harmful division in our society."

PACE is a decentralized organization, a network of local groups; it has a small central office which guides coordination and communication. There are presently about thirty local PACE groups, with a total of about two thousand members, but only fifteen to twenty of the groups are active.

Again, we need to remember that it is usual in Northern Ireland for Catholics and Protestants *not* to know one another, not to meet on any regular basis, and not to talk about issues which divide them. PACE was established to counter this trend. A group cannot affiliate with PACE unless there are Protestants and Catholics in it. The local group decides what activities it will take up. In the recent past, some of their activities have included sponsoring vacations for children outside Northern Ireland, organizing fund-raising events for a peace rally in local areas, planning a joint Christmas carol service, and hosting a number of speaking engagements. PACE offers an impressively long speakers' list, with topics that include the future of Ulster, the Third World, fire prevention, itinerants, violence, the media, Gaelic Ireland, drugs, and voluntary service. PACE issues a journal three times a year and occasionally sponsors large conferences. One such recent conference dealt with the "Needs of Children Today." The executive committee meets monthly and the council, consisting of representatives from local groups, meets quarterly.

To summarize, the main purpose of PACE is to inform its

members on important issues and to counter the sectarian divisions of Northern Ireland.

It has been criticized for being "middle-class and therefore irrelevant," since the major sectarian divisions most deeply affect working-class people. But since the climate of division affects everyone, PACE's work has been significant despite the class make-up of its membership. PACE is careful to state that it is non-political, in the sense that it does not make public statements on political issues, nor does it take part in any way in political party activities. PACE stands for the breakdown of sectarian divisions in Northern Ireland, for the sharing of responsibility between Catholics and Protestants, and for supporting the conviction that the causes of the conflict can be dealt with. It has helped move many toward the understanding which is the necessary base for a settlement of the Northern Ireland conflict.

Peace Forum

The Peace Forum, formed in May 1976, is an association of fourteen peace and community groups which meets monthly for the exchange of information and ideas. The forum has no decision-making powers at the present time. But in a situation where rumors often create misunderstandings, the opportunity to pool information is important. The forum's leading figures try to expand its concerns and its influence. Member organizations are the following (spring 1982): Corrymeela, Peace Point, Fellowship of Reconciliation, Protestant and Catholic Encounter, Action for Peace, Peace People, Pax Christi, Women Together, Glencree House, Dutch Northern Irish Advisory Committee, Lifeline, Dawn, Derry Peace and Reconciliation Centre, East Belfast Community Council, Campaign for Nuclear Disarmament, Witness for Peace, the Ulster Quaker Service Committee, and All Children Together.

Belfast Voluntary Welfare Society

The Belfast Voluntary Welfare Society (formerly the Belfast Council of Social Welfare) is a seventy-year-old umbrella group. The secretary is Peter McLachlan, formerly associated with the Community of the Peace People; he succeeded Denis Barritt. This organization seeks to provide social services that are not adequately provided by the government. Programs include:

holiday programs for children;
repairing of houses, making them available to tenants;
monthly social workers' luncheon, providing an opportunity for many social workers to meet each other, discuss common problems, and hear speakers;
Citizens' Advice Bureau, a network of advice centers (seven in Belfast alone) whose staff provide information on housing, landlord and tenant issues, personal problems, and consumer problems;
Voluntary Service Bureau, Belfast, which has over a hundred volunteers working in a broad range of activities. Its director is Sydney Stewart.

COMMUNITY ORGANIZATIONS

A great variety of community organizations exists. Many of them serve only one homogeneous neighborhood; others try to cut across the divides. For example, the Ballynafeigh Community Association in South Belfast serves both communities and both working and middle class people. Their housing association strives to help Catholics (thirty percent) remain in the neighborhood, against efforts to intimidate them into leaving. A June Festival has become a two-week high point, with a small circus and much local participation.

A second kind of community organization is the East Belfast Community Council, which provides important services in this mainly Protestant neighborhood. Its newsletter of late autumn 1976 included information about an annual carol service for peace in the area, an arts and crafts exhibition, a music festival for senior citizens, changes in the economic council, and an appeal for blankets for people unable to meet costs of food, electricity, and coal (they note that eight hundred blankets were distributed in the past). Winnie Jordan has lent her considerable skills to running the office—a task which includes an element of reconciliation work.

Another notable example was the Bogside Community Association (BCA) in Derry. The Bogside had about fifteen thousand residents, all Catholic. When heavy fighting began in 1969, residents sealed off the area and refused to allow police or the army to enter. Since many essential social services were therefore seriously hindered, people formed the Bogside Community Association in 1972, each district sending an elected representative to its council.

Besides its function of uniting the people against violence, BCA offered information on where to go for assistance; how to fix a broken back door; how to find housing; how to apply for social security benefits. It developed houses for homeless alcoholics and the Northland Centre (under separate direction) for the treatment of alcoholism.

Other BCA initiatives included organizing concerts and festivals, sports activities, and services for the injured. BCA organizers counted some weaknesses in their programs, but a number of other community projects developed from original BCA initiatives, in addition to the Northland Centre. The city created city-wide spring festivals; entertainment has once again come to Derry. The Bogside Community Association, however, closed due to lack of funds in 1981.

Cooperatives

Economic cooperatives enable local people to gain greater control of their lives. Cooperatives stimulate people's confidence and attract industries to an area. Economic development is seen as one part of community development in Northern Ireland. There is a large pool of unskilled labor in many areas; cooperatives enable people to learn skills while being employed. Economic cooperatives employ five percent of the total Northern Ireland work force. Although the cooperative movement cannot by itself eliminate unemployment, it can act as a stimulus and initiative against hopelessness, and as a spur for larger economic drives.

A recent development is Community Enterprise Northern Ireland (CENI), an amalgam of cooperatives and community projects aiming to develop employment and campaign for new legislation. People involved in CENI live in Derry, Omagh, Newry, Belfast, Strabane, and elsewhere.

Holiday Projects

Families and children living in poverty sometimes cannot afford any vacation. For years public-spirited groups, helped usually by public moneys, have arranged holidays for many. The Rotarians have bought and equipped Glebe House near Downpatrick. A Ballymurphy group has outfitted a place in County Leitrim. The Irish Children's Holiday Enterprise offers a Donegal home away from home. Many of the community organizations are involved in some way.

For instance, Holiday Projects West is one of the largest organizations devoted to providing holidays for children. Since 1972, it has served thousands of Protestant and Catholic children from grade-school age to teens. The holidays have been in Northern Ireland, in the Republic, in Britain, and in Holland, Belgium, Sweden, Germany and Iceland. Some have been purely for recreation; others have been work camps where participants have worked together to construct buildings, mend fences, and clear out storm-damaged fields, to give three examples. All the projects intend to include Protestants and Catholics, and increasingly, there is follow-up afterwards. It has been financed mainly by the Western Education and Library Board, which has aided many similar programs in Northern Ireland. In 1978 it won the Northern Ireland Witness for Peace Award.

Northern Ireland Civil Rights Association (NICRA)

The Northern Ireland Civil Rights Association is one of the oldest groups in Northern Ireland, since it was formed in 1968 to raise issues of civil rights in both communities. As the situation polarized, and infiltration by the Official IRA was alleged, NICRA lost much of its influence, but it has continued raising civil rights issues. More recently, NICRA has campaigned for a Northern Ireland Bill of Rights guaranteeing proportional representation, freedom to belong to any political party, and an end to discrimination in employment and housing based on religion, politics, sex, or race. In the U.S.A., its support group is the National Association for Irish Freedom (NAIF).

OTHER PEACE GROUPS

Witness for Peace, founded by Rev. Joseph Parker in 1972 after his son was killed in a bomb explosion, holds an annual service of remembrance, at Belfast City Hall, for all the victims of the strife. It also gives an annual peace award; recipients have included Corrymeela, the Alliance Avenue Community Shop, Saidie Patterson of Women Together, and Holiday Projects West.

Pax Christi Ireland is a small Catholic peace organization with a number of linked groups in different countries, including the United States, Great Britain, and the Irish Republic. The structure of Pax Christi Ireland includes local groups, a national office, and an annual meeting. Pax Christi explores a number of peace and war issues, concentrating on the causes of social conflicts. It has worked with other groups to try to develop peace initiatives in Northern Ireland, and established a Belfast chapter in 1979.

The Fellowship of Reconciliation is an international pacifist organization with branches in various countries, including the United States. The Northern Ireland and Great Britain offices have been actively addressing the issues of Northern Ireland since 1956. The FOR is best known there for organizing work camps for young adults, who have created playgrounds for children, repaired homes, and fostered communication across the sectarian divisions. For some years, its annual summer work camp has been located in Lurgan. The FOR has contributed to the activities of other groups, has supported vigils and other demonstrations for peace, and has publicized the issues of Northern Ireland among people who do not live there but who are concerned.

Faced with pessimism and hopelessness, it is amazing that these peace, reconciliation, and community action groups exist at all. Where despair and fear have led many people to take polarized positions, and the weight of bureaucracy has sometimes immobilized governments (at all levels), the reconciliation groups have often been the seedbed of small initiatives and new ideas. Sometimes the energy has not been available to sustain programs. Sometimes the analysis has been too weak to handle the criticisms. But no one can deny that volunteers and paid staff have cheerfully given their time and lives to see programs to their completion. In a situation where human considerations are often the last to be attended to—a cup of tea, a hand on the shoulder, a blanket—many reconciliation, peace, and community groups have been close enough to the grass roots to be responsive to human needs. It is the people who comprise these groups who make the recent history of Northern Ireland also a story of hope and bravery.

Derry Corner, in the Bogside in Londonderry. This sign was a symbol in the early 1970s of Catholic and Bogside pride and independence.

Chapter 7

The American Connection

There are several levels of connection between the United States and Northern Ireland. This chapter surveys some of these levels and tries to give an overall perspective. Activity at the governmental level has included congressional hearings and grand-jury investigations as well as statements by senators, congresspeople and governors. British troops received special training in the United States as NATO allies. The State Department has brought over key Northern Irish leaders for study tours.

American corporations have located and invested in Northern Ireland. Churches have sent volunteers and some funding. A number of colleges and universities work out exchanges of professors and students. The Irish American Cultural Institute brings over an excellent group of speakers and artists each year for an "Irish Fortnight" in many cities around the country. The Irish National Caucus has carried on public education campaigns and fund-raising drives. Irish Northern Aid (INA) has carried on extensive lobbying efforts in support of its "Brits out" position. News coverage, incomplete and partial, has added a special dynamic.

In addition to looking at these varied American connections, this chapter presents two case studies. The first examines a program for Northern Irish teenagers. The second case study deals with the Journey of Reconciliation in December, 1976, cosponsored by the National Council of Churches Ireland Program and Pax Christi U.S.A.

AMERICAN GOVERNMENT INITIATIVES

From 1937 to 1977, the American government followed a policy of avoiding public involvement in Northern Ireland because the province is an integral part of the U.K. But following Bloody Sunday in 1972, there were hearings before the Congressional subcommittee on Europe of the House Committee on Foreign Affairs. Testimony was given by individuals from Northern Ireland, the Irish Republic, and the United States.

Also, a story appeared in the *Philadelphia Evening Bulletin* on February 17, 1973, that an eight-hundred man commando unit of the British Royal Marine Commandos received training at Camp LeJeune in North Carolina for two months. An unidentified American Marine spokesman reported that the training included field firing and field training exercises. Before coming to Camp LeJeune, the British unit had been stationed in Belfast for four months and was scheduled to return to Northern Ireland for internal security duty after leave in England. (The North Atlantic Treaty Organization has an agreement that allows one country's military forces to be trained in another country.)

On March 17, 1976, President Ford and the prime minister of Ireland issued a joint statement which, in essence, appealed to the American and Irish people to refrain from supporting organizations involved in campaigns of violence in Northern Ireland.

On October 28, 1976, presidential candidate Jimmy Carter made a statement in Pittsburgh which expressed opposition to violence as part of the solution to Northern Irish problems, and voiced support for finding a just solution which would protect human rights. Some Irish-American groups interpreted his expression of interest in human rights as recognition of injustices suffered by the minority community. As president-elect, Mr. Carter denied any commitment to intervene in Northern Ireland.

Then on St. Patrick's Day, March 17, 1977, two important statements were issued. A joint statement was released by Secretary of State Cyrus Vance and the Irish foreign minister, Dr. Garrett Fitzgerald, reaffirming the traditional United States policy of non-involvement in the issue of Northern Ireland and stressing that a concern for human rights should not be misused by those who support violence for political ends in Northern Ireland.

On the same day, a joint statement was also released by Sen. Edward Kennedy, Sen. Daniel Moynihan, Rep. Thomas O'Neill, and Governor Hugh Carey of New York. In part, the statement said, "We appeal to all those organizations engaged in violence to renounce their campaigns of death and destruction and return to the path of life and peace. And we appeal as well to our fellow Americans to embrace this goal of peace, and to renounce any action that promotes the current violence or provides support or encouragement for organizations engaged in violence."

On April 22, Governor Carey made a controversial speech in Dublin in which he condemned the Official IRA as "Marxists" and the Provisional IRA as "killers," and noted that most Americans do not support the unification of Ireland through a military strategy.

The culmination of the impact of these statements was reached when President Carter made a statement about Northern Ireland on August 30, 1977, the first official statement about Northern Ireland made by an American president for many years. In part, he said:

". . . The United States wholeheartedly supports peaceful means for finding a just solution that involves both parts of the community of Northern Ireland, protects human rights and guarantees freedom from discrimination—a solution that the people of Northern Ireland, as well as the governments of Great Britain and Ireland can support. Violence cannot resolve Northern Ireland's problems; it only increases them, and solves nothing. I hope that all those engaged in violence will renounce this course and commit themselves to peaceful pursuit of legitimate goals. . . . I ask all Americans to refrain from supporting with financial or other aid, organizations whose involvement, direct or indirect, in this violence, delays the day when the people of Northern Ireland can live and work together in harmony, free from fear. . . . United States policy on Northern Ireland has long been one of impartiality, and that is how it will remain. We support the establishment of a form of government in Northern Ireland which will command widespread acceptance throughout both parts of the community. However, we have no intention of telling the parties how this might be achieved. . . . It is still true that a

peaceful settlement would contribute immeasurably to stability in Northern Ireland and so enhance the prospects for increased investment. In the event of such a settlement, the United States government would be prepared to join with others to see how additional job-creating investment could be encouraged. . . . "

The statement was generally well-received in Northern Ireland. The idea that U.S. investments would be encouraged in the event of a settlement was a new element.

On March 17, 1978, eighteen Democratic leaders, including the four from 1977, called for a more genuine commitment by the majority leadership in Northern Ireland, and by the British government, to end the "festering stalemate." Renewing the 1977 call, they asked for an end to killing and support for nonviolence. Similar statements were issued in 1979, 1980, and 1981.

Tip O'Neill's visit to Belfast in April 1979 created controversy. After he and sixteen other congressmen met with Northern Ireland political figures, O'Neill said publicly that Northern Ireland had been used as a political football by British political parties. (British politicians strongly and quickly issued denials.) Other American politicians from time to time have felt the need to make general public statements regarding Northern Ireland; Sen. Moynihan and Rep. Hamilton Fish each made such statements in June 1979.

In July 1979, Congressman Clement Zablocki, the House Foreign Affairs Chairman, announced intentions to hold hearings on the State Department decision to sell arms to the RUC. (Earlier, the State Department had announced it had agreed to sell three hundred magnum handguns and five hundred rifles to the RUC.) But a month later, the State Department announced it was banning the sale of arms until the policy was reviewed. The ban remains in effect as of early 1983.

In July 1980, an interesting event occurred which illustrates dynamics between the Republic of Ireland and the U.S. regarding Northern Ireland and Irish-American sentiments. Ireland's ambassador to the U.S., Sean Donlon, had strongly urged Americans not to contribute money to send arms to Northern Ireland. The Irish prime minister, Charles Haughey, was rumored to be taking steps to replace Donlon. The four most influential Irish-American politicians—Kennedy, O'Neill, Moynihan, and Carey—urged Haughey to keep Donlon as ambassador, on the ground that if he were removed a propaganda victory would be achieved by some Irish-American groups. Ambassador Donlon remained in the job. In March 1981, a new organization, Friends of Ireland, was set up by Kennedy, O'Neill, Moynihan, and Carey to promote peace in Northern Ireland.

IRISH-AMERICAN ORGANIZATIONS

Any town with a sizable Irish-American population will have one or more organizations—social, cultural, athletic—with names drawn from the counties and cities, saints and patriots of Ireland, or with more pedestrian titles like "Independent Irish Society." Many of them are connected with an Irish store, travel agency or pub glorying in names like Tara Irish Gift Shop, Lismore Travel, or The Plough and the Stars.

The largest associations are the Ancient Order of Hibernians and the Friendly Sons of St. Patrick. Until recently many towns had an "Irish" parish to go along with their "German" and "Italian" and "Polish" parishes. Urban migration has decimated these, so organizations connected with parish life have declined too.

The *Irish People* is a weekly newspaper printed in the Bronx which supports the Provisional cause; other Irish-American newspapers have a Nationalist perspective, considerably less aggressive than the *Irish People*. The *Irish Echo* regularly prints stories from the *Irish Times,* so its editorial viewpoint differs radically from the "I.P.", which draws much of its "news" from the Provisionals' propaganda arm, the Irish Republican Information Service. Americans who read only the latter are regularly bombarded with headlines like "Depraved Monsters . . . ," "Elizabrute," and such.

The Official IRA is linked to a national network of Republican Clubs dotted around the country. It has raised money for the Official IRA through dances, demonstrations and speeches.

The National Association for Irish Freedom (NAIF) is the support group for the Northern Ireland Civil Rights Association (NICRA), with an office in New York City.

The Irish National Caucus (INC) was formed in 1975 and claims as members about thirty Irish-American groups such as Northern Aid, the national office of the Ancient Order of Hibernians (AOH), the Irish Protestant Republican Club, the Irish Institute, Sons of Erin, and the New Jersey Gaelic Club. Its greatest success came when, in September 1977, an Ad Hoc Committee for Irish Affairs was formed by Congressman Mario Biaggi at the behest of Jack Keane, then national president of AOH. Soon over one hundred members of Congress gave their names to it, although it is not an official committee of Congress. One of its goals was to pressure for congressional hearings on Northern Ireland, or a "peace forum" of some kind; this was finally abandoned in September 1979. Biaggi insists that he does not support IRA violence; the Caucus says the same.

In January 1980, Irish Northern Aid (INA) held a dinner in New York City; the main speaker was Fr. Piaris O'Duill, chairman of the National H-Block Committee. Throughout the rest of 1980, INA increased activities around the H-Block issues. In November and December 1980, during a fast by numerous Republican prisoners, INA organized demonstrations on their behalf in at least twenty American cities.

INA has frequently given the impression to many that it has close ties with the Provisional IRA. This connection is one of the best known and the one which receives the widest media coverage. Many people claim that Irish Northern Aid raises money for the Provisional IRA and it is often alleged to send weapons. Recently, INA has claimed to support not violence, but only the welfare work of the Provisionals. Since INA publicly declares that this money sent for welfare frees up other money to be used for purchasing weapons and ammunition, they make a rather tenuous distinction between providing money for guns and providing it for "women and children." They hailed the Mountbatten murder as an "execution" of an imperialist soldier.

Irish Northern Aid has been registered as a lobby for a foreign group since April 1971. INA reported to the Justice Department that it had sent $11,500 to Northern Aid, Belfast, during its first six months. In January 1972, INA reported that it had sent $128,099 from July through December 1971. For January through June 1972, the amount given was $312,700. One claim is that the total sent by

INA up to 1977 was about three million dollars, but guesswork is the name of this claim. In July 1981, a U.S. federal court required Irish Northern Aid to register as an agent of the IRA. Two months later, Provisional Sinn Fein claimed that Irish Northern Aid had received donations of $250,000 from January to June 1981.

It is easy and not very helpful to speculate about the amounts of money that INA has raised. A conservative estimate suggests that a million dollars was raised in 1972, and decreasing sums since. Specific estimates are likely to be low, since accurate figures are not available.

The Justice Department has hit hardest at INA members. At least four separate grand jury hearings have been held since 1971 in San Francisco, Fort Worth, Baltimore, and Philadelphia. In all cases, the function of the grand jury was called into question by the defendants. Since some of those summoned were jailed for indefinite periods and without stated charges when they refused to testify, their lawyers insisted that constitutional guarantees of personal freedom had been violated. Meanwhile, Sen. Kennedy supported a move from the Justice Department to investigate the sale and shipment of arms to Northern Ireland. In 1979 and 1980, several incidents took place in the U.S. arising from accusations of illegal arms sales.

The U.S. government has denied visas as a way of trying to control further involvement of Irish-American groups in shaping American public opinion. In November 1979 (and at other times) Ruadhri O'Bradaigh was denied a visa, and in August 1980, Andy Tyrie was also refused a visa.

But visits continue. New Ulster Political Research Group members visited in winter 1976-79 and spoke to audiences about an independent Northern Ireland. In August, 1980, Fr. Daniel Berrigan and five other Americans kept a vigil outside the Maze prison near Belfast to draw attention to human rights issues.

Not all Irish-Americans, of course, support the Nationalist side. Many vigorously proclaim the Unionist position and organize into Ulster Clubs of different kinds. Orange lodges serve as gathering points in some American cities and towns, as well as Canada. Money is collected in support of the Ulster Defence Association or other paramilitary groups, as well as for the same worthy causes that Nationalists support: hospitals, orphanages, single-parent families, prisoners and their families.

GUNS FROM AMERICA

At one time seventy-five percent of Provisional IRA armaments were American-made. It is likely that some of the arms are bought in the Middle East. Some find their way from Vietnam through arms dealers in the Middle East and North Africa. Congressman Les Aspin in 1975 released a confidential Defense Department report saying that sixty-nine hundred guns and 1.2 million rounds of ammunition had been stolen by Irish militants from U.S. Army bases between 1971 and 1974.

Guns and other weapons were seized from passenger luggage from the liner *Queen Elizabeth II* when it docked at Cobh, Ireland, in October 1971. A gun dealer was traced and later arrested.

AMERICAN CORPORATE INVESTMENT

About thirty American firms in Northern Ireland account for a total investment of two hundred million dollars. About eighteen thousand people are employed in these firms, 3.7 percent of the total work force. Other foreign investment comes mainly from the Republic of Ireland and Germany. Three-fifths of foreign investment in Northern Ireland is American.

U.S. Subsidiaries in Northern Ireland

The U.S. parent company is listed in alphabetical order. Under each company within parenthesis are listed the U.S. subsidiary in Northern Ireland, the products produced and the date the company arrived in Northern Ireland.

American Brands Inc., N.Y.
   (Gallaher Ltd., Belfast: Tobacco, 1958)
Ames Textile Corp., Mass.
   (Ballymoney Mfg. Co., Ballymoney: Yarn, 1966)

Ball Corp., Indiana
  (Kent Plastics (UK) Ltd., Enniskillen: Plastics, 1967)
Brunswick Corp., Texas
  (Sherwood Medical Industries (UK), Ballymoney: Medical
  products, 1966)
Camco, Inc., Texas
  (Camco Ltd., Belfast: Oil well equipment, 1959)
Camp International, Michigan
  (S.H. Camp & Co., Ltd., Irvinestown: Surgical supplies, 1967)
E.I. Du Pont de Nemours & Co., Delaware
  (Du Pont (UK) Ltd., Londonderry: Synthetic fibers, 1960)
Ford Motor Co., Michigan
  (Ford of Europe, Belfast: Auto parts, 1965)
Fruehauf Corp., Michigan
  (Dennison Trailers Ltd., Newtonabbey: Trailers, 1966)
General Foods Corp., N.Y.
  (Windsor Foods Ltd., Portadown: Pet food, 1964)
Goodyear Tire & Rubber Co., Ohio
  (General Tire & Rubber Co., (GB) Ltd., Craigavon: Rubber &
  allied products, 1967)
H. J. Heinz & Co., Pennsylvania
  (Pickering Foods Ltd., Londonderry: Dairy, 1946)
Hughes Tool Co., Texas
  (Hughes Tool Co., Castlereagh: Oil well, drill bits, 1954)
Inmont Corp., N.Y.
  (Tennants Textile Colors Ltd., Belfast: Chemicals and dyes, 1949)
International Rectifier, California
  (International Rectifier Co., Ltd., Newry: Rectifiers, 1969)
International Telephone and Telegraph Co., N.Y.
  (Standard Telephone & Cables (NI) Ltd., Monkstown: Phone
  equipment, 1962)
Monsanto, Missouri
  (Monsanto Textiles, Coleraine: Acrylic fibers, 1958)

National Distillers & Chemicals, N.Y.
   (Bridgeport Brass Ltd., Lisburn: Tire valves, 1961)
Norton Co., Mass.
   (Norton Abrasives Ltd., Castlereagh: Industrial abrasives, 1953)
Oneida, Ltd., N.Y.
   (Oneida Silversmiths Ltd., Bangor: Tableware, 1961)
Plastic Capacitors, Inc.
   (Plastic Capacitors, Inc., Londonderry: Capacitors, 1968)
PX Engineering, Mass.
   (PX Nuclear Ltd., Belfast: 1977)
St. Joe Paper Co., Inc., Florida
   (Ulster Paper Products, Craigavon: Corregated board, 1967)
Synthetic Industries Inc., California
   (Synthetic Industries, Newry: Plastic tape, 1976)
Tenneco, Inc., Texas
   (Walker Manufacturing Co., Newtonbreda: Mufflers, 1965)
T R W Inc., Ohio
   (Mission Manufacturing Co., Castlereagh: Oil well equipment,
   1956)
Textron Inc., Rhode Island
   (Textron Ltd., Lisburn: Ball bearings, 1964)
United Technologies, Connecticut
   (Essex International: Auto parts, 1969)
V F Corp., Pennsylvania
   (Berkshire International (UK) Ltd., Newtonards: Stockings, 1947)
Warnaco Inc., Connecticut
   (Warner Bros (NI) Ltd., Dromore: Lingeries, 1963)

    Overseas investment is a controversial issue. On the one hand, Northern Ireland desperately needs jobs, and even with North Sea oil the British economy has been faltering for many years. Emigration from Northern Ireland in 1975 alone reached sixteen thousand. From 1968 through 1976, ninety-seven thousand emigrated, and recently the figure has hovered around eleven thousand annually.
    On the other hand, overseas investment can mean at most only a short-term solution, since transnational companies naturally are interested in profits which leave Northern Ireland. Given the present laws which govern foreign investment, a large share of profits goes

back to the investing countries and the long-standing issue of economic depression remains unaddressed.

How could overseas investments help deal with the issues of fairness and unemployment? The Carnegie Center for Transnational Studies suggests certain criteria for measuring appropriate compensation:

> The corporation should offer wages at least comparable to similar indigenous industries.
> Fair wages should be established through management-labor collective bargaining.
> Corporations should make sure that wages meet the minimum-wage standards established by the government.
> If the government has not established what appears to be an acceptable minimum living wage, then studies should be done to establish a non-governmental minimum wage.

The U.S. Congress has expressed interest in monitoring the performance of U.S. companies in Northern Ireland.

One development in the investment area has created interest—some might say a controversy—and it needs to be mentioned. In August 1978, the American firm, De Lorean, announced that it was establishing a car factory in West Belfast. De Lorean said it planned to produce an expensive car for export; these plans were initially criticized, since the factory would be capital-intensive rather than labor-intensive. Furthermore, De Lorean was faulted in March 1980 by local political figures for not hiring local people. With the Northern Ireland unemployment level rapidly rising, this was an important issue (see chapter 5 for an account of subsequent events).

NEWS MEDIA

Most of the American news media use releases from Great Britain. The army public relations office sends news through London. The British army has almost always been described as an impartial third party "keeping the two sides apart." American readers often think that only violent extremists inhabit Northern Ireland; the American press seldom mentions that most Northern Irish people are not extremists and do not carry guns. American wire services use stories sent by British news agencies because of their traditional links. They carry practically no analysis; if there is any, it is usually simplistic and general. A Belfast columnist in June 1978 speculated that U.S. media do not like a conflict that does not end, so they disregard Northern Ireland. He may well have a point.

This "British point of view" is often attacked by Irish-American readers, frequently IRA supporters, writing letters to the editor with "another point of view." Thus, we usually see only two limited themes: support the army or support the IRA. The civic tragedies and hopeful developments in Northern Ireland are never aired. The *New York Times,* the *Christian Science Monitor*, and a few periodicals occasionally carry a story or an editorial commenting on the latest political developments, but in general the only American coverage is of explosions and killings. Rarely do other Northern Ireland voices come through. The Irish-American weeklies supply a Nationalist view, but speak only to the "converted."

THREE DYNAMICS AT WORK

The twenty million Americans with Irish background see events unfolding in the North in a special way. It is valuable to understand their perspective.

The first obvious fact is that Irish-Americans identify to some degree with both sides of the struggle going on in Northern Ireland, but they are not directly a part of it in the sense of living there. They are often more bitter, angry, and rhetorical than the group they identify with.

There are several reasons for this. People living in the struggle see small changes which develop almost daily, and these forces tend to make them optimistic, whatever their political position. People on the scene are also able to *act,* rather than just support or watch. People at a distance can only know the headlines—almost always depressing. Finally, there is some degree of guilt and divided spirits among absentee combatants; they think they want to be fully a part of the struggle, yet they are not willing to join it in Northern Ireland.

A second dynamic has to do with the fact that Irish-Americans support civil rights for Catholics in Northern Ireland, but sometimes oppose civil rights for American minorities. Probably one reason for this is that working-class Irish-Americans and minority people often compete for the same jobs. Irish-Americans want to keep the economic security they have.

A third factor concerns the Irish-American self-image. The conflict has affected how Irish-Americans think of themselves, and also how other Americans think about the Irish. It seems fair to suggest that the news of bigotry and bombings tends to confirm old stereotypes of "the fighting Irish." News of peace movements may capture people's attention around the world for a time, as happened in 1972 and 1976, but tends to be quickly forgotten. No American media person worked full time in Northern Ireland, so emphasis is usually given to dramatic headlines or human interest stores. These do little to deepen understanding.

TWO CASE STUDIES

These case studies are two examples of constructive and on-going American projects which relate in profound ways to events in Northern Ireland. We offer them for study in the hope that they can stimulate other helpful projects in the future.

Joint Manchester Project

The Joint Manchester Project (JMP) was developed principally by the Reverend Stephen K. Jacobson, an Episcopal priest in Manchester, Connecticut. Through the efforts of St. Mary's Episcopal Church and St. James' Catholic Church, an effective ecumenical program has been created for teenagers from Northern Ireland. The purpose of the program is to develop leadership skills and enduring personal relationships between Protestant and Catholic young people which will contribute toward reconciliation in their home communities.

We must be clear on one point. This is *not* just another holiday program for children. It has been carefully designed to develop, enhance, and help sustain lasting personal relationships among young people who will in time be leaders in their own communities.

The participants range in age from thirteen to sixteen. Parish clergy in Northern Ireland select youngsters who:

have indicated an openness to the possibility of reconciliation
between Protestants and Catholics,
have a commitment to their parish church,
have demonstrated potential leadership skills.

1977 was the second year of JMP, involving thirty-eight participants from Belfast, Armagh, and Portadown.

Those selected meet together as a group for several orientation meetings on neutral ground in Ulster before coming to the United States. At these meetings, they and their parents begin to get acquainted with the other participants. This coming together of family groups from the different communities in Ulster sets the pattern for programs which take place once the young people have returned home from America.

Each participant is matched as carefully as possible with an American host teenager. This is facilitated by the use of a comprehensive "interests and activities" questionnaire which the Irish and American candidates are asked to complete. The Irish visitor lives as a member of his or her American host family. Care is taken to ensure that the visit is one which stimulates mutual sharing while maintaining normal family routines.

JMP is a six-week program which includes a planned series of events including:

Forum: a weekly learning and sharing experience utilizing methods adapted from group encounters and other appropriate educational models.
Trips: sightseeing in Boston, New York City, and Hartford.
Recreation: including picnics, pool parties, discos, concerts, and athletics.
Worship: in the two churches, respecting the consciences of all. In addition to the planned events, neighborhood activities and spontaneous get-togethers become a part of the experience.

The cost of the program is borne by the sponsoring committee. In 1977 this amounted to about eighteen thousand dollars, which was raised by direct-mail solicitation, especially of clergy. One-third came from institutional contributors and two-thirds came from individual gifts which averaged twenty dollars. A Hartford-based insurance company donated a comprehensive medical/surgical insurance policy for the participants, and another insurance company provided release-time to one of their employees, Mr. Odis Coleman, who served as director of the project.

In order to ensure effective follow-up in Northern Ireland once the participants returned home, an Irish staff traveled with the group to Manchester. The staff included a Roman Catholic priest from Armagh, a Church of Ireland priest from Portadown together with his wife, and four seventeen-year-olds who had participated in the project in 1975 and who have been especially active in the follow-up activities since that time.

A good question is: why is such a large amount of money spent on bringing the participants to the U.S.? The JMP offers three principal answers:

"1. The opportunities for an enduring learning experience are greatly enhanced when the participants are relieved of some of the pressures which exist in Northern Ireland. A new perspective on interpersonal relationships is the key to the success of JMP.
2. Funds for a project of this sort are relatively easy to raise because Americans seem eager to support non-political programs which seek reconciliation.
3. American social ideals are an important gift we have to share. We believe that those values, which are realized to a surprising extent in many American communities, include: commitment to individual liberty and the free expression of ideas; racial and religious integration; respect for the diversity of religious persuasions; above all, a belief that people of good-will can live together in harmony without losing their treasured cultural traditions. As our guests derive benefits from seeing these ideals at work, we derive the benefit of re-discovering the value of these ideals to our way of life which we often take for granted."

Follow-up evaluations suggest that most of the program objectives have been achieved. Perhaps the most universal and enduring impressions taken back are those of amazement, hope, and determination: amazement that Protestants and Catholics live and work so easily together; hope that this can one day be said of Northern Ireland; determination to begin to put it into practice personally in new ways.

A similar American program for teenagers is the "Ulster Project" sponsored by the Pacem in Terris organization in Wilmington, Delaware. There are also numerous holiday projects for children, and we wish to say a word on these.

Projects which take children out of Northern Ireland to Europe or America for brief times have been criticized on various grounds. Some holiday projects are poorly organized and do not fulfill promises made.

A list of questions is helpful in thinking through the factors involved. These queries are ones which Northern Irish people themselves have raised.

1. Is the project the result of extensive consultation with Northern Irish people?

2. Does the holiday experience raise expectations which are difficult or impossible to act on upon returning (e.g., living happily at home, keeping up with friendships across community divisions)?

3. Might the project hinder the children from understanding and loving Northern Ireland itself, where children and adults would otherwise spend their holidays?

4. Does the project have a special benefit from being located outside Northern Ireland? Enough to compensate for the disadvantages?

5. Is the project just a holiday, or does it provide learning experiences as well? (The latter seems to require teenagers rather than younger people.)

6. Is the project safe from the danger of being mainly an ego trip of an Irish person or of Americans who are generous but ill-informed?

7. Is there adequate preparation and orientation for the participants and their families?

8. Is there adequate follow-up for participants to continue a life of reconciliation when they return home?

9. Does the project continue the trend of encouraging people in Northern Ireland to rely too much on outsiders?

Journey of Reconciliation

The Journey of Reconciliation was a project cosponsored and organized by the National Council of Churches Ireland Program and Pax Christi U.S.A. One hundred eleven citizens of the United States and Canada took part in this trip to Northern Ireland and the Irish Republic from November 28 to December 5, 1976. Most participants represented churches and organizations.

The purposes of the journey were to listen and to learn more about Northern Ireland, to support the December 5 rally at Drogheda for reconciliation and peace with justice, and later to inform other Americans and Canadians about developments for peace, looking toward moral and financial support for these.

The trip was well received by people in Ireland. As one host told the guests: "In the past, some American money has gone to support violence. Your presence here today has greater value by far than monetary support, for we all know how much harder it is to give of one's self."

Participants had information briefings from leaders and visits to peace groups and community centers, including the Community of the Peace People, Peace Point, Glencree, and the East Belfast Community Centre. A highlight for most participants was staying overnight in the homes of the wonderful people of Belfast. The group visited Derry and Dublin as well. But the main focus was taking part in the final peace rally on the Boyne River in the Republic on December 5. The gathering was organized by the Community of the Peace People and represented a symbolic meeting of people from the Republic and Northern Ireland, all of whom expressed their commitment to peace and an end to the violence and bloodshed. They hoped to "un-battle the Boyne."

A few participants decided against attending the peace rally in Drogheda. Some of them made this decision because they felt they did not know enough about Northern Ireland to take a stand to support the aims of any particular group. Others felt they were unable to identify with the goals of the rally. It was unfortunate that Irish Northern Aid in the United States made propaganda use of this disagreement. It was not surprising that among over a hundred activists there were differences of opinion.

The main purposes of the trip were fulfilled. Almost all the participants were able to communicate the substance and excitement of the momentum for peace to Americans and Canadians. They wrote newspaper articles, gave television and radio interviews, made hundreds of speeches, often with slides or films they had taken.

Participation in a week's journey to Northern Ireland does not make anyone an expert, but does provide experience. Participants did learn that people in Northern Ireland were grateful for the personal support of Americans and Canadians. They learned a great deal about the issues behind the fighting. Most have continued to be active in learning more about Northern Ireland and supporting the momentum for peace there.

Like some other aspects of the American connection with Northern Ireland, the Journey of Reconciliation can be seen as an experience in nonviolent international support for peace. In that perspective, we need to find other such ways to support peaceful social change around the world. In each case, the American connection helps the most when it aids that search for alternatives.

ACTION SUGGESTIONS

When a social conflict is as complex as is the one in Northern Ireland, it is all too easy to let the apparent hopelessness of the situation take over. We might quickly conclude that any action we could take would be ill-informed or useless. In order to take useful, effective action, we need to dismantle the difficulties ahead of us one by one. If information and analysis are needed, we must inform ourselves. If one person alone is too weak, then we must join with others. Difficult social and political conflicts take some time to form; their resolution will not occur overnight. We need to be able to evaluate our actions, seek the long-term goals, and understand how short-term goals fit together with them.

The authors hope that this book has provided helpful information, analysis, and insights. We further hope it will help people to take considered and compassionate action—action that makes sense and is relevant at the time. We offer a number of action suggestions. But they are limited, since they are only the ideas we know to have been helpful in the past. Who knows what developments will occur, and how events will progress? Important opportunities will certainly arise in the future which may make these action suggestions appear narrow. In other words, we need to be alert to possibilities—and this means a fairly constant monitoring of events as they develop.

1. Pray for peace and justice at home, in our communities, and in Northern Ireland.

2. Read a variety of books, articles, newspapers—not just the accounts of one side. See the bibliography in this book and ask at your library and bookstore.

3. Subscribe to Northern Ireland periodicals, especially those of peace action and reconciliation organizations and quality independent publications (see appendix V).

4. Examine and challenge myths and stereotypes about Ireland and the Irish people.

5. Visit Ireland, South and North, to learn firsthand about Irish society in its richness and complexity from a variety of citizens, to get a balanced picture of the complicated situation in North and South.

6. Write letters to the editors of local newspapers and present your views.

7. Inquire of local media about their news sources for stories from Northern Ireland and the Irish Republic. No full-time American journalist is based in Northern Ireland; all news from Northern Ireland is channeled through London or Dublin.

8. Educate others about Northern Ireland by holding an event (e.g., an "Irish night") in your parish, school, church, or community.

9. Sponsor events which feature speakers from Northern Ireland when they travel through the U.S. In recent years, speakers have occasionally been available from the Fellowship of Reconciliation, the Society of Friends, and the Mennonite Church.

10. When Northern Irish speakers are available, arrange to have them interviewed by local media.

11. Become familiar with projects in the U.S. which enable Northern Irish young people to spend time here with Americans. If the programs are near you, consider how you might support them.

12. Enable volunteer workers to go to Northern Ireland or Ireland for a summer or a longer term by providing money for their transportation. Volunteers live with Irish people while working on short-term or ongoing programs. Over eighty Americans have worked this way in the 1970s.

13. If you are a young person, consider taking part in a summer program or consider volunteering for an ongoing program. The Fellowship of Reconciliation in Northern Ireland has organized summer workcamps, working with children, every year since 1969 (see appendix V).

14. Consider using an ecumenical channel for any funds you may raise or want to send to help relief programs or to support reconciliation programs in Northern Ireland.

Lynne Shivers

Children playing on MacGilligan Strand, a beach in County Londonderry. A frequent activity of workcamps led by peace groups is to help Catholic and Protestant children play together. This workshop was sponsored by the Fellowship of Reconciliation.

Chapter 8
Final Questions

This chapter includes questions which Americans have actually asked us. It also deals with some of the untidy issues that don't easily fit anywhere. The questions are not exhaustive, but they are frequently asked and they are important. It is fitting that these questions round out our discussion of Northern Ireland.

It's a religious war, isn't it? I get along with Catholics (Protestants) in my neighborhood. I just don't understand.

We Americans need to remember that "Protestant" and "Catholic" do not mean the same things in Northern Ireland as they do in the United States. Over there, these terms indicate not only one's church affiliation, but also the culture, lifestyle, social values, heroes and heroines, income to some degree, history, and more, of two distinct cultural groups. In other words, the terms have a quite different meaning and context in Northern Ireland from those they have in the United States. American media constantly use religious identities; we could easily conclude that religion is *causative* in the conflict, not merely descriptive of the combatants. Religion is not the cause of the conflict. But it is a factor that has been used to separate people of similar class backgrounds. Protestant working-class people and Catholic working-class people traditionally see each other as enemies, responsible to some degree for their oppresion. In this way, the religious labels have been used to divide people.

It might be helpful to realize that there are other regional conflicts which deal with religious identity: Lebanon is one striking example. Cyprus is another. So is the Philippines, in Muslim areas.

There is not space here to deal substantially with comparisons, but according to a United Methodist leaflet, these "... situations involve a conflict that is built into the entire social relationship of two communities, each of whom receives the occasional support and patronage of outside powers in a neo-colonial context. . . . Both places are concerned with finding formulae for the internal running of the country that coincide with the interests of larger, outside powers." Other comparative studies are enormously valuable, since we can learn from tragic errors as well as moderately happy successes. (See also the introduction for a fuller discussion of religious identity as the main issue.)

If the British troops left, the Northern Irish people could settle things for themselves, couldn't they?

Ever since 1921, when the Northern parliament voted itself a separate existence within the United Kingdom, Northern Ireland has legally been an integral part of the U.K., in spite of Republican sentiments to the contrary both in the twenty-six counties and in its own one-third minority. One can dispute eight hundred or three hundred or fifty-seven years of history, but the fact of Northern Ireland remains. The million people who form the majority want so far to remain in the U.K. Many of the majority feel that the British army is "their" army; their way of life is dear to them, and has existed longer than the "American way of life."

Some observers suggest that a parallel to Great Britain and Northern Ireland is the colonial relationship of France and Algeria in the 1950s and 1960s.

Some of the most vehement advocates of British withdrawal often live three thousand miles away and have no intention of getting involved in a civil war. No one can be sure that if British troops withdrew, the Northern Irish people could settle things for themselves. The brutality of the last ten years makes Northern Irish residents pause when they consider the thought of British troops withdrawing totally and immediately. Many fear that "settling things for themselves" would bring on the long-feared bloodbath. Few in Northern Ireland think it is worth the risk.

If the British troops left, there'd be a bloodbath! Aren't the troops necessary to keep the two sides from killing each other?

The question implies that the British army is an impartial protector for both majority and minority groups. We hold to the analysis that the army is not impartial.

Whether or not a civil war (or "bloodbath") would result should the army withdraw depends on many factors. No one can predict for sure what would happen. No one can give an accurate count, but combatants in the various paramilitary armies are a small number—perhaps two percent of the population. A guerrilla conflict can keep going with very few people doing the bombing and shooting. Northern Ireland is not a place where everyone is trying to kill someone else. It is our ignorance—due largely to neglect by the media—which projects that sort of civil war image.

The issue of whether or not British soldiers should be withdrawn hinges on one's expectations of what would follow. Members of the Provisional IRA continue to press for a troop withdrawal. Their insistence on this point is mainly based on their conviction that the British presence is the single source of oppression.

On the other hand, the British government is responsible for the security of its citizens, in this case people living in the North. They remember all too well the lawless mobs in 1969 entering neighborhoods, beating, terrorizing, and harassing. Until some alternative system of security is developed for all Northern Irish citizens, there is little chance of withdrawal by the British army.

It is important to note that the issue of troop withdrawal is often presented as an "either-or" case, losing a number of important points. Some British troops have been withdrawn since 1978; the military presence is smaller in 1983 than a few years ago. Results of troop withdrawal are not necessarily precipitous.

A few observers have suggested there is more than a little racism inherent in the position of maintaining British troops in Northern Ireland: "Paddy can't do it, but the Brits can," i.e., Northern Irish people themselves can't deal with the conflicts; the English are needed to do the job.

As much as anything else, the issue of British troop withdrawal is closely tied up with fears that horrible events which occurred in the past may be repeated. This residual fear is one of the great realities of such social turmoil, yet it is almost impossible to understand without having been on the spot. People in the South still have vivid memories of 1912-20, and Northerners have more recent vivid memories.

The Irish have always hated the British—the Irish love a fight anyway. There is no end to the war; it just goes on and on.

This statement is based on a stereotype of the Irish and their history. It's true, of course, that the Anglo-Irish conflict goes back a long way (see chapter 4). But we should not confuse past strife with the present conflict in the North, which is discontinuous with the past in many ways.

To say the Irish "love a fight" plays right into stereotypic thinking, something we should try to avoid. The "Fighting Irish" of Notre Dame University received their name from their reputation for never giving up in games, not from any habit of fisticuffs. The cartoon Irish of the nineteenth century look much the same as the cartoon Blacks of the early twentieth: ape-like, stupid, brawling. Both are disgraceful travesties, better left to oblivion.

If we perpetuate such an image, are we not in danger of identifying ourselves with one outdated aspect of our Anglo-Saxon heritage, at the expense of seeing another culture clearly?

We also need to remember that Irish history has been characterized by invasions and foreign rule. We accord other countries the right to national independence; we should extend that right to Ireland as well (setting aside for the moment the issue of how that independence might be achieved).

We should remind ourselves that, since the founding of the United Nations, the Irish have frequently been part of U.N. peace-keeping forces.

The Irish-American experience has been different from the Irish experience "at home." All the immigrant groups took their place at the bottom rung of the U.S. economic ladder and had to fight their way to economic self-sufficiency. The determination to survive and to hold on to one's self-respect is a powerful struggle in itself.

The Protestants are the invaders—they should go back to England where they came from.

To begin with, just about everyone on the island came as an invader! Second, the Protestants in Northern Ireland didn't all come from England. The seventeenth century settlers, or planters, came mainly from Scotland. But the impact of this question has to do with people's rights to live where they please. If this principle were applied to the U.S.A., all white people would have to go back to their ancestral homes in Europe or elsewhere, Blacks would have to go to Africa, and so on.

In other words, the question does not make sense any more. People whose ancestors moved to Ulster three hundred years ago have as much right to live there and call themselves "natives" as anyone else. More to the point, perhaps, is how Unionists and Nationalists of various political persuasions can learn to accommodate each other. An equitable solution is much more likely if we try to deal rationally with present conditions than if we postulate the total withdrawal of a whole population.

The history of Ireland proves that the Irish are essentially violent.

It is true that Ireland has a history of violence. So has every other country; it seems to be evidence for what many call "original sin." But it is also true that Ireland has, as well, a number of striking examples of nonviolent resistance to various forms of repression. The word "boycott" comes from Irish history (see chapter 4). When, during Penal times (1695-1829), the practice of Catholic Mass was forbidden, priests said Mass in the hills, thus bypassing rigid laws—all a part of nonviolent resistance. When formal education was forbidden for Catholics during the same period, "hedge schools" were established. O'Connell and Parnell advocated nonviolent action. In the North in 1971, the rent and rates strike to protest internment was a powerful example of a nonviolent economic boycott. The civil rights marches and protests were, at first, in the great tradition of Martin Luther King and Gandhi's nonviolent action. And since the present troubles began, many groups and organizations have advocated and implemented nonviolence programs.

The English are a fair and reasonable people. The British army is not brutal like some other armies. The violence must come pretty much from the temperamental Irish.

Most Americans think of Great Britain as the source of Western civil liberties and laws which protect individual rights. This is true, but not the complete truth about the army in Northern Ireland. There is a large gap between a tradition of civil liberties and the behavior of entrenched politicians, certainly of soldiers. Many observers suggest that the British army in Northern Ireland has generally been restrained in its activities, but others take a different view. Armed men trained to fight are unfit to do police work unless they receive special training or are exceptional individuals. The army is neither as bad as the hard-liners say, nor as good as uncritical admirers say. Violent troop behavior in Derry on Bloody Sunday and during the August 1971 process of internment has been found unjustified by impartial investigations. (Nevertheless, the Bennett Report, released in 1979, found that RUC detectives had ill-treated prisoners; see chapter 2). Certainly the ordinary soldiers have often shown extraordinary patience while being stoned and insulted; equally certainly, some have acted and reacted with undue violence. So, while it is probably true to say that the British army has usually acted with restraint, it is not true to say that the army has always acted without brutality.

I've heard there are communists in the North and South. Besides, the Soviet Union is involved.

The Communist Party in Northern Ireland, as well as in the Republic, is small, numbered in the hundreds. The implications of the question are more important than the actual fact of the presence of the Communist party. The question seems to imply that if communists are active in the North, then there is a moral imperative to fight to the death. One problem stemming from this attitude is that paramilitaries on both sides have visited Libya, sought weapons wherever they can be bought, and are just about equally suspect as "tools of Russia." Russian-made weapons have been used by the Provos; so have American-made weapons. Looking for the "red under the bed" can prevent us from looking at more explicit issues in the North such as injustice, unemployment, poor housing, and disregard for human rights. Our first priority should be doing what we can to help Northern Ireland be a place where life can prosper for everyone.

If people have had enough, why don't they emigrate?

They do! The latest figures the British government is willing to release show that sixteen thousand emigrated in 1976 and again in 1977. Emigration is a traditional Irish "solution" to unemployment, instability, and prejudice. Provisional leaders gave this as a reason justifying their violence: if so many after 1921 had not been forced to emigrate, the minority would be the majority by now! Americans may be surprised to learn that few emigrants go South; most go to the U.K., New Zealand, or Canada—where the social services are favorable. Recently, many emigrants have been young families from the Loyalist community.

Wouldn't it be possible to bring in a United Nations peace-keeping force?

This is possible only when the host government invites the United Nations to send in such a force. The British government has never issued such an invitation. A few times since 1969, especially when the situation seemed out of control, various political leaders in the North, in Ireland, in the U.S.A., and in Great Britain have suggested the idea, but it has never been taken up. In a private poll in Northern Ireland in 1974, only twenty-one percent said they favored replacing British troops with a U.N. peace-keeping force.

Wouldn't an independent Northern Ireland be viable and possible?

Debate about an independent Northern Ireland has grown over the past few years, especially since the NUPRG espoused it. The goal would be a *negotiated* independence, not a Unilateral Declaration of Independence (UDI), like Rhodesia's in 1965. The idea is attractive to many, since up to now the political debate has focused on which state Northern Ireland would be attached to: Great Britain or the Irish Republic—or both, in joint sovereignty. Pride in being "Ulster people" or even "Northern Irish" has grown over the past few years, as has irritation with the British since 1972's direct rule. So it is not surprising that some people are considering the idea of an independent six-county Northern Ireland. The discussion goes on not just among academics, but also among working-class people, clergy, and community leaders.

There are plenty of negative reasons for considering independence: political talks are deadlocked; all else has failed; the political vacuum ensures endemic violence; and so on. But there are also positive reasons: a common allegiance to "Ulster" could develop, partial achievement of the goals of both extreme parties could result; that is, the link with Britain would be broken, but so would dreams of a united Ireland.

Advantages include the freedom to pursue solutions directly geared to Ulster problems, the possibility of increased subsidies from the Common Market, and (for Republicans) the greater chance that independence might lead to closer ties with the twenty-six counties. Disadvantages include the greater difficulty of agreeing on power-sharing, eventual loss of U.K. subsidies, and (for Republicans) the danger that Loyalists might have greater control of political power. Nevertheless, the discussion continues, and Americans can benefit from understanding it. In August 1979, Corrymeela hosted a week-long forum on it, with participation of political figures, from North and South.

Why don't Unionists and Nationalists agree to share power?

The British have tried to force this on Northern Ireland three times; their efforts have been rebuffed, partly out of resentment Political and paramilitary extremists on both sides have been unwilling to compromise. They carry a major responsibility for the failure of power-sharing programs. Although the Provos have often said publicly that they wanted to sit down with the UDA, the latter has equally publicly refused to do so. They seem to have talked privately, on occasion. There is a fear, especially in the Unionist community, that one concession could lead to many. Following this train of thought, Unionist values could easily be eroded. The defense against this fear is the Loyalist tendency to hold rigid positions: "No surrender!" is the best-known rallying cry.

Why should Americans care about Northern Ireland? I'm not Irish. We have enough trouble right here.

Irish immigrants literally helped to build this country. The American-Irish link is strong and extends over generations.

In addition, we should realize that the U.S., by its power alone, has certain effects on the rest of the world. The U.S. impinges on small nations and smaller regions in ways we as Americans are not generally aware of. As a result, we have a special responsibility to at least become knowledgeable about Northern Ireland events.

The idea of an interdependent world is gaining a lot of support these days. In every part of the world people are experiencing the stresses and tensions of majority and minority groups living with each other. Prejudice, stereotyping, discrimination and serious economic disparity exist in many countries. So do segregated housing, employment, and schools. Lessons learned from Northern Ireland can help us understand our own problems, as well as the polarization that exists in other cultures.

All moral teaching proclaims that people are inherently equal as humans, different though they may be in location, nationality, cultural background, or language. Surely people in Northern Ireland are our sisters and brothers as much as are people in India, the Middle East, the Philippines, Nicaragua, El Salvador, and all around the world. We share a great deal with them, and in line with the title of this book, we share more than the troubles. We share our humanity. We share our love of justice, of peace, and of reconciliation.

APPENDIX I: PEACE EDUCATION—ITS RELEVANCE TO NORTHERN IRELAND

Joseph J. Fahey

So far in this book, we have offered readers information and analysis about Northern Ireland which will enable them to better understand events as they occur. This chapter applies themes dealt with earlier in this book to the concept of peace education.

Joseph J. Fahey, M.A., Ph.D., is director of the Peace Studies Institute at Manhattan College, Riverdale, N.Y. He was in Belfast during the summer of 1977 as an honorary research fellow in the Department of Further Professional Studies in Education at Queens University.

This article was originally published in The Northern Teacher, *November-December 1977, Queens University, Belfast. Two small sections are excerpts from an article originally published in* The Tablet: The International Catholic Weekly, *31 January 1976,*

Peace education in the United States, which is still in its beginning stages, began in response to the civil rights movement and the war in Indochina. Many teachers began to realize that while we were adequately preparing our students in the three "r's" and career preparation, we were not preparing them to deal with the personal, societal, and global conflicts which are the hallmark of our age. Further, some teachers believed that our schools must assist in the creation of a new culture characterized by unified diversity, nonviolence, and human justice. Some less idealistic teachers simply argued that aside from a moral imperative, peace education was practically necessary if we were to have a more functionally stable society. Peace education, in short, is an academic response to the problems of human violence and injustice which have never loomed so large as in our own century.

But what is peace education? This question can best be answered by looking at the meaning of the word peace itself. The Romans used the word "pax" to denote peace, and it essentially meant a pact or agreement not to fight. Thus, this definition is basically a negative one, and it refers to the absence of war as the chief characteristic of peace. The Greeks used the word "eirene" to define peace (Irene was the Greek goddess of peace), and this meant a state of harmony and communication in addition to the absence of violence. The Semitic word for peace is "shalom" (the Arabic word is "salaam"), and this word connotes the presence of internal and external physical abundance. For the Semitic mind, then, peace means an absolute minimum of violence and a maximum of justice, fulfillment and reconciliation. When we relate these words to education, it is obvious that a great deal depends on which definition we choose to relate to our students.

While all three definitions are relevant to classroom discussion, the best working definition of peace for educational purposes is that it is a positive condition of human cooperation and communication characterized by a high level of social, economic, and political justice, together with a minimum of physical and psychological violence. Almost any discipline or course of study is relevant to peace education. In addition, peace education can be taught at every level of our educational structures from primary school through university.

Areas of Concern

While there is a great variety of courses and programs which constitute Peace Studies, there is something of a consensus that peace education includes one or more of the following areas:

1) **Conflict Resolution.** Programs which have this focus tend to concentrate on the values and communications skills necessary to produce a creative response to the problem of human conflict. These courses deal with specific conflict resolution strategies which have been developed through the centuries and range from reconciliation through mediation and arbitration. (While the methods of violence should be explained, they should not also be encouraged!)

2) **Nonviolence.** Courses and programs in this area deal with both a philosophical and practical understanding of the nonviolence of such people as M.K. Gandhi and M.L. King, Jr. The study of history is relevant here, since there are abundant examples of nonviolent social change throughout recorded history. Contemporary anthropological studies also contribute to an understanding of the nonviolent behavior of preliterate societies which give something of an accurate picture of primitive human societies. Needless to say, there are many examples of nonviolent action in Irish society, and such study is clearly relevant to Northern Irish teachers and schools.

3) **War and Peace.** We can learn much about the path to peace if we study the causes of war. Courses in this area study both warlike and peaceful societies to determine the dynamics and strategies which lead to both. It is important, in this context, to study relatively peaceful societies and groups (and there are some!) to determine how they avoid war and violence and continue cooperation and communication even in stressful times.

4) **Social Justice.** Since true peace cannot exist apart from justice, it is imperative to study the kinds of political and economic systems which promote peace rather than war. We know that injustice is generally a prelude to violence. It should surprise no one that poverty, unemployment, and servitude lead to the frustration which causes violence.

5) **World Order.** Nationalism has never been so rife as in this century and often leads to alleged claims of racial superiority and dominance which are a prelude to war. We need to realize that we are common citizens of this earth and as such share a common and interdependent destiny which simply cannot be denied if we are to survive. The arms race and trade which is at present out of control needs some international body (like the United Nations) to ease the tensions between nation states and so provide ground for communication and cooperation. Courses in this area focus on these concerns and seek to develop the common concerns which bind us all. At the same time, the courses will realistically deal with the differences which are the causes of strife and possible violence.

Dealing With Myths

Despite the attempts of historians, sociologists, geographers and others to give an accurate picture of the human experience, many of us live with myths about human nature which must be dispelled if we are to have a peaceful world. Since we live as much by myth as we do by history, we must deal with the myths which surround us, which quickly have a way of becoming reality.

Perhaps the greatest myth which rules us is that we are genetically violent creatures. Robert Ardrey has expressed it this way:

*Man is a zoological group of sentient rather than sapient beings,
characterized by a brain so large that he uses rather little of*

it, a chin distinctive enough to identify him among related animals, and an overpowering enthusiasm for things that go boom.

Simply stated, Ardrey and others such as Konrad Lorenz and Anthony Storr have the view that we, indeed, are warlike creatures who must periodically erupt in violence lest we deny our genetic and psychological makeup. There are many scientists who disagree with this dour view of human nature, and René Dubos and Morton Hunt are representative when they tell us:

Man's propensity for violence is not a racial or a species attribute woven in his genetic fabric. It is culturally conditioned by history and ways of life. (Dubos)

The record of man's inhumanity to man is horrifying when one compiles it—enslavement, castration, torture, rape, mass slaughter in war after war. But who has compiled the record of man's kindness to man—the trillions of acts of gentleness and goodness, the helping hands, smiles, shared meals, kisses, gifts, healings, rescues? If we were no more than murderous predators, with a freakish lack of inhibition against slaughtering our own species, we would have been at a terrible competitive disadvantage compared with other animals. (Hunt)

We must have a better image of ourselves and come to see that despite our struggles and troubles, we are basically kind animals who thrive on love, joy, communication and sharing. The role of religion is particularly important here since the age-old message of the brotherhood of humankind is supported by a great deal of scientific and psychological truth.

Since its origins, humanity has laboured for peace and harmony and has always had those among its numbers (and if they were not the vast majority we would not have survived) who have practiced nonviolence in the face of violence and love in the face of hate.

In short, we must demythologize the doctrine of "original sin" and come to see that while humanity is not perfect it is perfectible and that while we do kill we can "choose life."

In some very violent cultures there was good reason to associate violence with virility because physical violence was the dominant sign of power and political control. In these cultures both physically weak men and most women were accorded second class citizenship and their strongest assets—reason, constructive judgment, and compassion—were either ignored or regarded as signs of weakness or inferiority. Peace education must challenge this superficial and degrading view of human nature (which is still so prevalent in today's "civilized" world). We must redefine words like "strength," "power," and "weakness" and ask ourselves whether in the last quarter of the 20th century the "weak" individuals and nations are not really the "strong," and whether the "powerless" may not be the "powerful."

It was a favorite saying of Mohandas K. Gandhi that "nonviolence is the weapon of the strong." Gandhi, who based his revolution on the premise that "soul" power was indeed stronger than violence, severely challenged the view that "God is on the side of the big cannon." It was no accident that Dr. Martin Luther King, Jr. based so much of his nonviolent thinking on Gandhi's thought. He learned from Gandhi that through nonviolence an oppressed minority could gain a new dignity and power which far surpassed that of a military force.

Another myth with which we must deal is the view that war makes peace and violence secures justice. No one should be so foolish to deny that war and violence have accomplished certain goals, but they very rarely have produced true peace or justice, and if they have, it has inevitably been through the denial of life and justice to others. Thus, even in the rare cases where war and violence have been effective, they have only been 50% so. In order to secure true peace and justice we must—in Gandhi's terms—make our means consistent with our end. That is, if we wish peace, the only way to it is through peaceful means. Just as a rose cannot be grown except through planting a rose seed, so peace cannot be developed except through peaceful means. War and violence, where they have been effective, have never brought peace but only the conditions which can lead to peace. Often the violent and oppressive attitudes that were built up during war continue on to affect a given society after war. Surely there are better ways. Peace education seeks to help us realize that nonviolence is the true sign of courage while violence is often a sign of cowardice and moral impotency. To paraphrase John F. Kennedy: war will be with us until that distant day when the person of nonviolence is as much respected as is the warrior today.

Surely there are nonviolent "heroes" in past and present Irish history, and it is time they received as much attention as the mythic "heroes" of ballads and poems which clearly are a source of cultural education of our young children.

Thirdly, there is the myth of alleged racial and cultural superiority which for so long has been a cause of fear, hatred, and violence. Human nature has developed various cultures, philosophers, languages, modes of dress, etc. The varieties of human experience should be viewed as a positive human trait rather than a negative one. Above all, we must stress that we share a common humanity which has been enriched by our diverse cultural heritage. Further, we have a great deal to learn from other cultures which can enrich our own and so contribute to a more humane society for us all. The Hindu proverb, "Truth is One: the paths to it are many," has great relevance here, since a peaceful world can only be created by the realization that all of us possess only partial—not absolute—truth, and that our truth must therefore be enriched by others if we are to have a more complete realization of truth. Education for cultural toleration and diversity is education for a more peaceful and just society. Unless our schools give a positive view of the diversity of the human endeavor, we shall continue to be ruled by the mistaken myth that our truth is the only truth by which all must live.

Finally, there are many who convincingly argue that peace will continue to be an illusion without fundamental reform of our economic system, which has clearly demonstrated its lack of concern for basic human justice and where, if the profit motive serves humanity, it is almost out of necessity, not choice. Any economic system based on profit before people must be morally questioned and politically challenged. That new markets and higher profits should contribute to exploitation and possibly war should surprise no one.

Clearly, we need more positive economic alternatives. If we try to avoid this problem, we must not revert to the old "liberalism" which thought we could reform society through the reform of individuals. Individual justice never guarantees group virtue, but group justice can at least provide a basis for individual growth and development.

The Advantages of Nonviolence

Some of the advantages of nonviolence which should find a place in our curricula are the following:

*The goal of nonviolence is to seek internal moral power rather than external physical power. In this context, the violence of the "brute" is seen as a sign of cowardice, whereas nonviolence is a sign of courage and strength.

*Nonviolence seeks to achieve victory for both sides in a conflict. Where violence must have a winner and loser, only nonviolence can provide a path through which both sides can win in a struggle. We must view compromise as a human virtue rather than a selling out of principle if both sides are to have a measure of justice. The oppressed normally gain economic and political freedom, and the oppressors gain moral liberation and ethical integrity.

*Nonviolence can achieve victory against great odds, since it relies on moral strength and an appeal to the good-will and conscience of the opponent. Further, anyone can join a nonviolent army, be they children, old people, or people who normally would be excluded from a military army.

*Nonviolence realizes that one's opponent is in possession of some truth and therefore seeks to work constructively with it. Nonviolence robs one's opponent of the self-righteousness which often leads to greater violence and oppression.

*The goal of nonviolence is justice, not victory. Both Gandhi and King often stated that it was not their goal to have a victory over the British or the whites, but rather to seek a common victory in the establishment of justice.

*Only in nonviolence are the "means" and "ends" convertible terms. The path to peace is sought actively through peaceful means.

It is important to remember that nonviolence usually is not successful at first, whereas violence often has immediate results. But nonviolence which is tenaciously held to after a series of failures, will, in the end, produce long-lasting justice, whereas violence only produces further and greater violence. Further, people who engage in violence to secure justice almost inevitably inflict violence on the very people they were seeking to liberate and so end up being unjust themselves. Nonviolent people who are just from the beginning are frequently just in the end.

The Relevance to Northern Ireland

Peace Studies can have a dual role in Northern Ireland. It must seek to relate the educational institutions to the immediate troubles and so examine the economic, political, and religious dimensions of the strife. The hope is that understanding will lead to practical and constructive action in ending the violence and building a more tolerant and just society. But Peace Studies has an equally important long range goal. Its goal is to heal the many scars which have been built up through the years of violence and so in the end to bring reconciliation to the various parties in these troubles. Even after the violence has ended—and history tells us that it will—there will still be a vital role of peace education in shaping the kind of society in which these difficulties will not be repeated. Violence is only a symptom of a deeper problem; unless there are long range strategies and programs to deal with that problem, there can be no true peace. Education must play a vital role here.

Conclusion

It has been said that we are giants when it comes to making war and mere pygmies when it comes to making peace. We are living in a violent age, and our response to it has often been to use greater and greater violence. We must break this endless cycle with the introduction of practical nonviolent strategies to solve our problems. Essentially we are educators for freedom, trying to make our students and society more free than it is by providing more nonviolent options to deal with our troubles. In the words of Dr. Ralph Abernathy, a close associate of Dr. King:

> *We are walking to freedom. We will walk without violence until, like the walls of Jericho, the walls of segregation tumble and fall. They can bomb our houses and our churches, they*

can put us in prison, but we will not hate. Like Moses we see the promised land. We may not enter into it but our children will. We are a freedom band walking with dignity to freedom.

Let us accept the challenge of freedom and nonviolence by our patient efforts to bring a peace dimension to our students and educational institutions.

APPENDIX II: ABBREVIATIONS

AOH	Ancient Order of Hibernians
DUP	Democratic Unionist Party
EEC	European Economic Community (Common Market)
ICTU	Irish Council of Trade Unions
INC	Irish National Caucus
INLA	Irish National Liberation Army
IRA	Irish Republican Army
IRSP	Irish Republican Socialist Party
ITGWU	Irish Transport and General Workers' Union
LEDU	Local Enterprise Development Unit
M.P.	Member of (British) Parliament
NATO	North Atlantic Treaty Organization
NCCUSA	National Council of Churches of the U.S.A.
N.I.	Northern Ireland
NICRA	Northern Ireland Civil Rights Association
NILP	Northern Ireland Labour Party
NUPRG	New Ulster Political Research Group
OIRA	Official Irish Republican Army
OO	Orange Order
OSSFWP	Official Sinn Fein Workers' Party
OUP	Official Unionist Party
PACE	Protestant and Catholic Encounter
PD	People's Democracy
PIRA	Provisional Irish Republican Army
RTE	Radio Telefis Eireann
RUC	Royal Ulster Constabulary
RUCR	Royal Ulster Constabulary Reserve

SAS	Special Air Service
SDLP	Social Democratic and Labour Party
SFWP	Sinn Fein Workers' Party
TD	Teachtai Dala (Member of the Irish Parliament)
UDA	Ulster Defence Association
UDR	Ulster Defence Regiment
UFF	Ulster Freedom Fighters
ULDP	Ulster Loyalist Democratic Party
U.K.	United Kingdom
UPNI	Unionist Party of Northern Ireland
USC	Ulster Special Constabulary
	Ulster Service Corps
UVF	Ulster Volunteer Force
UWC	Ulster Workers Council
UUAC	Ulster Union Action Council
UUUC	United Ulster Unionist Council
UUUM	United Ulster Unionist Movement
UUUP	United Ulster Unionist Party
VUM	Vanguard Unionist Movement
VUPP	Vanguard Unionist Progressive Party

APPENDIX III: FATALITIES SINCE 1969

	RUC/ RUC-R	Army	UDR	Civilian	Prison Officials	Total	Cumulative
1969	1	—	—	12	—	13	13
1970	2	—	—	23	—	25	38
1971	11	43	5	114	—	173	211
1972	17	103	25	322	—	467	678
1973	13	58	8	171	—	250	928
1974	15	28	7	166	—	216	1144
1975	11	14	5	217	—	247	1391
1976	23	14	15	242	3	297	1688
1977	14	15	14	66	3	112	1800
1978	10	14	7	48	2	81	1881
		Combined Army/UDR					
1979	14	48		51	—	113	1994
1980	9	16		50	—	75	2069
1981	21	23		55	—	99	2168
1982	12	28		57	—	97	2265

KEY: RUC   —Royal Ulster Constabulary
      RUC-R —Royal Ulster Constabulary Reserves
      UDR   —Ulster Defence Regiment

Sources: W.D. Flackes, *Northern Ireland: A Political Directory, 1968–79,* and Denis Barritt, *Northern Ireland: A Problem to Every Solution.*

APPENDIX IV: FACTS AND FIGURES

This appendix provides some background facts and figures for reference purposes.

Major sources:

Facts about Ireland. Department of Foreign Affairs, Dublin, 1978.
Facts and Figures about Northern Ireland. British Information Service (various years).
Ulster Year Book, 1976. Her Majesty's Stationery Office, Belfast, 1976.
Ulster Year Book, 1977. Her Majesty's Stationery Office, Belfast, 1977.

A. General Geography of the Island of Ireland

Location:	Part of the northwest continent of Europe, west of Great Britain—on the same latitude as Labrador.
Land Area:	35,595 square miles, or about the size of Maine.
Divided into:	twenty-six counties of the Republic; 27,136 square miles, or about the size of Massachusetts, New Hampshire, and Vermont. (83% of total land area.)
	six counties of Northern Ireland; 5,459 square miles, or about the size of Connecticut. (17 % of total land area.)
Greatest length:	(North-South): 302 miles
Greatest width:	(East-West): 171 miles
Climate:	Mild, due to position in the Atlantic, close to the Gulf Stream.
Temperature:	Winter average (Jan.-Feb.): 42 degrees F (low extreme: 15 degrees F)
	Summer average (July-Aug.): 59 degrees F (high extremes: 70-75 degrees F)
Rainfall:	Average: 30 inches per year (agriculturally significant)

Physical Features:	General configuration: central limestone plain surrounded by coastal highlands; "saucer-shaped."
Lakes:	Five major (greater than 30 square miles), numerous smaller Lough Neigh, 153 square miles, largest fresh-water lake in Europe.
Major rivers:	Seven (over 70 miles) including the longest: Shannon, 320 navigable miles.
Most important Mountains:	Wicklow, Croagh Patrick, Mourne, Sperrins.
Natural resources:	Oil deposits, offshore as well. Uranium, lead, zinc. Suitable agricultural climate. Favorable trade line location toward Europe (EEC). Tourist attractions and facilities; golfing, fishing, cycling, hospitality. Divided into a richer east and a poor west, almost on a line down the middle of the island.

B. Demography

Who are the Irish? How many are there? Some facts:

Population of the island: 4,497,888 (1971 census)

	Northern Ireland	Republic of Ireland
	1,519,640 (34% of total)	2,978,248 (66% of total)
Density:	291 per sq. mile	112 per sq. mile
Increase, 1926-71:	279,504 (18%)	6,256 (0.2%)

Religious Identity (1971 census):

Roman Catholic	477,921 (31.4%)	2,795,666 (93.9%)
Presbyterian	405,717 (26.7%)	16,052 (0.5%)
Ch. of Ireland (Anglican)	334,318 (22.0%)	97,739 (3.3%)
Methodist	71,235 (4.7%)	5,646 (0.2%)
Baptist	16,563 (1.1%)	591 (0.02%)
Others (incl. "no reply")	212,927 (14.0%)	59,921 (2.0%)
Jewish	959 (0.06%)	2,633 (0.08%)

Birthrate: 17 per 1000 in 1975   21.6 per 1000
                       (highest in U.K.)   in 1975

Deaths: 10.7 per 1000   similar to N.I.
                         in 1975

Marriages: 7.1 per 1000
                       (1975)   lower than in N.I.

Distribution
by age   under 15: 29%
          15-44: 40%
          45-64: 20%
        over 64: 11%

Emigration: 1922-1977: 360,000
  1968-1977: 97,000

C. Government in Northern Ireland

Status: Part of the United Kingdom of Great Britain and Northern Ireland (Section 1: "Northern Ireland Constitution Act 1973").

Authority: This Act provided for the division of powers between the sovereign and the parliament at Westminster, the U.K. government, the Regional Assembly at Stormont, and an Executive mostly drawn from the Assembly. Northern Ireland has been under **direct rule** from Westminster since the resignation of the last Northern Ireland Executive in May 1974. The "Northern Ireland Act 1974":
1. suspended the legislative functions of the Northern Ireland Assembly (Stormont);
2. provided for Northern Ireland administrative functions to be subject to the direction and control of the secretary of state for Northern Ireland in the United Kingdom cabinet.

Form: Part of the United Kingdom, with representation at Westminster (twelve members in the House of Commons). A member of Parliament is appointed secretary of state for Northern Ireland, and is a member of the cabinet.

Structure: **Northern Ireland Office** is one of the U.K. Government offices, composed of a secretary of state and four other ministers appointed by the Queen on the advice of the prime minister. This is similar to the provision for Scotland and Wales.

Secretary of State: responsible for political and constitutional matters, security police and operations, and major policy issues.

Departments: names of ministers are not included since they change frequently.

1. Dept. of Health & Social Services, also responsible for prisons, police administration, and compensation for criminal injuries.

2. Depts. of Finance, Manpower Services, and Civil Service.

3. Dept. of Environment.

4. Depts. of Commerce and Agriculture.

5. Dept. of Education: this minister is also responsible for handling all Northern Ireland matters in the House of Lords at Westminster.

Local Government: 26 District Councils, since 1973, with 526 ward councillors locally elected every four years in 98 PR areas, to

1. direct administration of local services;

2. represent local interests in regional matters;

3. oversee provision of street-cleaning, parks, cemeteries, consumer protection;

4. enforce building regulations, licensing, environmental rules;

5. promote local tourism and cultural life.

Area Boards: Five Education and Library Boards are responsible to the appropriate departments for local administration; four Health and Social Services Boards do likewise.

Elections: Parliamentary: at decision of government. Last held in June 1983.
Local: every four years. Last held in May 1977.
Franchise: everyone over 18.
Type: Proportional Representation (PR). See Electoral Law Northern Ireland Order 1978.
(Except for Westminster elections)

Civil Rights: Under U.K. law, every individual has the right to "personal liberty." Human Rights Provisions of 1973 Constitution provide that there be no discrimination based on religious belief or political opinion. No written Bill of Rights in U.K. (no written constitution either).

Legal System: Presumption of innocence; burden of proof on the prosecution; right to legal counsel and due process of law; in prosecution of persons charged with terrorist offenses, the right to due legal process is subject to "Northern Ireland Emergency Provisions Acts 1973," renewed in 1975 (see chapter 3).

Judiciary System: 1. Superior (supreme) courts:
— High Court of Justice; Court of Appeal.
2. Inferior courts:
— county; magistrate.

Judges are independent; appointment and removal of judges is by the Crown on advice of Lord Chancellor, not Northern Ireland Executive.

D. Economy and Industry

1. In 1974, 74 percent of imports and 82 percent of exports were traded with Great Britain; 12 percent of trade was with the Republic of Ireland.
2. Manufacturing industry employs 147,200 people. Of those, engineering and related industries employ almost 50,000. This includes shipbuilding and textiles.

E. Government of the Republic of Ireland

26 administrative counties in the four historic provinces, including three of ancient Ulster's nine.

Current Status:	Constitutional, sovereign, independent, democratic state.
Authority:	Constitution (*Bunracht na hEireann*) ratified by plebiscite, 1937.
Form:	Parliamentary democracy; bicameral British parliamentary model with parties and party cabinet governments.
Structure:	Parliament and prime minister. Parliament (*Oireachtas*) composed of 1. President (*Uachtaran*): **head of state,** popularly elected every seven years; maximum two terms. 2. Senate (*Seanad Eireann*): 60 members; 11 appointed by prime minister, 6 elected by graduates of universities (Ireland and Dublin); 43 elected by panels of representative vocational groups; 3. Dail (*Dail Eireann*): 148 members (called *Teachtai Dala*; "T.D.'s"); proportional representation (20,000 - 30,000 per T.D.) by those over 18; last elections held in June, 1983.

Members of the 21st Dail are in the three
parties which have predominated since 1922;
seats in 1978 were:
Fianna Fail: 84
Fine Gael: 43
Labour: 17
Independent: 4
Prime Minister (*Taoiseach*): **Head of
government,** nominated by Dail, appointed by
president.
Deputy prime minister (*Tanaiste*).
"bills:" presented by government to houses
which may amend them and make them laws,
called "acts."
Civil service: 16 departments, each under a
minister.

**Local
Government**   26 counties
— supervised by the civil service "Central
Department of Local Government";
— composed of county councils, city councils,
which are elected every five years and
administer local services through "managers."

Elections: National: every five years—sooner, if majority
wishes;
Local: every five years.

Civil Rights: Constitutionally protected; "inalienable rights
from the natural law:" private property,
equality before the law, freedom of speech and
association, right to due process.

**Legal
System:**   Founded on common law.
Administered by six-tiered judiciary (composed
of Supreme, High, Circuit, and District Courts).
Judges: appointed by president on advice of
government; dismissal only by *Oireachtas.*

Normal right to due process of law subject to Special Criminal Court established May 1972 (as part of High Court, Art. 38, Constitution) upon a decision by the government that "the ordinary courts were inadequate to secure the effective administration of justice and the preservation of public peace and order."

Security: Protective Services.
Garda Siochana, "Guardian of the Peace" (pl. *Gardai*)
   Administered by "Civil Service Department of Justice"
   Size of police force: 9,000
   Expenditure 1976-77: £ 60,180,000
   ($107,120,400)
   Size of army: 34,385
   Expenditure 1976-77: £ 85,223,000 (total defense expenditure)

APPENDIX V: ADDRESSES

A select list of organizations referred to in chapters 2 and 6, classified by country/province and function.

A. Northern Ireland: Peace, Reconciliation, and Community Development Groups

1. Ballynafeigh Community Development Association, 291 Ormeau Road, Belfast 7.
2. Belfast Voluntary Welfare Society, Bryson House, 28 Bedford St., Belfast BT2 7FE.
3. Community of the Peace People, 224 Lisburn Road, Belfast 7.
4. Corrymeela, Ballycastle, Co. Antrim; 8 Upper Crescent, Belfast BT7 1NT.
5. East Belfast Community Council. 198-200 Albertbridge Road, Belfast BT5.
6. Fellowship of Reconciliation, c/o Denis Barritt, 24 Pinehill Rd., Ballycairn, Lisburn.
7. Holiday Projects West, 14 Queen Street, Londonderry.
8. Irish Council of Churches, 48 Elmwood Avenue, Belfast 9.
9. North Belfast Community Council, at N. Belfast Resource Centre, 44 Alliance Ave., Belfast BT14.
10. Northern Ireland Civil Rights Association, 2 Marquis St., Belfast BT1 1JJ.
11. Pax Christi, c/o John and Margaret Watson, 126 Blacks Road, Belfast 10.
12. Peace Point, c/o Sheelagh Flanagan, 35 Marlborough Park North, Belfast 9.
13. Peace Forum, c/o Corrymeela, 8 Upper Crescent, Belfast BT7 1NT.
14. Protestant and Catholic Encounter, 103 University St., Belfast BT1 1HL

15. Ulster Quaker Service Committee (Religious Society of Friends), 22 Marlborough Park North, Belfast BT9 6HJ.
16. West Belfast Community Council, 234 Grosvenor Road, Belfast BT12 5AW.
17. Witness for Peace, 25 Beechlands, Belfast 9.
18. Women Together, Bryson House, 28 Bedford St., Belfast BT2 7FE.

B. The Republic: Peace and Reconciliation Groups

1. Co-operation North, 56 Fitzwilliam Square, Dublin 2.
2. Glencree Centre for Reconciliation, Enniskerry, Bray, Co. Wicklow.
   Glencree House Foundation, 1 Belgrave Square, Rathmines, Dublin 6.
3. Irish Mennonite Movement, c/o Mike Garde, 4 Clonmore Villas, 92 Ballybough Road, Dublin 3.
4. Pax Christi, 50 Lower Camden St., Dublin 2.
5. Southern Movement for Peace, c/o Col. W. J. Keane, Sonas, Garryneel, Killaloe, Co. Clare.

C. Northern Ireland: Political Parties and Other Organizations

1. Alliance Party, 88 University St., Belfast BT7 1HE.
2. Ancient Order of Hibernians, 23 Foyle St., Londonderry.
3. Democratic Unionist Party, 1a Ava Ave., Belfast BT7 3BN.
4. Northern Ireland Labour Party, One Cheviot Ave., Belfast 4.
5. Orange Order, 65 Dublin Road, Belfast 2.
6. Social Democratic and Labour Party, 38 University St., Belfast 7.
7. Ulster Official Unionist Party, 41/43 Waring St., Belfast BT1 2EY.
8. Unionist Party of Northern Ireland, 15 Chichester St., Belfast 1.

D. The Republic: Political Parties

1. Communist Party of Ireland, James Connolly House, 43 East Essex St., Dublin 2.
2. Fianna Fail, 13 Upper Mount St., Dublin 2.
3. Fine Gael, 51 Upper Mount St., Dublin 2.
4. Irish Republican Socialist Party, 34 Upper Gardiner St., Dublin 1.
5. Labour Party, 16 Gardiner Place, Dublin 1.
6. Sinn Fein (Provisional), 44 Parnell Square, Dublin 1.
7. Socialist Labour Party, 30 Chelmsford Road, Dublin 6.
8. The Workers' Party, 30 Gardiner Place, Dublin 1.

E. United States; Peace Groups and Groups Which Relate to Northern Ireland

1. Division of Overseas Ministries of the National Council of Churches of Christ of the U.S.A., Room 678, 475 Riverside Drive, New York, NY 10015.
2. Fellowship of Reconciliation, Box 271, Nyack, NY 10960.
3. Ireland Consultancy of National Council of Churches of Christ of the U.S.A., 5554 S. Woodlawn Ave., Chicago, IL 60637.
4. Pax Christi, 3000 N. Mango Ave., Chicago, IL 60634.
5. Peace People Charitable Trust, c/o Sally Leonard, College of New Rochelle, Rochelle, NY 10801.
6. Irish Childrens Fund, 5602 Hillcrest Road, Downers Grove, IL 60516

Ulster Projects - USA:

6. Mrs. David Foster, 240 Girard Park Dr., Lafayette, LA 70503.
7. Rev. Hunter Huckaby, 1030 Johnson, Lafayette, LA 70501.
8. Mr./Mrs. Patrick McMillan, 429 19th St., N.W., Massillon, OH 44646.
9. Mrs. Pat Spoerl, 6514 W. Wells St., Wauwatosa, WI 53213.
10. Rev. Monroe Wright, 15 Char Elm Dr., Manchester, MD 21102.
11. Charles Zoeller, Pacem in Terris (AFSC), 1106 Adams ST., Wilmington, DE 19801.

F. United States: Some Government Offices and Other Organizations

1. U.S. State Dept., Ireland Desk, Room 4511, 23rd St., Washington, DC 20520.
2. British Information Services, 845 Third Ave., New York, NY 10022.
3. British Consulate General, Suite 912, 225 Peachtree St., N.E., Atlanta, GA 30303.
4. British Consulate General, Suite 4740, Prudential Tower, Prudential Center, Boston, MA 02199.
5. British Consulate General, 33 North Dearborn St., Chicago, IL 60602
6. British Consulate General, Suite 2250, 601 Jefferson, Houston, TX 77202.
7. British Consulate General, Ammanson Center E. Bldg., 3701 Wilshire Blvd., Suite 312, Los Angeles, CA 90010.
8. British Consulate General, Equitable Building, 120 Montgomery St., San Francisco, CA 94104.
9. Embassy of Ireland, 2234 Massachusetts Ave., N.W., Washington, DC 20008.
10. Consulate General of Ireland, Chase Building, 535 Boylston St., Boston, MA 02116.
11. Consulate General of Ireland, 400 North Michigan Ave., Chicago, IL 60611.
12. Consulate General of Ireland, 580 Fifth Ave., New York, NY 10036.
13. Consulate General of Ireland, 681 Market St., San Francisco, CA 94105.
14. Ad Hoc Congressional Committee for Irish Affairs, c/o Rep. Mario Biaggi, House of Representatives, Washington, DC 20515. Attention: Bob Blancato.
15. Friends of Ireland, c/o Senator Edward Kennedy, 109 Russell Senate Office Building, Washington, DC 20510. Attention: Matthew Murray.
16. Irish National Caucus, 205 Pennsylvania Ave., S.E., Washington, DC 20003.

NORTHERN IRELAND ORGANIZATONS: CHRONOLOGY

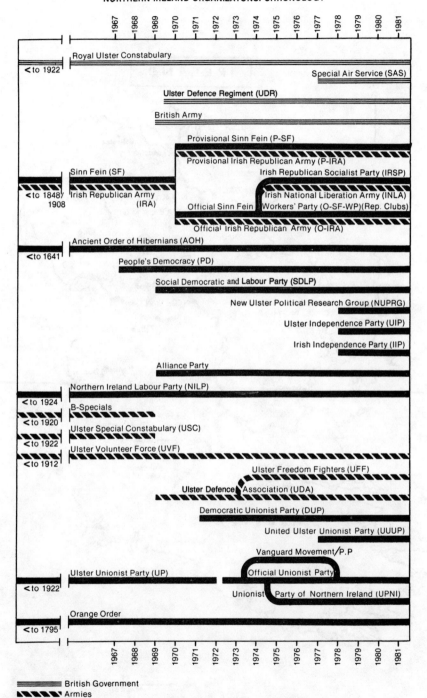

IRELAND

N.

CO. DONEGAL

Coleraine
● Londonderry
● Strabane

NORTHERN
IRELAND

LOUGH
NEAGH
Belfast
Lisburn

Sligo ●

Ballina ●

C O N N A C H T

▲ Croagh Patrick

● Galway

Athlone ●

Shannon ●

Limerick ●

Tralee

M U N S T E R

● Killarney

Cork ●

● Bantry

U L S T E R
CO. CAVAN

CO.
MONA-
GHAN
Armagh

● Newry

● Dundalk

Kells ●
● Drogheda

Maynooth Dublin ●
✳ Glencree

L E I N S T E R
■ The Curragh
● Portlaoise
Prison

Kilkenny ●

● Cashel

● Wexford

Waterford ●

0   15   50
MILES

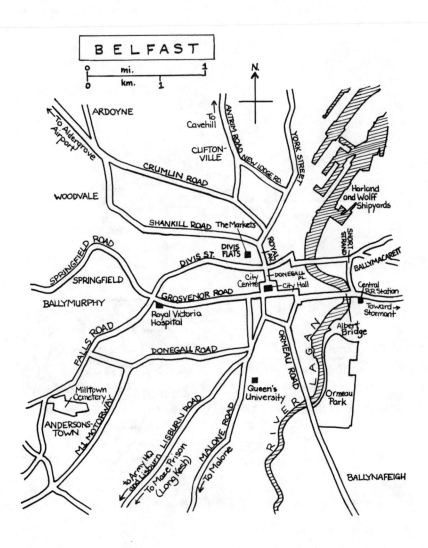

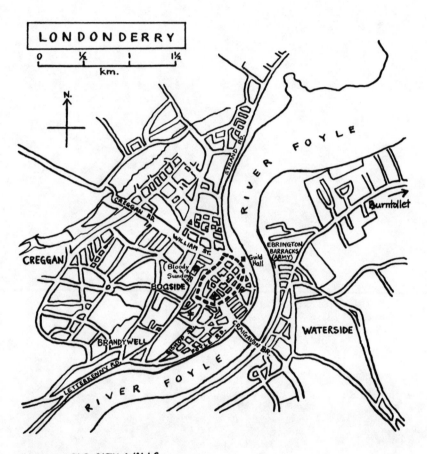

LONDONDERRY

0   ½   1   1½
km.

N.

RIVER FOYLE

STRAND RD.

CREGGAN RD.

WILLIAM ST.

CREGGAN

Guild Hall

Bloody Sunday

BOGSIDE

EBRINGTON BARRACKS (ARMY)

Burntollet

BRANDYWELL

LETTERKENNY RD.

BISHOP

FOYLE RD.

CRAIGAVON BR.

WATERSIDE

RIVER FOYLE

▪▪▪▪▪▪ OLD CITY WALLS
† ST. EUGENE'S CATHEDRAL
‡ ST. COLUMB'S CATHEDRAL

Bibliography

Five outstanding sources became especially important in writing this book. John Darby's book, *Conflict in Ireland,* is an excellent compendium, written with balance and sensitivity. Deutsch and Magowan's three-volume *Northern Ireland: A Chronology of Events,* was a constant reference. *Fortnight* magazine provided us not only with a continuation of a chronology but also with thoughtful articles on current issues. W.D. Flackes' book, *Northern Ireland: A Political Directory, 1968-79,* is an excellent reference book. Finally, *Violence in Ireland,* written by the working party appointed by the Irish Council of Churches/Roman Catholic Church Joint Group on Social Questions. Its capacity to raise questions and state issues provided a needed perspective. The book also offers suggestions and recommendations which we wholly support. The authors used these sources as well as most of the books, magazines, and newspapers listed below.

Arthur, Paul. *The People's Democracy, 1968-73.* Blackstaff Press, Belfast: 1974.
The only detailed, academic study of People's Democracy.

Barritt, D.P. *Northern Ireland: A Problem to Every Solution.* Quaker Peace & Service, London: 1982.
A 147-page balanced presentation of the issues.

Barritt, D.P., and A. Booth. *Orange and Green: A Quaker Study of Community Relations in Northern Ireland* (rev. ed.). Northern Friends Peace Board, 1972.
Brief but good in explaining the background of the conflict. Although this small book is dated, its balanced approach and brevity are useful.

Beckett, J.C. *The Anglo-Irish Tradition.* Faber and Faber, London: 1976.
Highly respected study.

Beckett, J.C. *The Making of Modern Ireland, 1603-1923.* Faber and Faber, London: 1966.
Respected historical survey.

Bell, Boyer. *The Secret Army, 1916-1970.* John Day Co., New York: 1971.
Historical study of the IRA.

Bell, Geoffrey. *The Protestants of Ulster.* Pluto Press, London: 1976.
Brief (144 pages) but useful study.

Bleakley, David. *Peace in Ulster.* Mowbrays, London: 1972.
A brief study of community initiatives for peace not available elsewhere.

Bleakley, David. *Saidie Patterson, Irish Peacemaker.* Blackstaff Press, Belfast: 1980.
Biography of a prominent Northern Ireland civil leader associated especially with Women Together.

Boulton, David. *The UVF, 1966-73.* Torc, Dublin: 1973.
The only study dealing specifically with the UVF.

Boyd, Andrew. *Holy War in Belfast.* Anvil, Tralee, Ireland: 1969.
Brief history of how "religious bigotry in the North of Ireland goes back many generations."

Clark, Dennis J. *Irish Blood, Northern Ireland and the American Conscience.* Kennikat Press, Port Washington, N.Y.: 1977.
A brief but thorough and well-documented study of Irish-American involvement in the Northern Ireland conflict.

Coogan, Tim Pat. *The I.R.A.* Fontana, Collins, London: 1970.
Historical account of the IRA.

Coogan, Tim Pat. *On the Blanket: The H-Block Story.* Ward River Press, Dublin: 1980.
The only study dealing specifically with the H-Block issue.

Dangerfield, George. *The Damnable Question: One Hundred and Twenty years of Anglo-Irish Conflict.* Little Brown and Co., Boston: 1976.
Highly praised scholarly history; relates in detail Anglo-Irish relations, 1800-1921.

Darby, John. *Conflict in Northern Ireland: The Development of a Polarized Community.* Barnes and Noble Books, New York: 1976.
Information is arranged to help the reader learn basic background. Helpful reference; important bibliography.

DePaor, Liam. *Divided Ulster*. Penguin, Baltimore: 1970.
One of the most respected brief histories.

Deutsch, Richard. Trans. Jack Bernard. *Mairead Corrigan, Betty Williams*. Barron's, Woodbury, N.Y.: 1977.
The only sizable account of the Community of the Peace People and two of its leaders.

Deutsch, Richard, and Vivien Magowan. *Northern Ireland, 1968-73: A Chronology of Events. Volume 1, 1968-71*. Blackstaff Press, Belfast: 1973.
Volume 2, 1972-73. Published in 1974.
Volume 3, 1974. Published in 1975.
Unique and major contribution in that the three volumes are primarily a chronology of events in Northern Ireland, 1968-74.

Devlin, Bernadette. *The Price of My Soul*. Pan, London: 1969.
Important and moving autobiography. Unfortunately, the book ends as the author becomes a central political figure in Northern Ireland (1969).

Fisk, Robert. *The Point of No Return: The Strike Which Broke the British in Ulster*. Times Books, Andre Deutsch, London: 1975.
Sizable study of the Unionist workers' strike in 1974; the only detailed study generally available.

Flackes, W.D. *Northern Ireland, A Political Directory, 1968-79*. Gill and MacMillan, St. Martin's Press, New York: 1980.
Easy-to-use succinct reference book. Entries arranged alphabetically. Special sections on election results and security.

Fraser, Morris. *Children in Conflict*. Penguin, Baltimore: 1973.
The best study done on the social and psychological effects of the Ulster violence on children and adults. Respected and useful.

Gray, Tony. *No Surrender: The Siege of Londonderry, 1689*. MacDonald and Jane's. London: 1975.
Detailed study of this mythologized event.

Hezlett, Sir Arthur. *The 'B' Specials: A History of the Ulster Special*
Unique brief study of this influential group.

Holland, Jack. *Too Long a Sacrifice: Life and Death in Northern Ireland Since 1969*. Dodd, Mead, & Co., New York: 1981.

Kitson, Frank. *Low Intensity Operations*. Stackpole Books, Harrisburg: 1971.
Prominent book on British military analysis and strategy in middle-level military engagements.

Lyons, F.S.L. *Ireland Since the Famine* (rev. ed.). Fontana, Glasgow: 1973.
A respected long history of Ireland since 1850. Well-documented; bibliography.

MacEoin, Gary. *Northern Ireland: Captive of History*. Holt, Rinehart, and Winston, New York: 1974.
Readable and helpful study.

Marlow, Joyce. *Captain Boycott and the Irish*. Andre Deutsch, London: 1973.
Detailed study of the boycott campaign and the background of the land league campaign.

McCreary, Alf. *Corrymeela: The Search for Peace*. Christian Journals Limited, Belfast: 1975.
The only study of this length (119 pages) on Corrymeela.

McGuffin, John. *Internment!* Anvil, Ireland: 1973.
The only study dealing specifically with internment.

Moody, T.W. *The Ulster Question, 1603-1973*. Mercier Press, Dublin: 1974.
Brief history by a prominent Irish historian, with the focus on the historical roots of the Northern Ireland conflicts.

Murphy, Devla. *A Place Apart*. Penguin, Baltimore: 1978.
Readable and engaging prose treatment of impressions and thoughts by a sensitive southern woman journalist.

O'Brien, Conor Cruise. *States of Ireland*. Vintage Books, Random House, New York: 1973.
Widely-read and readable book by a popular figure in Irish political and cultural life.

O'Donnell, E.E. *Northern Irish Stereotypes*. College of Industrial Relations, Dublin: 1977.
Dissertation which focuses on how Protestants and Catholics in Northern Ireland see each other.

Riddell, Patrick. *Fire Over Ulster*. Hamish Hamilton, London: 1970.
This book articulates moderate Unionist views and is worth reading because of it.

Rose, Richard. *Governing without Consensus: An Irish Perspective.* Beacon Press, Boston: 1971.
Major landmark study of opinions and background of Northern Ireland.

Sunday Times Insight Team. *Ulster.* Penguin, Baltimore: 1972.
Major study done for the London *Sunday Times,* written by respected investigative journalists. Readable and informative.

Sweetman, Rosita. *'On Our Knees': Ireland 1972.* Pan Special, London: 1972.
Interviews with prominent and articulate people; provocative and stimulating.

vanVoris, W.H. *Violence in Ulster: An Oral Documentary.* Univ. of Massachusetts Press, Amherst: 1975.
Unique because of its oral-history approach, based on long interviews with prominent and ordinary people.

Violence in Ireland: A Report to the Churches. Christian Journals Limited, Belfast: 1976.
Prominent study and forthright presentation of issues; challenging action suggestions.

Woodham-Smith, Cecil. *The Great Hunger.* New English Library, London: 1962.
One of the best historical studies of the Irish famine, 1845-49.

PAMPHLETS

Boserup, Anders. *Who Is The Principal Enemy? Contradictions and Struggles in Northern Ireland.* Independent Labour Party, London: 1972.
The author challenges the analysis that the Northern Ireland conflict deals with British-Irish or Protestant/Catholic issues. Discussion of myths and contradictions.

Committee for Withdrawal from Ireland. *Ireland: Voices for Withdrawal.* n.p. 1980.
Anthology favoring withdrawal of the British army.

Lampen, John, compiler. *Will Warren: A Scrapbook.* Quaker Home Service, London, 1983.

Designed as peace education for children, this 49-page pamphlet has quotations by and about Will Warren.

McKeown, Ciaran. *The Price of Peace.* Community of the Peace People, 224 Lisburn Rd., Belfast: 1976.
Articulation of the vision of the Community of the Peace People.

Time for A Change: The Case for the Repeal of the Emergency Provisions Act. Belfast, 1980.
Contribution from the Community of the Peace People on the Northern Ireland criminal justice system.

MAGAZINES FROM NORTHERN IRELAND (conversion: 1 pound equals roughly $1.50.)

Dawn, focusing on nonviolent action, civil liberties, and movements for change. Monthly published from Belfast and Dublin. Subscriptions £6.00 minimum for ten issues airmail, £3.50 in Europe or surface. Also publishes the occasional, more theoretical *Dawn Train.* Airmail £3.00 for 4, Europe/surface £2.00 for four. Address: 1 Belgrave Square, Rathmines, Dublin 6.

Fortnight, an independent review for Northern Ireland. Originally came out every two weeks, now comes out monthly. A liberal review of politics and the arts in Northern Ireland. Subscriptions: 10 pounds airmail to the U.S. 7 Lower Crescent, Belfast 7.

PACE Journal, published by Protestant and Catholic Encounter three times a year. Fifty cents a copy plus postage. PACE, 103 University St., Belfast 7.

Peace by Peace, magazine of the Peace People, usually published every two weeks (less often in the summer). Covers the political situation and other groups to some extent in addition to Peace People news and views. Subscriptions: 10 pounds in Ireland or Britain, overseas airmail 12.50 pounds. 224 Lisburn Road, Belfast 9.

Scope, a review of voluntary social work and community development in Northern Ireland, published ten times a year by the

Community Information Service of the Northern Ireland Council of Social Service. Twelve-month subscription £ 5.50 in Ireland/Britain, airmail £ 13.00. Community Information Service, 2 Annadale Avenue, Belfast BT7 3JH.

Corrymeela and Glencree also publish newsletters which are sent to "friends" and which may contain interesting and useful material. Inquire to Corrymeela House, 8 Upper Crescent, Belfast 7 and to Glencree, 1 Belgrave Square, Rathmines, Dublin 6.

AMERICAN NEWSPAPERS

The Irish Advocate, 15 Park Row, New York, NY 10038.

The Irish Echo, 1860 Broadway, New York, NY 10023.

The Irish Edition, 134 W. Coulter St., Philadelphia, PA 19144.

The Irish People, 4951 Broadway, New York, NY 10034.

The Irish World, 853 Broadway, New York, NY 10003.

Irish American News, P.O. Box A-66218, Chicago, IL 60666.

Index

More Resources From New Society Publishers

WOMEN IN DEVELOPMENT: A RESOURCE GUIDE FOR ORGANIZATION AND ACTION
by ISIS Women's International Information and Communication Service.

A lavishly illustrated book, with 122 photographs, five years in the making. Women scholars from all over the world contributed to make this one of the most comprehensive and beautiful books of its kind ever published. Sections on women and multinationals, women and rural development, women and health, education, tourism, migration, etc.

Annotated resource lists, bibliographies. 240 pages. 1984.
Hardcover: $39.95
Paperback: $14.95

THE EYE OF THE CHILD
by Ruth Mueller

A brilliant healing myth for a world gone mad!

"Of all the creatures to whom the great mother had given birth all were a part, not apart, but one. Yes all but one flowed as she flowed, born of her womb, dying in her bosom, struggling, true, but never against their own life support. One, only one, capable of standing apart, imagining self above and outside, turning to rend, turning to overpower, to subdue, to conquer the vessel of life itself, creation's own embodiment. Had she not labored for aeons to give birth to a triumph of joy and beauty as fair as dawn, a creature of light to share the glowing consciousness of the whole, one of understanding as deep as her deeps are deep, of laughter as divine as tears and of tears as cleansing as laughter, one who was no alien to mercy, capable of new visions above predation, a familiar to the art of healing, above all a creature of tongues, creation itself no longer mute to express—to express—
"What had gone wrong?"

Ecological speculative fiction of the highest order.

240 pages. 1984.
Paperback: $7.95

To Order: send check or money order to New Society Publishers, 4722 Baltimore Avenue, Philadelphia, PA 19143. For postage and handling: add $1.50 for the first book and 40¢ for each additional book.

More Resources From
New Society Publishers

GANDHI THROUGH WESTERN EYES
by Horace Alexander

"This book stands out as an authoritative guide: clear, simple, and straightforward, both to Gandhi's personality and to his beliefs. As a Quaker, Mr. Alexander found it easy to grasp Gandhi's ideas about nonviolence; the author's prolonged and intimate friendship helped him to know the Mahatma as few men were able to do, and to appreciate that he was something far greater than a national hero of the Indian independence movement—a man, in fact, with a message that is intensely relevant for the world today. Nothing that has so far been published about Gandhi is more illuminating than this careful, perceptive and comprehensive work. It is not only comprehensive—it is convincing."

—Times Literary Supplement

Letter, Index. 240 pages. 1984.
Hardcover: $24.95
Paperback: $8.95

A MANUAL ON NONVIOLENCE AND CHILDREN
compiled and edited by Stephanie Judson; Foreword by Paula J. Paul,
Educators for Social Responsibility

Includes "For the Fun of It! Selected Cooperative Games for Children and Adults"

Invaluable resource for creating an atmosphere in which children and adults can resolve problems and conflicts nonviolently. Especially useful for parents and teachers in instilling values today to create the peacemakers of tomorrow!

"Stephanie Judson's excellent manual has helped many parents and teachers with whom we have worked. An essential part of learning nonviolent ways of resolving conflicts is the creation of a trusting, affirming and cooperative environment in the home and classroom. This manual has a wealth of suggestions for creating such an environment. We highly recommend it."

—Jim and Kathy McGinnis,
Parenting for Peace and Justice,
St. Louis, Missouri

Anecdotes, exercises, games, agendas, annotated bibliography.
Illustrated, large format. 160 pages. 1984.
Hardcover: $24.95
Paperback: $9.95

WE ARE ALL PART OF ONE ANOTHER; A BARBARA DEMING READER

"I have had the dream that women should at last be the ones to truly experiment with nonviolent struggle, discover its full force."

Essays, speeches, letters, stories, poems by America's foremost writer on issues of women and peace, feminism and nonviolence, spanning four decades. Lovingly edited by activist-writer Jane Meyerding; Black feminist writer Barbara Smith, founder of Kitchen Table Press, has graciously contributed a foreword. A book no activist of the '80s will want to be without!

"Barbara Deming is the voice of conscience for her generation and all those to follow, measured in reason, compassionate, clear, requiring: the voice of a friend." —Jane Rule

"Wisdom, modesty, responsiveness, love: all of these qualities live in her writings, a treasured gift to the world." —Leah Fritz

320 pages. 1984.
Hardcover: $24.95
Paperback: $10.95

REWEAVING THE WEB OF LIFE: FEMINISM AND NONVIOLENCE
edited by Pam McAllister

". . . happens to be one of the most important books you'll ever read."
—*The Village Voice*

"Stressing the connection between patriarchy and war, sex and violence, this book makes it clear that nonviolence can be an assertive, positive force. It's provocative reading for anyone interested in surviving and changing the nuclear age." —*Ms. Magazine*

More than 50 Contributors – Women's History – Women and the Struggle Against Militarism – Violence and Its Origins – Nonviolence and Women's Self-Defense – Interviews – Songs – Poems – Stories – Provocative Proposals – Photographs – Annotated Bibliography – Index

Voted "Best New Book—1983"—*WIN MAGAZINE ANNUAL BOOK POLL*

448 pages.
Hardcover: $19.95
Paperback: $10.95

To Order: send check or money order to New Society Publishers, 4722 Baltimore Avenue, Philadelphia, PA 19143. For postage and handling: add $1.50 for the first book and 40¢ for each additional book.

More Resources From New Society Publishers

"This is the bravest book I have read since Jonathan Schell's FATE OF
THE EARTH." —Dr. Rollo May

DESPAIR AND PERSONAL POWER IN THE NUCLEAR AGE
by Joanna Rogers Macy

Despair and Personal Power in the Nuclear Age is the first major book to examine
our psychological responses to planetary perils and to lay the theoretical founda-
tions for an empowering, personally-centered approach to social change. Included are sections on awakening in the nuclear age, relating to children and
young people, guided meditations, empowered rituals, and a special section on
"Spiritual Exercises for a Time of Apocalypse." As described and excerpted in
New Age Journal and *Fellowship Magazine.* Recommended for public libraries
by *Library Journal;* selected for inclusion in the 1984 Women's Reading Program, General Board of Global Ministries, United Methodist Church.

200 pages. Appendices, resource lists, exercises. 1983.
Hardcover: $19.95
Paperback: $8.95

RAINBOWS NOT RADIATION! BANANAS NOT BOMBS!
GRAPES NOT GUNS! XYLOPHONES NOT X-TINCTION!

**WATERMELONS NOT WAR! A SUPPORT BOOK FOR PARENTING
IN THE NUCLEAR AGE**
by Kate Cloud, Ellie Deegan, Alice Evans, Hayat Imam, and Barbara
Signer; Afterword by Dr. Helen Caldicott.

Five mothers in the Boston area have been meeting regularly for four years, to
give each other support, to demystify nuclear technology—weapons and technology—into terms parents, *and children,* can understand, to find ways of acting
which will give their children a future. The result is WATERMELONS NOT
WAR! A SUPPORT BOOK FOR PARENTING IN THE NUCLEAR AGE.

—As written up in *Ms. Magazine, Whole Life Times, Sojourner.*

Large format. Beautifully illustrated. Annotated Bibliography.
160 pages. 1984.
Hardcover: $19.95
Paperback: $9.95